From the Series Editor:

Sams Publishing is excited and proud to announce that *Sams Teach Yourself Lotus Notes R5 in 10 Minutes* is part of our new integrated series of books on Lotus Notes and Domino R5.

As illustrated in the User Pyramid (see facing page) this series is not merely a collection of books but a carefully planned succession of tutorials and reference material. Our building block approach to Lotus Notes and Domino R5 gives corporations the ability to identify the right book for each of their users. Individuals "graduate" to the next level of proficiency with confidence that the topics and depth of coverage are appropriately expanded and enhanced.

The lead authors in our series are Certified Lotus Notes Professionals (CLP) and/or Certified Lotus Notes Instructors (CLI) with real-world product experience. They represent the professional Lotus Notes and Domino community, and they understand your need to augment skills commensurate with new product releases and evolving user community needs.

I hope you enjoy our series of R5 books as much as we have enjoyed our collaborative efforts to deliver them to you. Thank you.

Sincerely,

Jane

Jane Calabria

Series Editor

SAMS

Teach Yourself

LOTUS NOTES® R5

Jane Calabria, CLP,
Dorothy Burke, CLI
with Barbara
Anderson, CLS

in 10 Minutes

SAMS

201 West 103rd St., Indianapolis, Indiana, 46290 USA

Sams Teach Yourself Lotus Notes® R5 in 10 Minutes

Copyright © 1999 by Sams

All rights reserved. No part of this book shall be reproduced, stored in a retrieval system, or transmitted by any means, electronic, mechanical, photocopying, recording, or otherwise, without written permission from the publisher. No patent liability is assumed with respect to the use of the information contained herein. Although every precaution has been taken in the preparation of this book, the publisher and author assume no responsibility for errors or omissions. Neither is any liability assumed for damages resulting from the use of the information contained herein.

International Standard Book Number: 0-672-31419-3

Library of Congress Catalog Card Number: 98-86481

Printed in the United States of America

First Printing: July 1999

03   02   01   4   3

Trademarks

All terms mentioned in this book that are known to be trademarks or service marks have been appropriately capitalized. Sams cannot attest to the accuracy of this information. Use of a term in this book should not be regarded as affecting the validity of any trademark or service mark.

Lotus Notes is a registered trademark of IBM.

Warning and Disclaimer

Every effort has been made to make this book as complete and as accurate as possible, but no warranty or fitness is implied. The information provided is on an "as is" basis. The authors and the publisher shall have neither liability nor responsibility to any person or entity with respect to any loss or damages arising from the information contained in this book.

EXECUTIVE EDITOR
Dean Miller

DEVELOPMENT EDITOR
John Gosney

MANAGING EDITOR
Brice Gosnell

PROJECT EDITOR
Sara Bosin

COPY EDITOR
Michael Dietsch

INDEXER
Mary Gammons

PROOFREADER
Andrew Beaster

TECHNICAL EDITOR
John C. Palmer, CLP

INTERIOR DESIGN
Gary Adair

COVER DESIGN
Aren Howell

COPY WRITER
Eric Borgert

LAYOUT TECHNICIANS
Brandon Allen
Timothy Osborn
Staci Somers

Contents

About the Authors

Jane Calabria is the *Series Editor* for the Macmillan Computer Publishing (MCP) series of Lotus Notes and Domino R5 books. She is a Notes R5 Principal Application Developer, CLP (Certified Lotus Professional). She is also a *Certified Microsoft User Specialist* at the Expert level in Word and Excel. She and her husband, Rob Kirkland, own Stillwater Enterprises, Inc., a consulting firm located near Philadelphia, Pennsylvania. Jane and Rob are preeminent authors, speakers, and trainers on the topic of Lotus Notes and Domino and they conduct national training sessions and seminars.

Dorothy Burke is a *Certified Lotus Notes Instructor* (CLI) and a Notes R5 Principal Application Developer, CLP (Certified Lotus Professional). She teaches Domino system administration and application development and has been an independent consultant and trainer since 1988.

Together, Jane and Dorothy have co-authored over 18 Macmillan books including Que's *Certified Microsoft Office User Exam Guide*(s) for Microsoft Word 97, Microsoft Excel 97 and Microsoft Power Point 97. Also, *Microsoft Works 6-in-1, Microsoft Windows 95 6-in-1, Microsoft Windows 98 6-in-1, Using Microsoft Word 97, and Using Microsoft Word 2000.* Their Lotus Notes and Domino titles include Que's *Ten Minute Guide to Lotus Notes 4.6,* the *Ten Minute Guide to Lotus Notes Mail 4.6,* and *Lotus Notes and the Internet 6-in-1.* Their new titles for Release 5 of Lotus Notes and Domino include *Sams Teach Yourself Lotus Notes R5 in 10 Minutes, How to Use Lotus Notes R5,* and *Sams Teach Yourself Lotus Notes and Domino R5 Development in 21 Days.*

Barbara Anderson is a *Certified Lotus Notes Specialist,* and a Lotus Notes Project Manager with InterFusion, Inc., a Lotus Premier Partner located in Merchantville, NJ just outside of Philadelphia. Barbara is responsible for Domino corporate infrastructure planning, as well as developing and deploying Notes applications. Along with developing Notes courseware for customized applications, Barbara has delivered Notes end user training throughout the United States.

John Palmer (Technical Editor) John C. Palmer is an *R5 Certified Lotus Professional*, certified as an Application Developer and as a System Administrator. He owns John Palmer Associates in southeast Pennsylvania, providing Lotus Domino consulting services to medium and large size companies in the Delaware Valley. His expertise is in integrating Domino and web technologies, and developing complex Domino applications. John Palmer Associates is a Lotus Business Partner and can be found on the World Wide Web at www.jpassoc.net.

Dedication

We dedicate this book to Monique Campbell, and thank her for a great summer of '98, and a successful Camp Spring Creek!!

Acknowledgments

A lot of hard work went into completing this project, and we'd like to thank all of those involved. First and foremost, our gratitude goes to Sams Publishing for becoming the leader in Lotus Notes and Domino books. Their commitment to provide quality books in a timely fashion to the Notes/Domino community makes this a very exciting time to be writing and working with their dedicated staff. Thanks too, to our new Notes and old Notes teams at Sams: John Pierce, Dean Miller, Sean Dixon, Sara Bosin, Michael Dietsch, Andrew Beaster, and Mary Gammons. A special thanks to John Gosney for agreeing to work with us again – gosh, we've missed you. And lastly, but hardly least, a special thanks and welcome to John Palmer, our technical editor, and Janet Crawford, who always works herself into the position of Inspector General. We salute you Janet and thank you for your attention to detail.

Tell Us What You Think!

As the reader of this book, *you* are our most important critic and commentator. We value your opinion and want to know what we're doing right, what we could do better, what areas you'd like to see us publish in, and any other words of wisdom you're willing to pass our way.

We welcome your comments. You can fax, email, or write me directly to let me know what you did or didn't like about this book—as well as what we can do to make our books stronger.

Please note that I cannot help you with technical problems related to the topic of this book, and that due to the high volume of mail I receive, I might not be able to reply to every message.

When you write, please be sure to include this book's title and author as well as your name and phone or fax number. I will carefully review your comments and share them with the author and editors who worked on the book.

Fax: 317.581.4666

Email: feedback@samspublishing.com

Mail: Sams Publishing
201 West 103rd Street
Indianapolis, IN 46290 USA

Introduction

Many people considered Lotus Notes to be *the* groupware product of the '90s. Perhaps Lotus Notes R5 will be *the* universal client for the millennium. Ever evolving to meet the collaboration, communication, and Internet needs of businesses, Release 5 of Lotus Notes focuses on the Notes client to create a seamless, universal client from which you can access mail, the Internet, your intranet, and so forth. The new look and functionality of the R5 client is the topic of this book.

Welcome to *Sams Teach Yourself Lotus Notes R5 in 10 Minutes*

This book focuses on the basics of Lotus Notes and Domino; introduces general groupware, Notes, and email concepts; and shows you some advanced features of the program. You can work through the book lesson by lesson, building on your skills, or you can use the book as a quick reference when you want to perform a new task. Features and concepts are presented in lessons that take 10 minutes or less to complete.

If you are new to Notes, start at the beginning of the book. If you've used Notes before, you might want to skip the first few lessons and work from there. Use the Table of Contents and select the lessons that cover features of the program you haven't yet used. If you travel with Lotus Notes on your laptop, the compact size of this book is perfect for fitting into your laptop or notebook case.

Who Should Use This Book

Sams Teach Yourself Lotus Notes R5 is for anyone who

- Has Lotus Notes installed on their PC or laptop
- Needs to learn Notes quickly
- Wants to explore some of the new features of Lotus Notes R5
- Needs a task-based Lotus Notes tutorial
- Requires a compact Notes reference guide

Conventions Used in This Book

In telling you to choose menu commands, this book uses the format *menu title*, *menu command*. For example, the statement "choose **File, Properties**" means to "open the File menu and select the Properties command."

In addition, *Sams Teach Yourself Lotus Notes R5* uses the following icons to identify helpful information:

 Plain English　New or unfamiliar terms are defined in "plain English."

 Timesaver Tips　Look here for ideas that cut corners and confusion.

 Caution　This icon identifies areas where new users often run into trouble and offers practical solutions to those problems.

From Here...

For more information on Lotus Notes, try these other Macmillan Computer Publishing books:

- *How to Use Lotus Notes R5*—A full color visual tutorial for beginning Lotus Notes users.

- *Sams Teach Yourself Lotus Notes R5 in 24 Hours*—In-depth coverage of the topics found in Sams Teach Yourself Lotus Notes R5 in 10 Minutes and more! Here you find lesson questions and answers and lesson summaries.

- *Special Edition Using Lotus Notes and Domino 5*—The ultimate Lotus Notes companion for the advanced user, help desk personnel, consultant, administrator, and developer.

- *Sams Teach Yourself Domino Application Development in 21 Days*—The comprehensive way to learn the important development features of Lotus Notes and Domino R5, with a lesson-a-day format.

- *Lotus Notes and Domino R5 Development Unleashed*—The long-awaited high-end reference and learning guide to the advanced features of Domino development.

To learn about all of the MCP Lotus Notes books, visit our Web site at www.samspublishing.com.

For Lotus Notes press releases, technical information, and new product information, visit the Lotus Web sites. The following Lotus sites contain information relevant to the Notes client:

- www.Lotus.com   The Lotus home page, where you can find information on all Lotus products and services, including support and access to other Lotus Notes sites.

- www.lotus.com/education   The Lotus Education site, where you can find course descriptions, schedules, locations, certification information, and Lotus Authorized Education Centers for Lotus Notes and other Lotus Products.

- www2.lotus.com/learningcenters   To learn about Notes features, take a take a Notes guided tour.

LESSON 1

Getting Started with Notes

In this lesson, you learn about Lotus Notes concepts, how to start and move around in Notes, how to change your password, and how to exit Notes.

Understanding the Notes Client

Lotus Notes is based on client/server technology, which enables you to access, share, and manage information over a network. The network can consist of five or ten computers in your office building, cabled together, or it can consist of 30,000 computers across the United States, connected to one another in various ways. Your PC is the Lotus Notes client. It requests and receives information from the server, called the "Domino" server.

You communicate with the Domino server through a series of wires and cables (hardware) and networking software. The information you request is in Lotus Notes applications, or databases. The Domino server usually stores these databases so that many clients can access them at one time. In most cases, when you click a database bookmark, you are actually opening a database that is stored on the server. Your client (your PC) requests that database from the server, and when the database opens, the database that resides on the server appears.

This is similar to the connection you might have at work to your file server. Often, you store work that you have created in other software programs (other than Lotus Notes) on the file server on your network at the office. For example, you might create a Lotus 1-2-3 spreadsheet or a Word document and save them on your F: drive, which is actually space that is dedicated to you for storage on the file server.

Lotus Notes applications typically support or automate business functions by helping you create, collect, share, and manage almost any kind of information. Notes applications can incorporate information from external sources (such as Lotus spreadsheets), export data to external databases (such as Approach), or contain documents (such as Word). Notes *applications* are a collection of one or more *databases* that are designed to perform a specific function or work process (workflow). It is not unusual for people to use the terms *application* and *database* interchangeably.

Starting Notes

Start Notes from the Windows 95, Windows 98, or Windows NT desktop. Notes is also available for Macintosh computers and works almost exactly as it does in Windows, but in this book the instructions apply to non-Macintosh PCs. After starting Notes, you can leave it onscreen or you can minimize the Notes window so that it's easy to access anytime during your workday. To start Lotus Notes, follow these steps:

1. From the desktop, select the **Start** button.

2. Choose **Programs**, **Lotus Applications**, **Lotus Notes**. If Lotus Notes is not in the Lotus Applications folder, it will be in the folder your system administrator set for you or the folder you specified during installation.

3. Enter your password as assigned to your by your network administrator. Passwords are context sensitive, so be certain to enter the password exactly as it was given to you. (You will learn more about passwords later in this lesson, including how to change your password.)

 Caution   If you are not attached to your network when you start Notes, the Choose Location dialog box might appear. Choose **Home** as your location and continue to work through this lesson, or go to Lesson 20, "Setting Up for Mobile Use," and see the section "Creating Location Documents."

This book assumes that you're using the Office (Network) connection to a Domino server; however, most of the procedures and tasks in this book are similar, however, no matter which location option you choose.

If you are starting Notes for the very first time, the Lotus Notes Welcome screen appears with the default style (called Basics) selected, as shown in Figure 1.1.

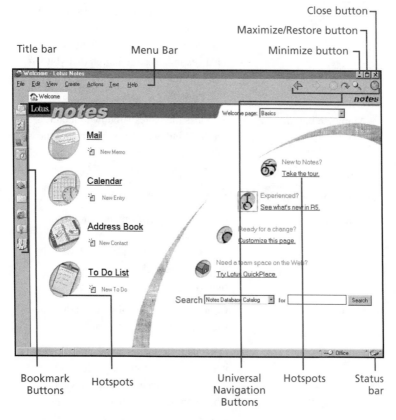

FIGURE 1.1   The Lotus Notes Welcome Page is your starting point to access mail, calendar, and all features of Notes.

Through hotspots and bookmark buttons, the Welcome page provides access to mail, calendars, Address Books and To Do lists. The Welcome page is customizable and you can add your favorite Web sites or newsgroups. From here, you can also search databases or Web sites, take a tour of Notes, and see what's new in Lotus Notes R5. Table 1.1 describes the elements of the Notes window.

Table 1.1 Notes Window Elements

Element	Function
Maximize button	Enlarges the Notes window to cover the Windows desktop; when the window is maximized, the Maximize button changes to a Restore button that you can click to return the window to its previous size.
Minimize button	Reduces the Notes window to a button on the Windows taskbar; to restore the window to its original size, click the button on the taskbar.
Close (X) button	Closes (exits) the Notes program.
Title bar	Contains program's name, and if you are in a database, describes where you are in that database; also displays a description of selected menu commands.
Menu	Contains the menus of commands you use to perform tasks in Notes.
Status bar	Presents information about the selected item, shows error messages (if any), displays your location, and indicates when you have new mail.
Hotspots	Text or picture that you click on to perform an action or follow a link.
Bookmark Buttons	Each button opens bookmark page or a list of bookmarks to access documents, sites, or databases.

Element	Function
Bookmark	Opens a database or task when you click the bookmark.
Universal Navigation buttons	Provide the means to navigate through Notes, going forward or backward, stopping an activity, refreshing pages, searching, or opening URLs.

Navigating in Notes

There are several tools for moving around and opening tasks or databases in Notes. They include hotspots, as you find on the Basics page of the Welcome screen, navigation buttons, and bookmarks.

The hotspots on the Welcome page are pretty self-explanatory: Click on the Mail hotspot to open your mail database, or click on the New Memo text hotspot to open a new mail memo, ready for you to fill in.

Navigation buttons are located in the upper-right corner of the Notes window. When you point at one of the buttons, a tip appears to tell you the name of the button and the keyboard shortcut that performs the same function. Table 1.2 provides a short explanation of each button.

TABLE 1.2   The Navigation Buttons

	Go Back	Returns to the previous page, document, or task. Right-click to see a drop-down menu of places you can go back to; select one to go there.
	Go Forward	Takes you to the task, page, or document that was displayed prior to your clicking Go Back. Right-click to see a drop-down menu of the places you can go forward to; select one to go there.

continues

TABLE 1.2   Continued

	Stop	Interrupts the current program activity.
	Refresh	Refreshes the current document, page, or view with the latest data.
	Search	Displays a drop-down menu of search choices to find what you need. You can search the current view, document, or page; your Notes domain; or the Web.
	Open URL	Displays a box with the URL (Web address) of the current page. Type in a new URL to open that Web page. Click the pin to keep this box onscreen.

Bookmark buttons are located on the left of the Welcome window. From here you can also open your mail, calendar, and to do list (just as you can by clicking a hotspot). Bookmark buttons link to databases, bookmark pages, or even Web pages. Bookmark buttons are customizable; you learn how to add bookmarks throughout this book. Table 1.3 describes the default bookmark buttons that are found on the Welcome page.

TABLE 1.3   The Default Bookmark Bar Buttons

Click Here	To
	Open your **Mail** database. From here you can view your Inbox, create new mail, and so forth. You learn about the mail database in Lessons 3–6.
	Open the **Calendar** where you manage your appointments, access the calendars or free time of other people (given permission, of course), invite people to meetings, accept invitations, and so forth. You learn about calendar functions in Lessons 8–10.

Click Here	To
	Open your **To Do** list. You learn how to work with To Do tasks in Lesson 11, "Working with Tasks."
	Open the **Replicator** page, which is useful if you are working remotely or disconnected from the server. You learn about the Replicator page in Lesson 21, "Using Notes Remotely."
	Open the **Favorites Bookmarks** page. Favorites contains links to the databases and pages you visit frequently, such as your mail, address book, calendar, To Do list, and the Replicator Page (if you are a mobile user). Databases you visited recently also have bookmarks here
	Open the **Databases** bookmark page. If you upgraded to Notes R5, all the databases you had on your workspace now appear on this bookmark page. To add a new bookmark to the page, drag the task button onto the bookmark page. To remove a bookmark from a page, right-click the bookmark and select **Remove Bookmarks**.
	Open the **More Bookmarks** bookmark page, where you add any additional bookmarks that you want to use.
	Open the **Internet Explorer** page. If you have Internet Explorer installed, the bookmarks for the Web browser appear here. If you have **Netscape Navigator** installed, the bookmarks for the Netscape Navigator appear here. If you have both of these programs installed, you see one bookmark for each program.
	Opens your Address Book where you keep information on contacts.

If a bookmark opens a task such as a database, a document, or mail, it opens the task in a new window and creates a new task button (See Figure 1.2). Opening a new window for each task is similar to the way a word processing document works—it opens a new window for each document you have open, or for each document you are creating. To move from window to window click on the task button. In Figure 1.2, several tasks are open and several task buttons are displayed. When you hold your mouse over a task button, the task close button appears as shown in Figure 1.2. Close a task by clicking the close button located on the task button.

Task Buttons

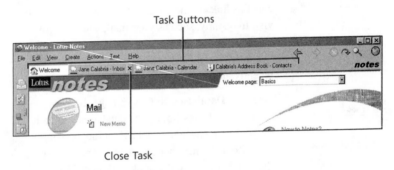

Close Task

FIGURE 1.2   Here, the Welcome Page is the active page. Note that the Welcome task button is highlighted. Other open tasks include the Inbox, Calendar and Address Book, all of which are represented with task buttons.

Create a bookmark from a task by dragging the task onto the Bookmark bar or into a folder that is located on the bookmark bar.

Opening Menus and Selecting Commands

As with most Windows applications, Notes supplies pull-down menus that contain the commands you use to work in Notes. Each menu contains a list of commands that relate to the operation of Notes. For example, the Edit menu contains commands such as Cut, Copy, Paste, and Clear. In addition, some menus change, depending on the task you're performing; for example, Notes adds the Attachments menu to the menu bar if you have an attachment in the document.

Pull-Down Menu   A menu that includes a list of related commands or actions. You pull the menu down by activating it with the mouse or the keyboard.

To open a menu with the mouse, click the menu name in the menu bar. To open a menu with the keyboard, press the **Alt** key and then press the underlined letter in the menu name. (For example, to open the File menu, you can press **Alt+F**.) Either way, the menu drops down to display a list of related commands (see Figure 1.3).

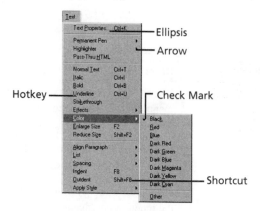

FIGURE 1.3   Pull-down menus contain the commands you use to work in Notes.

To select a command with the mouse, move the pointer to the menu command and click it. To activate a command with the keyboard, press the hotkey of the command you want. If selecting a command leads to a secondary menu, click a command in the secondary menu or press its hotkey to activate it.

Hotkey   The underlined letter in a menu name, command, or other option that you press (often in combination with the Alt key) to activate that option. This also is referred to as the accelerator key.

Menus can contain a number of elements along with the commands. For example, some commands have hotkeys that you can use to access the command from the keyboard, and some have keyboard shortcuts with which you can bypass the menu altogether. In addition, certain symbols might appear in a menu to indicate what happens when you activate the command. Table 1.4 describes the command indicators you might see in a menu.

TABLE 1.4   Command Indicators

Element	Description
Arrow	Indicates that another menu, called a submenu or cascading menu, appears when you select that command.
Ellipsis	Indicates that a dialog box or Properties box appears when you select that option.
Hotkey	Marks the letter key you press to activate the menu or command using the keyboard.
Check Mark	Indicates that an option or command is selected or active.
Shortcut	Provides a keyboard shortcut you can use to activate the command without accessing the menu; you cannot use the shortcut if the menu is open.
Dimmed command	Indicates that the command cannot be accessed at the current time. (For example, you cannot tell Notes to delete unless you've selected something; if nothing is selected, the Delete command is not available.)

Cancel a Menu To cancel a menu, point to any blank area of the workspace and click once. Alternatively, you can press the **Esc** key twice.

Viewing SmartIcons

Some people prefer to click on icons to perform program functions in lieu of accessing the menu. In most programs that are designed to run under Microsoft Windows, icons can be found on the windows toolbar. Lotus refers to their icons as SmartIcons and, by default, these SmartIcons do not display. SmartIcons are context sensitive, and they change depending upon the task you are performing in Notes. For example, one set of icons appears when you are reading a document, and another set appears when you are editing a document. To display the SmartIcons, choose **File, Preferences, SmartIcon Settings,** and then click the **Icon Bar** check box. Click **OK,** and the SmartIcon set appears on your toolbar as shown in Figure 1.4.

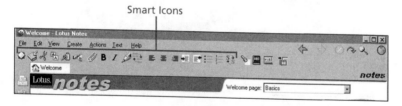

FIGURE 1.4 SmartIcons appear in black and white below the menu bar. For full color SmartIcons, choose **File, Preferences, User Preferences** and change the Icon color scheme to **Full color.**

When you hold a mouse over one of the SmartIcons, a brief description of the icon appears. You learn how to customize and change the position of SmartIcons in Lesson 22, "Customizing Notes." To turn off the display of SmartIcons, choose **File, Preferences, SmartIcon Settings**, and deselect the **Icon Bar** box.

Using Dialog and Properties Boxes

Often, selecting a menu command causes Notes to display a dialog box, but right clicking an item usually presents a menu from which one can choose **Properties** and display a Properties box. Dialog boxes and Properties boxes function similarly in that they both enable you to set options and make specific choices related to the object with which you are currently working. Each type of box contains certain elements that you need to understand in order to use it.

Figure 1.5 shows a sample dialog box. The User Preferences dialog box, which you access by choosing **File**, **Preferences**, **User Preferences** from the menu, contains many of the elements common to Notes dialog boxes. In fact, many of the elements are common to Windows dialog boxes, as dialog boxes are really an element found in all products designed to run in Windows. Table 1.5 describes those elements and explains how to use them.

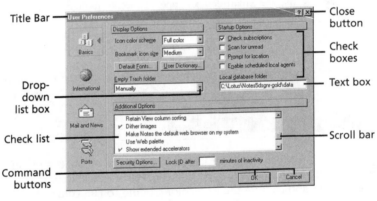

FIGURE 1.5   Use dialog boxes to make additional choices related to the selected menu command.

TABLE 1.5   Dialog Box Elements

Element	Description
Title bar	Indicates the name of the dialog box (such as the Open Database dialog box).
Drop-down list box	Displays one option from a list; click the arrow to the right of the box, and the box drops down to display the entire list.
List box	Displays a list of options so that you can see more than one choice at a time.
Scroll bar	Enables you to display additional items in a window or list box; click the up or down arrow to see more.
Text box	Enables you to enter a selection by typing it in the box.
Command button	Completes the commands or leads to another related dialog box that contains more options.
Close (X) button	Closes the dialog box without saving changes.
Check boxes	Enables you to select or deselect options individually; when the option is selected, a check mark appears in a small square box beside the option.
Radio buttons	(Not shown in figure) Enables you to select or deselect from a group of options. Unlike check boxes where you can select more than one option, radio buttons allow you to select only one option.
Check list	Enables you to select one or more items from a displayed list of options; click an option to select or deselect it, and a check mark appears beside it or disappears, respectively.

To use a dialog box, make your selections, as described in Table 1.5, and then choose a command button. The following list describes the functions of the most common command buttons:

- **OK** or **Done**—Accepts and puts into effect the selections you've made in the dialog box, and then closes the dialog box. Pressing the Enter key on your keyboard has the same effect as clicking the OK or Done button.

- **Cancel**—Cancels the changes you've made in the dialog box and closes it (as does the Close (X) button at the right end of the title bar).

- **Browse**—Browse (or any other button with an ellipsis following the button's name) displays another dialog box.

- **Open**—Open (or any other button with only a command on it) performs that command.

- **Help**—Displays information about the dialog box and its options.

 I Can't Get Rid of the Dialog Box   After you've opened a dialog box, you must cancel or accept the changes you've made and close that dialog box before you can continue to work in Notes. Use the command buttons or the Close (**X**) button to close the dialog box.

Like a dialog box, a properties box also presents options that are related to the menu commands. However, you work with a properties box in a different way than you work with a dialog box. A properties box displays only the properties of a specific item, such as selected text or a database. properties are types of information about an item such as its name, location, settings, design, size, and so on. When you make a selection in a properties box, it takes effect immediately—even though the Properties box remains onscreen as you work.

Properties boxes contain tabbed pages that offer various options for the item you have selected. Figure 1.6 shows the properties box for a database.

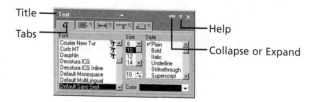

FIGURE 1.6 Use a Properties box to change the properties or attributes of selected items.

Properties boxes have many of the same elements that dialog boxes have: drop-down lists, list boxes, text boxes, and check boxes, for example. However, Properties boxes also contain the additional elements described in Table 1.6.

TABLE 1.6 Properties Box Elements

Element	Description
Title of Properties Box	All Properties boxes begin with the word *Properties*. You select the element for which you want to change the properties in the drop-down list in the title bar.
Tabs	Named flaps that represent pages of options related to the selected element.
Help	Click this button to launch context-sensitive help.

Because a Properties box can remain onscreen while you work, you might want to reposition it on your screen. To move a Properties box, click the title bar and drag it to a new position.

Collapse and Expand   Click the **Collapse** icon on the title bar of a Properties box to collapse it. Collapsing hides all but the title bar and the tabs, and it frees up space on the workspace. When it is collapsed, the icon becomes the Expand icon. Click the **Expand** icon to expand the Properties box back to its original view and size.

Changing and Locking Your Password

When you first open Lotus Notes, the password you enter is the one assigned to you by your Notes Administrator. Change your password so that no one else can use your user ID to access shared Notes databases.

A password can have any combination of keyboard characters, as long as the first character is alphanumeric and you don't use spaces. When you change your password, your new password needs to contain at least eight characters unless your Notes Administrator tells you otherwise. Be careful about how you capitalize your password, though, because *PASSWORD* is different from *password*.

Use the following steps to change your password:

1. Choose **File**, **Tools**, **User ID** from the menu.

2. Enter your current password in the box (see Figure 1.7) and click OK.

FIGURE 1.7   As you enter your password, you see are a series of X's.

3. When the User ID dialog box appears, click **Set Password**.

4. Enter your current password and click **OK**.

5. In the Set Password dialog box, enter your new password (see Figure 1.8). Be sure to type it correctly because you can't see the characters you type. Click **OK**.

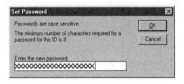

FIGURE 1.8   Enter a new password, keeping in mind that the default setting requires a minimum of eight characters and no spaces. Check with your Notes administrator if you want to use fewer than eight characters.

6. Enter the new password again to confirm it. Click **OK**.

7. Click **Done** to close the User ID dialog box.

Always protect your password. Don't share it with anyone, and don't write reminders to yourself that you leave in obvious places (such as the Post-It note on your monitor).

Someone Is Accessing My Mail!   Don't give your password to others, and never give your User ID file to others! If someone has your ID, changing your password does not stop him from accessing your mail because the password is stored in the User ID file. For further security, it's also a good idea to change the password that was assigned to you by your Notes administrator. Typically, the administrator assigns a password that is easy for him (and you) to remember so that you can get up and running on Notes. It's not unusual for that password to be the same password that is assigned to all Notes users. Shortly after you become familiar with Notes, take the time to change your password—and keep it to yourself!

Locking Your ID

After you've opened the Lotus Notes program and have been working with it, your personal information is at risk if you walk away from your desk and leave Lotus Notes running. You've already entered your password, so anyone who walks up to your desk can access any data that you can, including your mail database.

When you leave your desk, lock your ID so that no one else can access your Notes files without first entering your password. To lock your ID, choose **File, Tools, Lock ID** from the menu; or press **F5**; or click the **Lock ID** SmartIcon if it is displaying. You can't always predict when you're going to be pulled away from your computer, and you might not have time to manually lock your ID. Notes can automatically lock your ID for you after a specified time period. To set up this automatic lock, choose **File, Tools, User Preferences** from the menu to open the User Preferences dialog box. Enter the number of minutes in the Lock ID After_____ Minutes of Inactivity field. Click **OK**.

Exiting Notes

When you're finished with Notes, you can close the program in several different ways:

- Choose **File, Exit Notes**.
- Double-click the application's Control menu button.
- Click the application's Control menu button, and choose **Close** from the menu.
- Press **Alt+F4**.
- Click the Close (**X**) button at the right end of the Notes title bar.

In this lesson, you learned how to start Notes, navigate the Notes window, open menus, use dialog boxes and Properties boxes, change your password, and exit Notes. In the next lesson you learn about working with databases.

LESSON 2
Working with Databases

In this lesson, you learn how to open a database, use views, and read the Status bar. You also read the About and Using this Database documents.

Reading the About and Using Documents

Everything that is stored in Lotus Notes is stored in a database—for example, your mail is contained in a mail database, and when you click on **Help** you open the Help database. Lotus Notes is much more than email, however, and its real purpose and function is as a groupware tool—a place for you and your co-workers to come together for discussions, sharing and editing of documents and information, communication through email, and so forth. In this lesson you learn how to open a database and use those elements that are common to all databases, such as views and supporting help documentation. The mail database is used in the example here, but if you have access to another database created by your company, you can use that database while working through this lesson.

To open a database from a bookmark, click on the Databases button on the Bookmark Bar to display the Databases bookmark page. Click the bookmark to open a database. The first time you open a database, the About this Database document might appear, stating the purpose of the database.

You can view the About document whenever you are in the database or when you select the database. To view the document, choose **Help, About this Database** from the menu. Figure 2.1 shows the About this Database document for a discussion database. To close the document, press the **Esc** key.

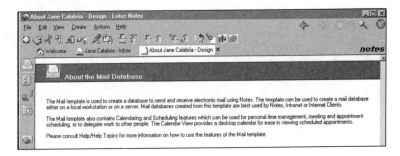

FIGURE 2.1   Read the About This Database document to learn about each database you use.

A database can also contain a Using This Database document. The Using document provides more detailed information on using the database. To access the Using document, open the database or select it on the bookmark page and select **Help**, **Using this Database** from the menu. To close this document, press the **Esc** key. Figure 2.2 shows the Using this Database document for the Personal Address Book database.

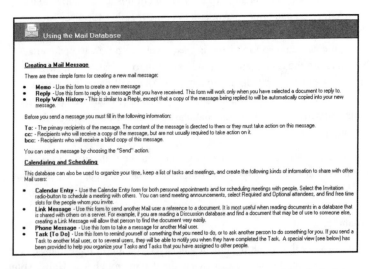

FIGURE 2.2   The Using This Database document provides helpful information on how to use a database.

Working with Views

When you open a database, Notes displays the contents of the database in a list, called a view. Each line in the database represents one document. Databases often contain more than one view or more than one way of listing information. Some views can be sorted.

Figure 2.3 shows a list of views and folders that are available in the Notes Mail database. From the Mail database, you can send, receive, forward, delete, read, and answer messages. To move from view to view, click the view name in the navigation pane on the left of the mail database workspace.

Often, you can expand or collapse views. A green triangle next to the view name (called a *twistie*) indicates that you can expand or collapse the view.

A triangle next to the column title indicates that you can sort the view. In Figure 2.3, you can sort the Who column in ascending order and the Date column in descending order.

To open a document, double-click the document in the view pane. To preview a document without opening it, open the preview pane by dragging up toward the view (see figure 2.3). Adjust the size of the preview pane by dragging its top border up or down. You learn more about the Mail database in Lessons 3–6, and more about the Preview pane in Lesson 3, "Reading Mail."

To close a document and return to the database list of views, choose **File**, **Close** or press the **Esc** key. Repeat these steps to close the database.

Action bar
View pane

Navigation
pane   Sort Button   Document

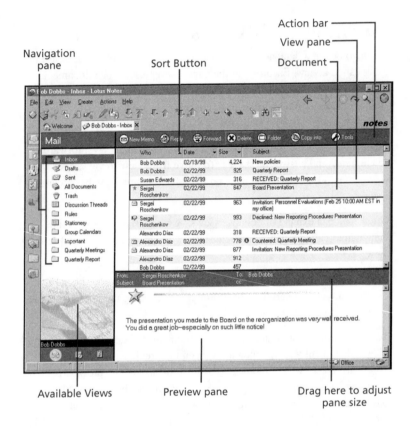

Available Views   Preview pane   Drag here to adjust
                                                pane size

FIGURE 2.3   A view lists the documents of a database; most databases contain more than one view.

Reading the Status Bar

The Status bar, located at the bottom of the Notes window, displays messages, icons, and other information you use as you work in Notes. The
Status bar is divided into sections; some of these sections display messages, and others lead to a pop-up box or pop-up menu. When a pop-up
menu appears, you can select from the menu to make changes in your
document or location. Figure 2.4 shows the Status bar with the recent
messages displayed in a pop-up box.

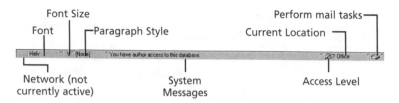

Font Size   Perform mail tasks
Font   Paragraph Style   Current Location

Network (not   System   Access Level
currently active)   Messages

FIGURE 2.4   Use the Status bar for shortcuts and information.

The Status bar is context-sensitive, and the available features depend on the task you are currently performing and the area of Notes in which you are working. Throughout this book, available options on the Status bar are referred to when they apply to the task you are performing. As you can see in Figure 2.4, each section of the Status bar is a button with a specific function. Table 2.1 describes the Status bar buttons and their functions.

TABLE 2.1   Status Bar Buttons

Button	Description
Network	Displays a lightning bolt while Notes is accessing the network; otherwise, the button label is blank. Absence of the lightning bolt does not mean you are not connected to the server. The bolt displays only when the server and your workstation are actively talking to each other.
Font	Displays a pop-up menu of fonts from which you can select. When the button label is blank, font selection is not an option.
Font Size	Displays a pop-up menu of font sizes you can assign to text in a document. When the button label is blank, font size selection is not an option.

continues

TABLE 2.1   Continued

Button	Description
Paragraph Style	Displays a pop-up menu of paragraph styles (preformatted headings, subheads, and so on) that you can apply to text in a document. When the button label is blank, paragraph style selection is not an option.
System Messages	Displays system messages about Notes activities. This box is never labeled and is always active. Clicking the messages section displays the last nineteen system messages.
Access Level	Displays a dialog box that shows your status—or level of access—to a database. Clicking the access level displays the level of access you have, as well as the groups and roles that are defined for the database.
Location	Displays your current location. Click the button to see a pop-up menu with choices to change your location.
Perform mail tasks	Displays a pop-up menu from which you can choose Mail options without having to open the Mail database first.

Understanding Local Versus Server

As you work with databases, you'll find that some databases are *local* databases, or files stored on the hard disk of your computer. These databases are available whenever you need them, regardless of whether you are connected to the Domino server.

Other databases are stored on the Domino server. This enables you and others in your organization to access information centrally and share it. When you are working on a server database, the changes you make are immediately seen by anyone else who is also accessing that database.

If you are a mobile user, which means your computer is not connected to the server at all times, the local databases you have might be *replica* of databases on the server. A replica is a specialized form of copy that maintains a link back to the original on the server. When you make changes to your local replica of the database, you are working on your computer with a database that is saved on your hard disk. However, at some point the changes you make to the database are transmitted to the server, and the modifications to the server version of the database are transmitted back to your replica. This process is called *replication*. When you replicate, your computer and the server only exchange the modified or new database documents—not the entire database file. See Lesson 19, "Understanding Replication," to learn more about replication.

Adding a Database to Your Bookmarks

Opening any database that you have opened before is a simple matter of clicking its bookmark. But what do you do if you want to open a database for which you don't have a bookmark? In that case you must use the menu commands:

1. Choose **File**, **Database**, **Open** from the menu.

2. In the Open Database dialog box (see Figure 2.5), specify the computer on which the database is stored by selecting **Local** or the name of a server from the Server drop-down list.

3. From the Database list box, select the name of the database. If you don't see the name of the database on the list, click **Browse** and locate the database file.

4. If you aren't sure which database you need, click **About** to see the About This Database document.

5. To open the database, click **Open**. The database opens to the About This Database document. Press **Esc** to continue. After you've opened the database, point to the task button and drag it to a bookmark page to create a bookmark for the database. Click on the bookmark page to release it.

To add a bookmark for the selected database, click **Bookmark**. When you choose Bookmark, the dialog box stays open so that you can select other databases and add them to your bookmarks. Click **Cancel** to close the dialog box. The new bookmark shows up on the Databases bookmark page.

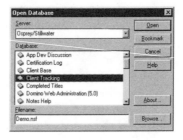

FIGURE 2.5   The Open Database dialog box.

Deleting Databases

Here's the first rule in deleting databases: Don't try to delete databases on the server. Chances are, you don't have the authority to do so anyway. Deleting databases on the server is usually the province of the system administrator, not you. If you want a database removed from the server, contact your system administrator.

Deleting a database is not the same thing as removing the database bookmark from your bookmark pages. If you want to remove a database from your bookmarks, right-click it and choose **Remove Bookmark**. When you do this, the database disappears from your list of bookmarks. However, the database file still exists on your computer or on the server.

Deleting databases on your own computer is entirely within your control. If you truly want to get rid of a database file on your hard disk, select the bookmark and choose **File**, **Database**, **Delete**. When the warning appears that the action can't be undone, click OK.

Using the Help Database

Help is only a click away. When you need help with a Properties box or dialog box, click the Help button in the box or press **F1**. A window opens displaying a Help document that relates to the box you have open. This is called *context-sensitive* help. Any time you need some assistance with a task you are performing, pressing **F1** accesses the Help database (see Figure 2.6).

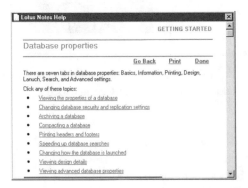

FIGURE **2.6**   This window opened when the Help button on the Database Properties box was clicked.

Looking up information on your own is very similar to using any database except that you can access the Help database by choosing **Help, Help Topics** from the menu. When the Help database opens, the Contents pane displays. The topics listed there are like chapter headings (see Figure 2.7). You click a topic and the document appears.

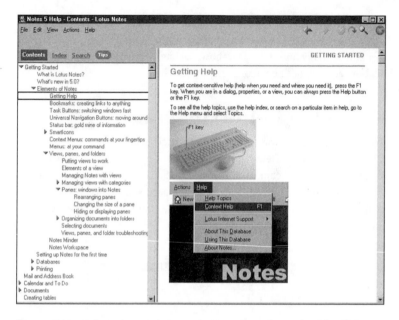

FIGURE 2.7 Select the topic you want to view from the View Pane and read the document in the right pane. Hotspots on the document lead to related information.

Another way to view the list of covered topics is alphabetically. Click the Index hotspot to see the list. To quickly search for a topic, start typing the word. A dialog box opens for you to enter the topic (see Figure 2.8). Click **OK**, and the first topic that matches the characters you typed opens.

FIGURE 2.8 Type the name of the item you want read about and click OK to open the first matching topic on the index list.

To search for a word or phrase in Help, click the Search hotspot to see the titles of every document in the database. In the Search bar at the top, type a word or phrase and then click Search (see Figure 2.9). If Notes finds the topic, the related document opens.

To <u>search</u> effectively, your database must be indexed. If the Not Indexed indicator is filled in, you need to index the database. You learn more about searching and indexing in Lesson 7, "Searching and Indexing Databases."

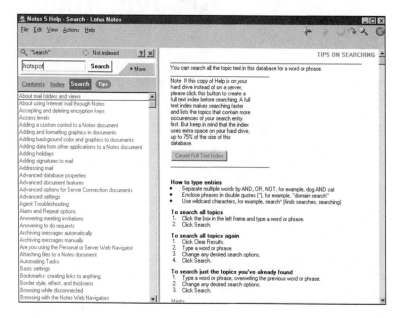

FIGURE 2.9   To search for specific text, enter the text and click Search. Click More to see more options to refine your search.

In this lesson you learned how to open and close a database. You also learned how to read the About and Using this Database documents, as well as how to read the status bar. In the next lesson, you learn how to read your mail.

LESSON 3
Reading Mail

In this lesson, you learn to open your mail inbox, select and read messages, use the preview pane, and close the mailbox.

Opening Your Mail Inbox

All the information that is found in Lotus Notes is stored in a database. Mail is no exception. Lotus Notes stores your mail in your *mail database*. The stored mail includes copies of messages you've received and sent, as well as some specialized documents such as calendar entries and tasks. To open your mail database, click on the mail hotspot on the Welcome page or click the **Mail** bookmark.

When you first open a Lotus Notes database (such as Mail), the display is split into two large panes called the Navigation Pane and the View Pane. The titles of the available views are displayed in the pane on the left, also known as the Navigation Pane, and the specific information is displayed in the View Pane on the right.

If you were looking at a database that contained a list of clients, you might want a quick way to look at those clients by company name, salesperson, or contact name. Views provided for you might be called "By Company," "By Salesperson," and "By Contact Name."

The Navigation Pane

The Favorite Bookmarks Navigation Pane, which lists labeled icons that represent mail, calendar, tasks, and other databases to which you have access, is displayed when you click on the Favorite Bookmarks Button. To

open your mail, click either the envelope icon or your name to the right
of the envelope icon. The Favorites Navigation Pane is instantly replaced
with the Mail Navigation Pane.

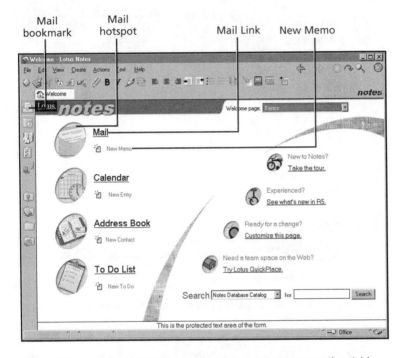

FIGURE 3.1 Notes provides several ways to open your mail quickly,
using hotspots or bookmarks. From the Welcome Page, choose a
Mail link, hotspot, or to start a new memo, click New Memo.

The Mail Navigation Pane (see Figure 3.2)lists views, such as the Inbox,
Drafts, Sent views, and Folders, that you create to organize your mail
messages. At the bottom of the Mail Navigation Pane are icons that bring
up the Calendar Navigation Pane and the To Do Navigation Pane when
they are clicked.

Views   Incoming Mail   Action Bar

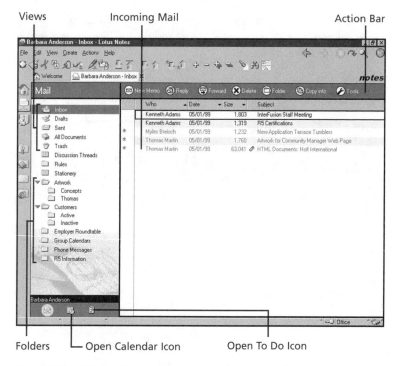

Folders   └─ Open Calendar Icon   Open To Do Icon

FIGURE 3.2   The Mail Navigation Pane with the Inbox view selected.

Resizing the Panes   You can change the size of the
Navigator and View panes to see more of one side or
the other. Point to the line that separates the two
panes until your mouse pointer turns into a two-
headed arrow, separated by a black line. Drag that
line to the left or right. You also can resize the
columns in the View pane. Use the method that was
just described for resizing panes, but drag the lines
between columns.

The View Pane

As you select different Navigator icons in the Navigation Pane, the documents that are listed in the View Pane change. For example, when you

click on the Inbox view, your incoming mail messages are visible in the View Pane on the right. When you click on the Sent view, however, your outbound mail messages are visible.

Click on the Inbox view to see your incoming mail messages. You can see who sent the message, the date it was sent, and the size and subject of the message. All unread messages have a red star in the selection bar to the left of the message (see Figure 3.2).

 No Mail?   If you don't see mail, make sure that you have clicked the Inbox at the top of the Favorites Navigation Pane. If you are new to Notes, it's entirely possible that no mail has been sent to you, so no documents are listed in the View Pane.

Table 3.1 describes the views that are found in the Mail Navigator pane.

TABLE 3.1   Mail Database Views

View	Description
Inbox	Displays mail that has been sent to you.
Drafts	Stores mail messages you're working on but have not sent yet; also contains any mail you create but choose to save as a draft.
Sent	Stores copies of messages you have sent (if you choose to keep a copy of the messages).
All Documents	Displays all messages, including those you've sent, received, saved in folders, and so on.
Trash	Holds messages that are marked for deletion until you empty the trash or permanently delete the message.

continues

TABLE 3.1   Continued

View	Description
Discussion Threads	A list of mail messages organized by conversation, with an initial message listed first and the responses to that message listed directly below it.
Rules	Displays a list of mail rules you have created. If you are new to Notes, this view shows no rules. You learn more about rules in Lesson 6, "Using Mail Tools."
Stationery	Displays a list of custom stationery you have created and saved. If you are new to Notes, this shows no stationery. You learn more about stationery in Lesson 6.
Group Calendars	Displays a list of group calendars you have created. You learn how to create group calendars in Lesson 10, "Working with Meetings and Group Calendaring."

The Action Bar

The Action Bar (see Figure 3.2) contains command buttons to assist you with your current task. For example, when you select a mail message in the View Pane, you can click one of these buttons to delete a message or to reply to a message. Like the menu bar and SmartIcons, the Action Bar buttons change depending on in the task you are performing.

Selecting and Marking Mail

Before you can read, delete, print, or otherwise manipulate a mail message, you must first select it. One message is already selected when you open your mailbox. The selected message has a rectangle (usually black) around the name, date, and subject of the message. That rectangle functions as a selection bar.

To select a different message in the list, click the message or use the up and down arrows on your keyboard to move to it. To select multiple messages, press and hold the **Shift** key and click the messages. A check mark appears in the selection bar to the left of each selected message.

You can also use the menu commands **Edit, Select All** to select all the messages in the view, and you can use **Edit, Deselect All** to remove all the checkmarks from the messages in the view.

If you accidentally select a document, you can deselect it by clicking on the check mark again.

What a Drag!   If you want to select multiple messages, place your mouse cursor in the selection bar to the left of the messages. Click and hold down the mouse button and drag down the selection bar. This places check marks next to all the messages you drag past. You can deselect messages the same way.

Reading and Previewing Your Mail

You can select any message in your Inbox to read at any time. To read a mail message, double-click the message or press the **Enter** key on a selected message. Figure 3.3 shows an open mail message.

Every mail message, or memo, contains the following elements:

- **Heading**—The heading includes the name of the person who sent the message, as well as the date and time it was sent. In addition, if you're on a Windows NT network, you might see the domain name, company name, or other information beside the sender's name.

- **To:**—The To: line shows the name of the person to whom the message is being sent. Again, the domain name might be included. If the message is coming to you, your name is displayed in the To: line.

- **cc:**—The cc: (carbon copy) line displays a list of any others who received a copy of the message.

- **Subject**—The subject describes the topic of the message, as defined by the sender of the message.

The rest of the message is the body field. The mail body field is a *rich text field*. If you cannot view all of a message onscreen at once, use the mouse in the vertical scroll bar, or use the Page Up, Page Down, and arrow keys on your keyboard to view more of the message.

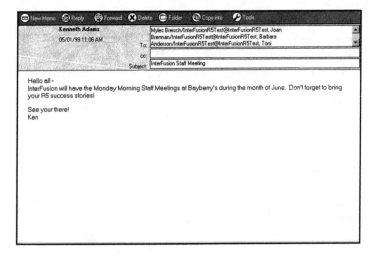

FIGURE 3.3   Messages display in the Mail Memo form.

    Shortcuts   You can press **Ctrl+End** to go to the end of a long message or **Ctrl+Home** to go to the beginning of a message.

Rich Text Field Information that is stored in Lotus Notes is stored in fields. A rich text field is the only type of field that can accept multiple data types: text, numbers, graphics, file attachments, and so forth. It is also the only kind of field in which you can assign text and paragraph attributes. The only time you can bold, italicize, or change a font is when you are in a rich text field.

When you finish reading a message, press the **Esc** key to return to your Inbox, or click on the **X** at the top right of the message task button.

Understanding Read Marks

By looking at the messages in your Inbox, you can tell at a glance which messages you've read. Mail messages you haven't read appear in red and have a red star located in the selection bar to the left of the mail message. After you open and read the message, the star disappears, and the mail message appears in black. Figure 3.4 shows both read and unread messages in the inbox, as well as messages that are marked, or selected. By marking messages, you can perform tasks such as deleting to multiple messages at one time.

Using the Preview Pane

You might prefer to read your mail by using the *Preview pane*, which enables you to read most of your messages from the Inbox view without opening them. To see the Preview pane, place your cursor on top of the black horizontal bar at the bottom of the View pane. The cursor turns into a double-headed arrow. Drag the mouse up the screen to open the Preview pane. The Inbox view is now split into three panes, as shown in Figure 3.5.

Marked messages   Selection Margin

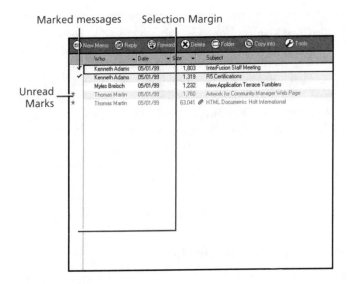

Unread
Marks

FIGURE 3.4   Red stars display in your Inbox indicating which messages have not been opened, and checkmarks appear next to messages that have been marked.

With the Preview pane activated, the mail message that is selected in the
View pane is the message that displays in the Preview pane. To navigate
through mail while using the Preview Pane, you can do the following:

- Use the up and down arrow keys on your keyboard

- Use the Navigator SmartIcons on the toolbar

- Use your mouse to select a mail message

Previewing is Not Reading   By default, Lotus Notes
does not consider previewed mail as having been
read. Unread marks continue to display until you open
individual mail messages. To change this default,
choose **File, Preferences, User Preferences** from the
menu. In the **Additional Options** box, place a check
mark next to **Mark documents read when opened in
preview pane.** Click **OK.**

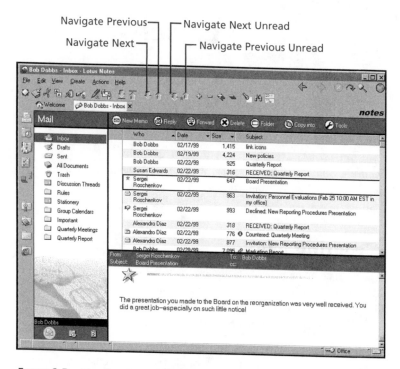

Navigate Previous — ┌─ Navigate Next Unread
Navigate Next — ┌─ Navigate Previous Unread

FIGURE 3.5 The Preview Pane enables you to read most mail messages quickly. If you prefer, press the Enter key to view your mail message, and use the navigation SmartIcons to navigate through your mail.

In this lesson, you learned how to open and close your mail database, and how to read and navigate through your incoming mail messages. In the next lesson, you learn to navigate through mail with such tasks as sorting, deleting, printing, and using folders.

LESSON 4

Creating and Sending Mail

In this lesson, you learn to create, send, reply to, and forward an email message. You also learn how to select, copy, and move text, to set delivery options, and to create drafts.

Creating Mail

The most common type of email message is the memo. It's a good idea to keep mail messages as short as possible because this helps ensure that recipients read your messages. Notes mail messages can contain formatted text, tables, graphics, attachments, graphs, and embedded objects.

You can create mail messages from any area of Notes, even when you are working in other databases. Use one of the following methods to create a mail message from your Inbox:

- Click the **New Memo** button on the Action bar.

- Choose **Create**, **Memo** from the menu.

A blank memo like the one in Figure 4.1 appears. Your name and today's date and time are displayed in the Heading of the email. A separate task button labeled New Memo displays to the right of the Inbox task button. The message is split into two parts: The *heading* is the top part and the *body* is the bottom.

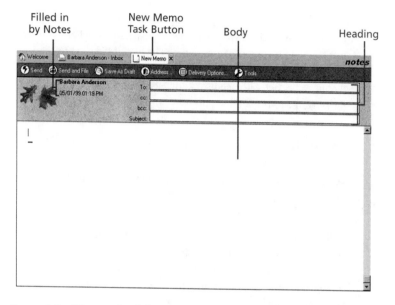

Filled in by Notes

New Memo Task Button

Body

Heading

FIGURE 4.1 The sender information is automatically filled in when you create a new email message.

Filling in the Heading

The heading of the mail memo consists of fields; you begin your email by filling out those fields. Follow these steps to complete the heading information:

1. Type the name of the person to whom you want to send the memo in the **To** field. When you need to send to multiple recipients, separate the names in the **To** field with a comma.

2. As you type, Notes searches your personal address book and a company-wide address book called a Directory to find a match for the name as you type it in. This feature, called quick-address, continues to search as you type until it finds the unique name you want. Quick-address searches for both first names and last names. If you don't like this feature, it can be disabled in the Mail section of your Location document. See "Creating Location Documents" in Lesson 20, "Setting Up for Mobile Use," for more information.

3. (**Optional**) Use the Tab key or your mouse to move to the **cc** (carbon copy) field. Type the name of the person to whom you want to send a copy of the message. The cc field is used to send a copy of a message to someone who is not directly affected by the message, but who needs to know about the contents of the message for informational purposes only. Quick-address works in this field, too.

4. (**Optional**) Click in the **bcc** field and type the name of the person to whom you want to send a blind carbon copy. The recipients of the message, and those listed in the carbon copy field, do not know that the person who is listed in the blind carbon copy field received a copy of the message.

5. In the **Subject** field, enter a descriptive title for your message. It is extremely important that you fill in a Subject because it appears in the recipients' Inbox views, telling them the purpose of your message. To create multiple lines within the subject line, press the **Enter** key.

Email Etiquette   It's important to understand email etiquette (what's acceptable, what's considered rude, and what's proper use of email at work). If email etiquette is something you've never heard of, please refer to Appendix B, "Email Etiquette." Learning proper use of email now can save you embarrassment later.

Using Address Books

Most Notes clients use two *address books*: the *Personal Address Book*, which is usually stored on your local hard drive, and at least one of the *Directories* stored on the Domino server. Like everything else in Notes and Domino, these address books are databases. You are the only person who has access to your personal address book, and your last name is usually part of the database name (for example, "Burke's Address Book"). The Directory is accessible to everyone in your company and usually contains the name of your company (for example, "InterFusion's Address

Book") in the title. The directory is managed by your company's system administrators; you manage the content of your personal address book.

While you're writing a memo, you can use the Address books to add people to your **To**, **cc**, and **bcc** fields. If you aren't sure of a person's last name or the spelling, look him up in either Address Book. Use the following steps to access the Address Books from a new mail memo:

1. Click the **Address** button on the Action bar. The Select Addresses dialog box appears, as shown in Figure 4.2. Table 4.1 lists the options in this dialog box.

2. Select the Address Book you want to access. If you are using the Notes client for the first time, your Personal Address Book is probably empty at this point, but it can be easily populated using the Copy Local button. In order to access the company-wide Directory, you have to connect to the Domino server.

3. Select the names of the individuals or groups from the available list of names. To select one person, click on that person's name; to select more than one person, click once in the margin to the left of the person's name to place a checkmark next to their name.

4. Click on **To**, **cc**, or **bcc**, depending on which address field you want to complete. Or you can click the **Copy Local** button to add this person or people to your Personal Address Book.

5. Click **OK**.

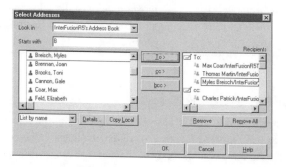

FIGURE 4.2   Choose your address book and mail recipients in the Select Addresses dialog box.

TABLE 4.1   The Select Addresses Dialog Box

Prompt	Description
Look In	The names of all the Address Books to which you have access.
Starts with	Type in the first letter of the name you are looking for to jump to the names that begin with that letter.
List by name	Pull-down choices enable you to change the order of the display of the names in the address books. Other choices include by Notes name hierarchy, Corporate hierarchy, and categorized by language and initial letter of last names.
Details	Opens up the person document in the Directory, where additional information is stored about the individual. If you select a group, the members of the group are displayed.
Copy Local	The names you select are copied into your Personal Address Book.
To, cc, bcc	Fills in the heading fields with the names that are selected.
Remove, Remove All	Removes either just the selected names, or all the names from the Recipients window.

Completing the Message

Type the message you want to send in the lower half of the screen, which is known as the *body* (see Figure 4.1). Unlike the fields in the heading, the text and the paragraphs in the body of the message can be formatted. This is known as a *rich text field*. Rich text fields can also contain file attachments, graphics, tables, links, and embedded objects. You learn more about rich text formatting in Lesson 15, "Editing and Formatting Text and Fields," and more about attachments in Lesson 17, "Working with Attachments."

Using Spell Check

Spell Check compares your text against a stored spelling dictionary of tens of thousands of words. If any of your words aren't in the spelling dictionary, Spell Check tells you that the word is possibly misspelled. In addition to your misspellings and typos, Spell Check also alerts you to proper names and unusual words that might be spelled correctly, but that are not in the spelling dictionary.

Lotus Notes looks in two dictionaries for correctly spelled words. The main dictionary is extensive, covering most of the common words in American English. Proper names, acronyms, and business jargon that are not included in the main dictionary are then looked for in your user dictionary. The user dictionary is one to which you can add words.

Spell Check reports duplicate words, such as *the the*, but it won't look at single-character words such as *a* or *I*, or words that are longer than 64 letters. It also ignores text that doesn't have any letters, such as the number 1,200,543.

Unlike other programs, for example some word processing programs, Spell Check does not operate on-the-fly. When you want to check the spelling in your message, you must be in edit mode. Edit mode enables you to change the text in the document in which you are currently working. When you're *creating* a new mail message, you're automatically in edit mode.

To run Spell Check, follow these steps:

1. Choose **Edit, Check Spelling**, or, if you have SmartIcons displayed, click the **Check Spelling** SmartIcon. If Spell Check finds a questionable word, the Spell Check dialog box appears, as shown in Figure 4.3.

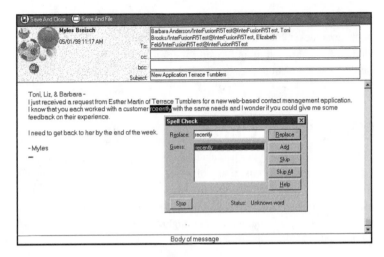

FIGURE 4.3 From the Spell Check dialog box, you can add new entries to your personal dictionary, correct spelling errors, and skip words.

2. When Spell Check finds a word it doesn't recognize, the word appears in the **Replace** box of the dialog box. You can then choose one of the following options:

- **Replace**—Enables you to change an incorrect spelling to a correct one. If the correct spelling of the word shows up in the Guess box, click the correct guess and then the **Replace** button. If Spell Check provides no suggestions and you know the correct spelling, click the **Replace** box and make the correction by deleting or adding characters. Then, click **Replace** to make the change in your message.

- **Add**—Enables you to add the word to your user dictionary. After the word is added, Spell Check recognizes it as correctly spelled.

- **Skip**—Ignores the misspelling and goes on to the next word. Use this option when the word is spelled correctly.

- **Skip All**—Tells Notes to ignore all the instances of this word in the message. This is useful when a correctly spelled proper name crops up several times in a memo.

3. After Spell Check finishes, click **OK**.

By default, Spell Check checks your entire mail message. If you want to Spell Check one word or a paragraph, select the word or text with your mouse; then start the Spell Check using the previously outlined process. Running Spell Check doesn't guarantee a perfect mail message. If you accidentally type the word *form* when you wanted to type *from*, for example, Spell Check won't catch it because *form* is a word that is in the dictionary. Also, Spell Check doesn't catch incorrect punctuation or missing words. There is also a possibility that a word was not added correctly to the user dictionary. To change words that you added to your user dictionary, follow these steps:

1. Choose **File**, **Preferences, User Preferences**. In the User Preferences dialog box (see Figure 4.4), click the **User Dictionary** button.

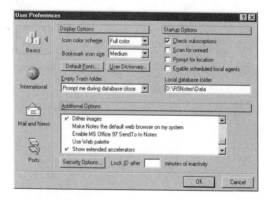

FIGURE 4.4   The User Preferences dialog box.

2. You can then make any of the following changes:

- To delete the incorrectly spelled word, select it and click **Delete**.

- To change a misspelled word, select it from the list, enter the correct spelling in the small text box at the bottom of the dialog box, and then click **Update**.

- To add a word, enter it in the small text box and click **Add**.

3. When you finish, click **OK**. Then, click **OK** to close the User Preferences dialog box.

 Automatic Spell Checking   You can set a user prefer- ence to automatically perform a Spell Check on every mail message you create. It is highly recommended that you set this option. Choose **Actions, Preferences** from the menu bar. On the Basic tab of the Mail sec- tion, place an **X** in the **Automatically check mail mes- sages for misspellings before sending.** Click **OK** to close the window.

Sending Mail

When you have completed spell check (see Figure 4.5), you can send the message or you can save it as a draft to send later.

To send the message, click the **Send** button or the **Send and File** button in the Action Bar:

Send	Notes sends the message to the recipient's mailbox and, by default, saves a copy of your message in the Sent view.
Send and File	In addition to sending the message, you are given the option of storing a copy of the mes- sage in a folder. For more information about creating folders, see Lesson 5, "Managing Mail."

Send   Send and   Save as
       File   Draft

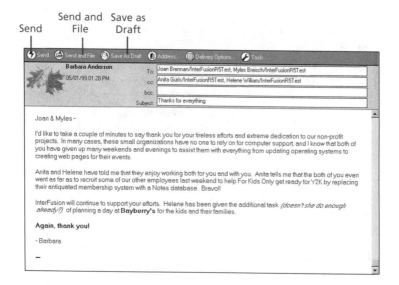

FIGURE 4.5   A completed message can be sent or saved in the drafts folder. The body of the message is a rich text field and can contain formatted text as shown here.

To save a message as a draft, click the **Save As Draft** button in the Action Bar. Your message is stored in the Drafts folder. At a later time, you can open the message by double-clicking the message from the Drafts view. The document is automatically opened in edit mode. When you're ready, send the message by choosing **Send** or **Send and File** (which allows you to choose a folder in which to save your copy)

Choosing Delivery Options

You control how and when each of your mail messages are delivered through the **Delivery Options** button on the Action Bar. Delivery Options, as described in Tables 4.2 and 4.3, have to be set prior to sending the message. If you are sending mail via the Internet to non-Notes users, some of these features do not work, and they are marked as such with an asterisk (*) in Tables 4.2 and 4.3. See Figure 4.6 to see the Delivery Options dialog box, which appears when you click the Delivery Options button on the Action Bar. To learn more about Notes and Internet mail, refer to Que's *Special Edition Using Lotus Notes and Domino 5.*

TABLE 4.2   Basic Delivery Options

Option	Description
*Importance	Choices: Normal, High, or Low. If this is set to High, an exclamation mark appears to the left of the message in the recipient's Inbox. The envelope icon to the left of the message in the sender's Sent view is red. Otherwise, no icon appears.
Delivery report	Tells Notes to place a report in your mailbox that indicates how the delivery of your message went. The default option is Only on Failure. Your system administrator might ask you to change this option if you are experiencing mail problems. Otherwise, there is no need to change this option.
Delivery priority	Marks the message as Normal, High, or Low priority. Priority governs how quickly the mail is delivered. When you send a message to a recipient on the same Domino server, it is not necessary to choose a priority—Normal priority delivers it immediately. When you send a Notes message to a different Domino server or to the Internet, High priority causes your Domino server to deliver it immediately, instead of at the scheduled delivery set by your systems administrator. Low priority means that the mail will be delivered in the middle of the night, during off-business hours.
Return receipt	Places a receipt in your mail Inbox that tells you the time and date at which the recipient received the message.

Option	Description
*Prevent copying	Prevents the recipient from forwarding, copying, or printing your message. Use this if the information is highly confidential.
Sign	Adds a unique digital code to your message that identifies you as the sender.
Encrypt	Encodes the message so that no one but the intended recipient can read it.
*Mood stamp	When you select a mood from the pull-down list, a graphic is added to the top of your memo and appears to the left of the message in the recipient's Inbox.

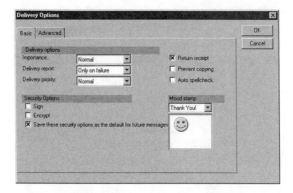

FIGURE 4.6   Set your delivery preferences in the Delivery Options dialog box. Please check with your Domino System Administrator before you send mail High priority. It might not be necessary for you to select that option for important mail.

You can find less frequently used delivery mail options by choosing the **Advanced** tab of the Delivery Options dialog box. For example, you can set mail expiration dates and request where and when you want replies to messages to be sent. Figure 4.7 shows the advanced options for sending mail.

Encrypt Sounds like you need to put on your magic decoder ring! When you choose to encrypt a message, Lotus Notes scrambles the message, and only the recipient has the key to unscramble it. Because your message travels from your PC to the Lotus Notes server and then to the PC of the recipient, encrypting the message prevents anyone who might be working at the Lotus Notes server from reading your message.

Why Is He Mad at Me? Lots of new Notes users think that the Flame mood stamp indicates that a message is "hot" (important). In the true Net Etiquette sense, flaming is an indicator that you are truly angry at someone, and is considered insulting. You might want to think twice about using this mood stamp.

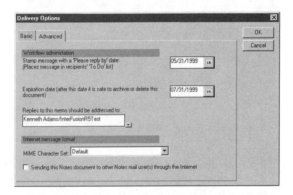

FIGURE 4.7 The Advanced Delivery Options are not used as frequently as the Basic Delivery Options. For most of your mail, you can leave these options set at their default settings

TABLE 4.3   Advanced Delivery Options

Option	Description
Stamp Reply by Date	Select the date from the calendar. The message is placed in the recipient's To Do list. It is also marked in the heading with the requested reply date.
Expiration date	Set Rules to automatically delete or archive mail messages based on an expiration date. More information on rules can be found in Lesson 6, "Using Mail Tools."
Send Replies to	Choose the individual to whom you want the replies to be sent. This is especially useful if you want someone else to manage the replies to a particular message.
MIME Character Set	Select the MIME character set you need to use when sending messages over the Internet. Unless your System Administrator instructs you to change this, leave the setting as Default.
Sending Notes to Notes	Check this if you are sending to a Notes user over the Internet to ensure that Notes-centric formatting is preserved.
Internet Message Format	HTML Only is the default setting. More information about HTML mail can be found in Lesson 13, "Navigating the Web."
Encoding for Attachments	Determines how attachments are to be encoded for delivery to an Internet account. **Accept Administrator's default** is the default setting, and it is recommended that you don't change this without talking with your Notes Administrator first.

Replying to Mail

After you've read your mail, you can choose from various reply options. To reply to a mail message, start by selecting the message to which you want to reply in the view pane, or open the message. Click the **Reply** button in the Action Bar. Select **Reply** from the pull-down list. Follow these steps to reply to mail:

1. The New Reply window appears. When you reply to mail, Notes fills in the header information of your mail message. You can make changes to the header information if you want.

2. To send a carbon copy of the message to other parties, type the names in the **cc** field.

   To send blind carbon copies, type the names in the **bcc** field.

3. Position the mouse cursor in the message body and begin typing your reply message.

4. Click the **Send** or **Send and File** button on the Action Bar.

Reply with History   Clicking **Reply with History** attaches a copy of the original message to the bottom of the reply. Use this option when you want to respond to a lengthy message, providing the recipient with a copy of the original message.

Don't Forget Others!   Use the **Reply to All (**or the **Reply to All with History)** option on the pull-down list when you are replying to mail that originally included others in the header fields. This is a courtesy that saves you time later, when you discover that you have not informed everyone in the original distribution list of your reply.

Forwarding Mail

You can forward any mail message (that has not been restricted with the "Prevent copying" feature) to another person, and you even can add your own comments or reply to it. To pass a message on to someone else, click the **Forward** button in the Action Bar. The New Memo window appears (see Figure 4.8).

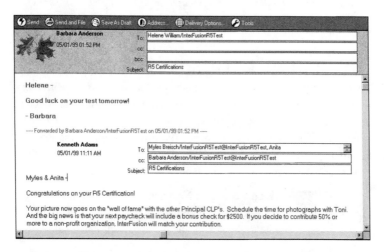

FIGURE 4.8 You can add comments to forwarded messages, explaining your purpose for sending this message.

Forwarding a mail message inserts one mail message into another so that the original header information stays intact. Complete the To: and Subject: lines and add your comments above the Forwarded by line. Click the **Send** or **Send and File** button in the Action Bar to send the message.

In this lesson, you learned how to create, reply to, and send mail. You also learned how to use Spell Check and set delivery options. In the next lesson you learn how to sort, manage and print mail.

LESSON 5
Managing Mail

In this lesson, you will learn to navigate through mail, sort messages, delete messages, use folders, and print mail.

Navigating Through Mail

There are two ways to navigate through your Inbox: Press the **Enter** key to open a message and again to read the next message, the **Backspace** key to read the previous message, or the **Esc** key to return to the Inbox view. Alternately, continue to read unopened (unread) messages using the SmartIcons. There are four SmartIcons that help you navigate through your mail without returning to the Inbox:

 Use the Navigate Next and Navigate Previous SmartIcons (plain up and down arrow icons) to navigate to the next or the previous mail message.

 Use the Navigate Next Unread and Navigate Previous Unread SmartIcons (up and down arrows with stars) to navigate to the next or the previous unread message.

Sorting Mail

By default, the Inbox view is sorted by date in ascending order, which means that the older messages are at the top of the view and the newer messages are at the bottom. You can temporarily change the sort order of the documents in a view by clicking on the view column headers. However, not all the columns in the view can be changed. How can you tell whether or not you can sort a view column? The column headers have little triangles on them. For example, in the Inbox view, the Who column header has an up triangle that indicates that this column can be resorted in ascending order (alphabetically, from A–Z). The Date column has a down triangle, which means this column can be resorted in descending order (from most recent to oldest). The Size column has a down triangle, indicating that the messages can be resorted by size, with the largest messages first.

The Inbox does not have any columns that can be sorted both ways—that is, first in ascending order, and then, when you click the column heading again, in descending order. However, you might see that sort option in other views for other databases. If the option to sort both ways is available in a view, there are two triangles in the column heading—one points up and the other points down.

FIGURE 5.1   Sorting columns on-the-fly can help you find messages quickly.

Deleting Mail

To keep your Mail database manageable, make it a practice to clear out old messages periodically. If you're not sure if you'll need the message again, either archive it or store it in a folder. If you know that you don't need the message anymore, delete it.

Deleting messages is a two-step process. First, mark the message for deletion; then, remove it by emptying the Trash.

Oops! Can I Get the Message Back? After you have emptied the trash or confirmed deletion of the message, it is *permanently* deleted from your mail database. You cannot get the message back. It cannot be recovered from your operating system recycling bin.

You can mark messages for deletion while you're reading them, or you can do it from the view pane. Use the following steps to delete a message while you are in read mode:

1. In the opened message, click the **Delete** button on the Action bar or press the **Delete** key on your keyboard.

2. Lotus Notes marks your open message for deletion and closes the message, and your next message appears.

3. Continue reading the rest of your messages, deleting those that you don't want to keep.

You Didn't Mean to Click the Delete Button   So far, you've only *marked* the message for deletion. If you didn't mean to do this, hit the **Esc** key to go back to the view. A blue trash can appears in the selection bar to the left of the messages that are marked for deletion. Select the message and then press the **Delete** key again to remove the mark.

To mark messages for deletion while you are in the Inbox or while you are in some other view, you must first select the message or messages you want to delete. This can be done using one of the methods for selecting documents that were described earlier in this lesson.

After the documents have been selected and a check mark appears in the selection margin, press the **Delete** key on your keyboard or click the **Delete** button on the Action Bar. A blue trash can appears in the selection bar to the left of each item you mark for deletion. A message that is marked for deletion remains in the view until you empty the trash from the Trash view or exit the database.

To permanently delete the message, open the **Trash** view in the Mail Navigator pane. You'll see the messages you marked for deletion in the View pane, as shown in Figure 5.2.

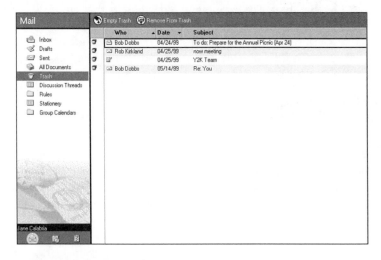

FIGURE 5.2   The Trash view displays messages that are marked for deletion in the View pane.

Click the **Empty Trash** button in the Action Bar to delete messages in the Trash view.

Change Your Mind? If you decide that you do not want to permanently delete the message, you can click the **Remove From Trash** button in the Action Bar. The deletion marks that appear next to messages are then removed. Messages disappear from the Trash view at this point, but they are visible in their original view.

All for one, one for all   A view is just a means of organizing the same set of messages in your mail database. For example, the documents that are contained in your Inbox are also contained in your All Documents view. Be careful! When you delete a message from *one* view, it is deleted from *all* views.

Using Folders

Each time you select another view in the Mail Navigation Pane, you see different documents in the View pane, or you see the same documents sorted in a different way. If you want to save a mail message, assign it to an existing folder by dragging it to that folder. Alternately, select the message and choose **Folder**, **Move to Folder** from the Action Bar and select a folder from the list of folders.

Deleting from Folders   Be careful when deleting documents from your folders because this action deletes those documents from your mail database. When you place a document in a folder or folders, it does not make a new copy of the document for each location; you are actually creating a pointer to that one document in the database. If you no longer want a particular document in a folder, select it and click on **Folders** in the Action Bar and then **Remove from Folder** from the pull-down list.

To remove mail from a folder, don't delete the document unless you mean to delete if from the database. Although you will be prompted by Notes (you know the routine…"are you *sure*?") when you delete the document, it disappears from all views except the Trash folder. And depending on your setup, it might not even be in the trash folder.

Instead of deleting, remove the memo from the folder by choosing **Folder**, **Remove from Folder** on the Action Bar.

Creating and Deleting Folders

If you don't like the choice of existing folders, create your own folders in which to save your mail. To save mail in a folder, follow these steps:

1. Choose **Folders, Create Folder** from the Action Bar.

2. In the Create Folder dialog box, type the name of the new folder directly over the word *Untitled* in the Folder name box. Figure 5.3 shows The Create Folder dialog box in which a folder named "Human Resources" is being created.

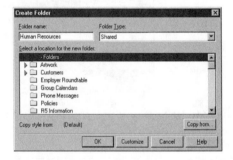

FIGURE 5.3   Type the name of the new folder in the Create Folder dialog box.

3. The default folder type is **Shared**. Leave this default as your choice.

4. Select the location for the new folder. The default location is **Folders,** but you can place your new folder within an existing folder by selecting an existing folder. For example, create a folder called Customers, and then create two folders under Customers called Active and Inactive (see Figure 5.4).

5. To select a design for your folder, click on the **Copy From** button. By default, the design is the All Documents view, so all messages can be displayed in your new folder. But you might want your new folder to look like your drafts folder, where the column header information differs from the Inbox folder. When you click the **Copy From** button, select a folder on which to base your new folder.

6. Click **OK** to save your changes and see your new folder in the Mail Navigation Pane (see Figure 5.4)

Nested folders

Figure 5.4   The Mail Navigation pane, showing nested custom folders.

The newly created folder immediately appears in the Mail Navigation pane under Other Folders. You can open it at any time by clicking on it; its contents appear in the View pane. You also can move and add messages to folders by clicking and dragging selected documents to folders you have created.

You may be wondering why we didn't tell you to create a *Private* folder. Private is one of the selections in the folder type field of the Create New Folder dialog box. Well, any *shared* folder you create in your Mail database is essentially private unless you've given rights to someone to read your mail (as described in Lesson 8, "Setting Mail and Calendar Preferences"). If you have given rights to your mail database to someone else, he can't see Private folders you create, but he can see the All Documents view of mail, which displays all documents in the database. Of course, if you *encrypt* your mail, those with access to your All Documents view cannot read the mail message. The other two types of folders that we haven't discussed are the *Shared, private on first use* folder and the *Shared, desktop private on first use* folder. These two folder types do not apply to your mail database. Our point is that there really is no point to creating any kind of folder except the default *Shared* folder when it comes to your mail database.

To delete a folder, remove it from the Navigation Pane by selecting it and choosing **Actions**, **Folder Options**, **Delete Folder** from the menu (not the Action Bar). Any memos that are contained in the folder at the time you delete the folder remain in the All Documents view of the Mail database; they are not deleted when you delete the folder.

You have rights to create private folders for most of the databases to which you have access. For example, if your company gives you access to work in a database in which they track clients or propose new products, you might create your own private folder. Follow the instructions here, but note that the Create Folder dialog box will undoubtedly present you with the option of creating a *Private* folder only. You won't see the choices for *Shared* folders and so forth.

Printing Mail

You can print one or many mail messages at a time. As with many Windows products, you can activate the Print command in several ways.

However, like deleting and moving, you have to first select the messages
in the view pane by placing a check mark in the selection bar to the left of
the messages. Then print using one of the following methods:

- Hold down the **Ctrl** key while pressing the letter **P**.

- Select **File**, **Print** from the menu.

- Right-click on the unopened mail message and then click on
  Print at the bottom of the shortcut menu (see Figure 5.5).

All three of these options present the Print dialog box (see Figure 5.6),
which enables you to select the printer, print a view, print selected documents with various page break and form options, select the pages to print,
and print multiple copies.

FIGURE 5.5   Right-click on the message to access the shortcut menu.

At times, it's useful to print a view. For example, you might want to print
out a listing of the messages that have been sent to you by one person.
The printed listing only shows the data that is displayed in the view pane,
such as Who, Date, Size, and Subject. To print a view, choose **File**, **Print**
from the menu. In the View Options portion of the Print dialog box, click
Print View. Click **OK** to print.

When you choose the **Print** command, the File Print dialog box that is
shown in Figure 5.6 appears. Table 5.1 describes the Print dialog box
options in detail.

FIGURE 5.6   Set print options in the Print dialog box. Unless a document is selected or opened before you bring up the Print dialog box, the default setting is to print the view. Be careful and be certain you are printing what you want to print.

TABLE **5.1**   Common Print Options

Option	Description
Printer	Select this button if the printer that is listed in the box is not the correct one. In the Print Setup dialog box that appears, choose the printer you want to use.
Print View	Select this option to print a listing of documents that appear in a view.
Print selected documents	Choose this option to print the selected messages.
Print range	Select All to print all pages of the message, or select From and To and enter the beginning and ending page numbers for the document you want to print.

continues

TABLE 5.1 Continued

Option	Description
Draft quality	Select this option if you don't need a letter-quality copy (dark text and nice looking graphics). Draft quality enables the printer to print more quickly. This feature might not apply to all printers.
Graphics scaled to 100%	Select this option if there are pictures in the message and you want them to appear full-sized on the printout.
Copies	Enter the number of copies of the message you want to print.
Preview	Click this button to see an onscreen preview of the document you are ready to print.

In this lesson, you learned how to navigate through mail, sort mail, delete mail, set print options, print mail and views, and use folders. In the next lesson, you learn how to create stationery, rules, and out of office notices.

LESSON 6

Using Mail Tools

In this lesson, you learn how to create stationery, select a letterhead, use bookmarks, and activate an Out of Office Message. You also learn how to send a phone message.

Creating Stationery

You can use stationery time and time again saving you from having to re-create the same mail message, addressed to the same group of people. You design how you want your stationery to look, including graphics and even a list of recipients. Stationery is stored in your Stationery folder, and you can create as many different stationery designs as you need.

Most stationery is based on the Personal Stationery template, as are the instructions in this lesson. Different from Memo Stationery, the Personal Stationery template has a total of three rich text fields to support graphics and formatting at the top and the bottom of the document. The Memo Stationery has only one rich text field.

Use the following steps to create stationery:

1. Open your mail database and click the **Stationery** folder to open it.

2. Click the **New Stationery** button on the Action Bar.

3. Choose **Personal Stationery**. Blank stationery appears (see Figure 6.1).

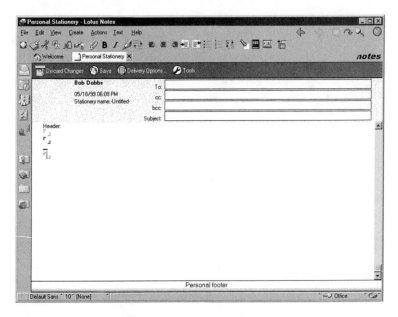

FIGURE 6.1   Blank stationery, ready for your customization. When you make changes and save this stationery, all fields are in edit mode at the time you create memos using this stationery, so changes to the fields can be made "on-the-fly."

4. Fill in the header information—the To, cc, bcc and Subject lines—if you want them to remain the same each time you use this stationery. These important fields are part of the purpose of creating stationery. Information you put into these fields is saved with the form.

5. Fill in the first rich text field that appears in the body of the memo. This is an optional step; however, if you leave this field blank, it appears as a blank field at the time you create a memo using your stationery. In other words, you can't make this field disappear from the form by leaving it blank. Include any graphics or formatted text. This field name (Header) is misleading, since the *header* area of the memo is the area that you completed in the previous step (number 4). Unfortunately, we think Lotus made a bad call when they named this field Header. The result is that this stationery has two headers: one is the header area, the other the header field and they are not at all related.

6. Fill in the body field (optional). It's the second rich text field contained on this form. This is an optional step but leaving the field blank does not delete the field from your saved form.

7. Fill in the third rich text field: the footer field. This is an optional step but leaving the field blank does not delete the field from your saved form.

8. Click the **Save** button on the Action Bar.

9. A dialog box appears, as shown in Figure 6.2. Enter a name for the stationery in the What Would You Like to Call This Stationery? box, and then click **OK**.

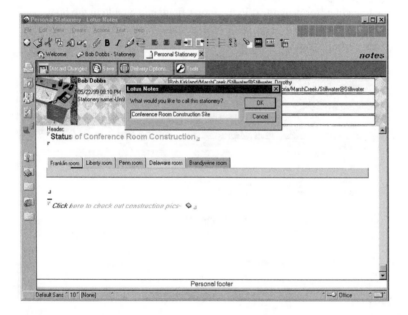

FIGURE 16.2   This Personal stationery contains information that will be used again and again, each time a status report is created. When saving your stationery create a descriptive and meaningful name so you can easily identify the correct stationery to use in the future.

10. The stationery is stored in the Stationery folder (see Figure 6.3).

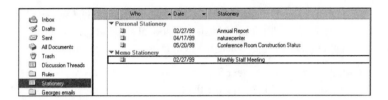

Figure 6.3　The Stationery folder is the only view that shows a list of stationery you have created and saved. You don't need to be in this view to use with your stationery, but you need to be in this view to create *new* stationery.

Figure 6.4 is an example of a Personal Stationery template with a formatted heading, formatted text in the footer field, and a table in the body field. With this kind of design leverage, you can use your stationery for many reports, such as weekly expense or sales reports.

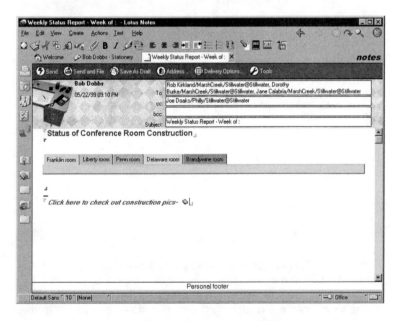

Figure 6.4　Taking advantage of the rich text fields on the Personal Stationery form, this stationery contains formatted text, a table, and even a database link.

To use your new stationery, go to the Inbox, Drafts, Sent or All Documents view and click the **Tools** button on the Action Bar. Select **New Memo—Using Stationery**. The Select Stationery dialog box appears (see Figure 6.5). Select the stationery template you want to use and then choose **OK**. A new mail message appears, including the elements you incorporated into your template. All fields are in edit mode, so you can make changes to the fields at this time. Note that your changes will not be saved as changes to the form itself; they are only reflected in the memo you are creating. Enter your information and send it as you send any other mail message.

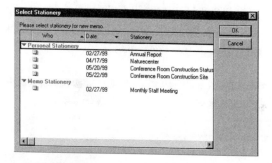

FIGURE 6.5 Choose the stationery for your new memo from the Select Stationery dialog box.

To change your stationery design, select it from the Stationery folder and click the **Edit Stationery** button on the Action Bar. Make your changes and save the document. To delete stationery, select it in your Stationery folder and press the **Delete** key.

Remember that *Memo* stationery differs from *Personal* stationery in that the Memo stationery uses the Mail Memo template. This template contains only one rich text field—the body field—and has no header or footer fields. To create memo stationery, follow the preceding instructions for creating Personal stationery, but choose **Memo Stationery** from the **New Stationery** button on the Action Bar.

Since the Memo stationery uses the Mail Memo template, a quick way to create stationery is to create a memo as you would any mail message, by clicking the **New Memo** button on the Action Bar. When you have completed the fields you'd like to save, choose **Tools, Save as Stationery**, from the Action Bar. This saves your memo as Memo Stationery.

Working with Rules

Rules determine how Notes handles your incoming mail. You create a rule by defining an action for Notes to take upon receiving a memo. With the rule turned on, Notes acts on any incoming mail that meets the conditions of the rule. For example, if a memo has the subject "National Convention," a rule can move it immediately upon receipt into your "Convention" folder, and you don't have to sort through incoming mail for memos on the topic of National Convention.

Use the following steps to create a new rule:

1. Open your mail database and then open the Rules folder.

2. Click the **New Rule** button on the Action Bar. The New Rule dialog box appears (see Figure 6.6).

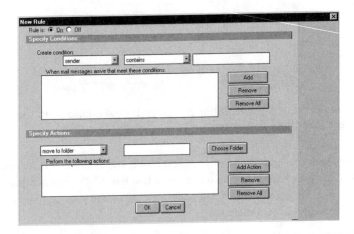

FIGURE 6.6   The New Rule dialog box.

3. Under Create Condition, select the elements of the rule's condition: From the first drop-down list, select the item to look at (sender, subject, importance, To, cc, and so on). From the second drop-down list, select the condition "contains," "does not contain," "is," or "is not" (except for Size, which has conditions relating to size). In the third box, type or select the value for which you are looking.

4. Click **Add**.

5. (Optional) To create other conditions for the rule, select
   Condition and then choose **AND** or **OR**—AND to match both
   conditions, OR to match either. Then enter the second condition.
   Click **Add**.

6. (Optional) To create a condition under which the rule doesn't
   apply, select **Exception**. Select or enter the appropriate conditions. Then click **Add**.

7. Under Specify Actions, define what action to take when a memo
   meets the conditions you set. Click the first drop-down list to
   select an action such as Move to folder or delete. If you want to
   move or copy the memo to a folder, click **Choose Folder** to
   open the folders dialog box (see Figure 6.7), where you select a
   folder and then choose **OK** (you can also create a new folder).
   Click **Add Action**.

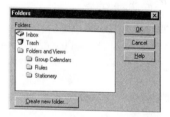

FIGURE 6.7   Select a folder from the Folders dialog box or create a
new one by clicking the **Create new folder** button.

8. After your conditions, exceptions, and actions are defined,
   click **OK**.

The Rules folder lists rules in order of precedence. To position your new
rule where it belongs in the list, select it and then click the **Move Up** or
Move Down button on the Action Bar.

To make changes to the Rule, select it in the Rules folder and then click
Edit Rule on the Action Bar. The New Rule dialog box opens again so
that you can change your settings. Make your modifications to the conditions or actions and then choose **OK**.

If the rule is getting in the way of your mail management or if you are missing an element that you need when the rule runs, turn the rule off before opening it to edit.

Using Out of Office Notices

The Out of Office message enables you to respond to incoming mail messages while you are away from the office. You create a standard message that is automatically sent as a response to incoming messages, notifying others that you are away. This is a good tool to use when you are away from the office for long periods of time without access to your mail. You can even create a unique response message to individuals or groups so that some people receive one type of response and others receive a different response.

Use the following steps to create an Out of Office message:

1. Open your mail database. Click the **Tools** button and choose **Out of Office** from the menu.

2. The Out of Office dialog box appears. There are four tabs on this dialog box. On the **Dates** tab, add the dates for **Leaving** and **Returning**. Figure 6.8 shows those fields.

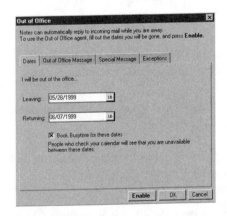

FIGURE 6.8   Out of Office dialog box with Leaving and Returning dates. The Book Busytime option is selected by default. Leave the X in the box so others will see that you are not available when they are searching for free time on your calendar. You learn about free time in Hour 9.

3. The Out of Office Message page provides a place for you to type the Out of Office message (see Figure 6.9) that will be delivered to all people except those who you will list on the Special Message and Exceptions pages. Note that this message will actually be delivered to all people unless you indicate otherwise.

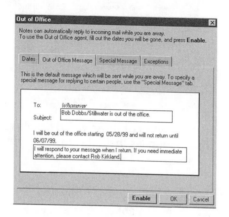

FIGURE 6.9 The basic message is sent to most of the people who send you mail while you're away.

4. (Optional) The **Special Message** tab enables you to provide a message for a special person or a group of people. To select people for this group, press the down arrow key next to the **To** box. When the dialog box appears, select people from your address book, and type your message, as shown in Figure 6.10.

5. On the **Exceptions** page, indicate the people and groups who are not to receive any notification in the **Do not automatically reply to mail from these people or groups** field. Click the drop-down arrow key and select people or groups, type the names directly into the field, or leave the field blank if you have no such exceptions.

6. While you're away you might also get mail that is addressed to a group of which you are a member, and you won't want Out of Offices responses going out to the senders. In this case, enter the names of those groups in the **Do not automatically reply to mail which is addressed to these groups** field.

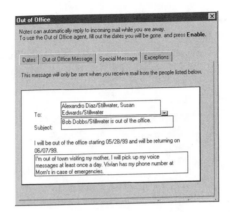

FIGURE 6.10   Select the names of those you'd like to receive a special message. Notes supplies the dates for your out of office message.

7. You may be a member of an automatic mailing, in which you don't want to reply with out of office messages. Examples are notices of company meetings or agents that search databases and notify you with automatic emails. In these cases you might not know who will be sending the notices, and therefore, you can't include them in your exclusions list. However, you can exclude notification by using words or phrases. In the **Do not automatically reply if the subject contains these phrases** field, enter words or phrases (such as *meetings*) you want Notes to look for in the subject line of incoming messages. Note that this applies only to words in the subject line of incoming messages and that these terms are case sensitive, so you want to enter both *meetings* and *Meetings*. Note too, that this does not apply to Internet mailings, for those go to the next step.

8. Consider placing an X in the **Do not send notices to Internet Addresses** field only if you have automatic mail sent to you from Web sites, list groups, and so forth and you do not regularly receive mail from others via the Internet. If you regularly receive Internet mail, you'll want to leave this field deselected. (See Figure 6.11.)

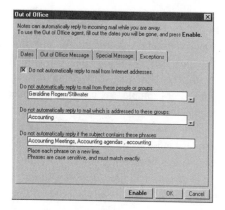

FIGURE 6.11   Enter or select people or groups who are not to receive Out of Office notices.

9. Click the **Enable/Disable** button. A dialog box confirms that the agent is enabled. Click the **OK** button. If you receive a message indicating that you should contact a developer or administrator because you are not allowed to run agents, contact your Notes Administrator for assistance.

If you return to the office on the date that you indicated in the Out of Office dialog box, you don't need to disable Out of Office. If you return before that date, disable the message using the following steps:

1. Open your mail database. Choose **Actions**, **Tools**, **Out of Office** from the menu.

2. When the Out of Office dialog box appears, click the **Enable/Disable** button.

Don't Forget to Replicate!   If you are a remote user and you have created an Out Of Office message from your remote PC, be certain to replicate your Mail database before leaving for your trip. Otherwise, the server is not notified that this Out of Office agent needs to run. Refer to Lessons 19, "Understanding Replication," and 20, "Setting Up for Mobile Use," for remote user information.

Creating a Link Message

Link Messages are used to send a document link to Notes mail correspondents. By using the Link Message feature of Notes, you also use a special mail template that fills the entire mail message in for you, except for the To, cc, and bcc fields. For example, say a new client appears in your Customer Tracking database and you want to bring that to the attention of a Mail Memo recipient. Create a Link Message and send that message to your co-worker. Understand something important about link messages: They are a feature of Notes Mail, but you won't use this to link to messages contained in your own mail file. The link will fail because only those with access to your mail database can see the document to which you are linking. If you want others to see a mail message from your inbox, *forward* that message. Use link messages when you are certain that the document to which you are linking is accessible by all the recipients listed.

In order for a Link Message to work, remember that others must have access to the database to which you are linking. Use the following steps to create a Link Message:

1. Open the document to which you want to create a link for your mail correspondents. The document can be a Notes document or a Notes database or view.

2. Choose **Create**, **Mail**, **Special**, **Link Message** from the menu. A Link Message document opens (see Figure 6.13).

3. Enter the name of a recipient in the To field, change the Subject if necessary, and then use the action buttons to add Delivery Options and Send the message as you would any other mail message.

When your recipient gets the bookmark in the mail, she opens it and clicks the link icon to open the document you wanted to share with her.

 Access Required   Your recipient must have access to the database, Notes server, or an Internet location that contains the document for which you sent the link. If not, she can't open it.

Document link

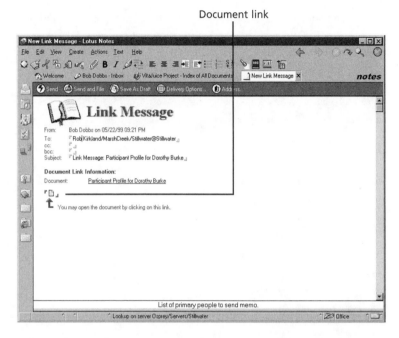

FIGURE 6.12   A Link Message sends a document link to the recipient. Notes completes all fields except the recipient field. You can add other information to the memo field and change or edit the Subject field if you like. In this example, we have filled in the To field only.

Creating Phone Messages

Phone messages are simple, straightforward forms that you use to send telephone message information via Notes. Phone messages work in the same manner as mail messages—fill out the form and click the **Send** button on the Action Bar, and the message is mailed to the person or persons in the To, cc, and bcc fields. Use the following steps to create a phone message:

1. With your Mail database open, choose **Create**, **Special**, **Phone Message** from the menu. From another database, choose **Create**, **Special**, **Phone Message**.

2. The Phone Message form appears, as shown in Figure 6.13. Fill
   in the To field and any other information that you want to supply
   with this message.

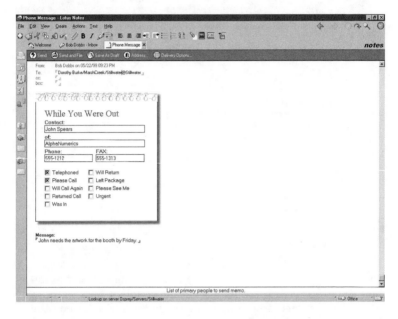

FIGURE 6.13   Add message text to the Phone Message form or simply check the boxes and add the phone number if necessary.

3. Use the rich text field, **Message**, to type any additional information that the caller supplied with his message.

4. Click the **Send** button on the Action Bar to send the message.

In this lesson, you learned how to create and customize stationery. You
also learned how to create, enable, and disable an Out of Office message;
create a phone message; and send a message link. In the next lesson, you
will learn how to work with Notes utilities and use the Help database.

LESSON 7
Searching and Indexing Databases

In this lesson you learn how to index a database and how to search a database. You also learn how to search using conditions and how to display and save search results.

Index a Database

For Notes to find information within a database, that database must be indexed. The Notes Administrator usually indexes any databases on the server (except your Mail), and then the server updates each index nightly. You won't be able to index most of the databases on the server because you need Manager or Designer access to the database to create a full-text index for it.

You are responsible for indexing any local databases and your mail database. You create a full-text index only once per database, and Notes takes care of updating the index thereafter.

How do you know when a database has a full-text index or when you need to create one? One way is to check the Database properties box. View the Database properties box for an open database by choosing **File, Database, Properties** from the menu. For a database that's not open, right-click the bookmark, and choose **Database, Properties** from the shortcut menu.

Select the **Full Text** tab in the Database properties box. If the database needs to be indexed, "Database is not full text indexed" appears at the top of the Full Text page (see Figure 7.1).

FIGURE 7.1   There is no question that this database needs to be indexed. Click Create Index to make one if you have Manager or Designer access. Otherwise, contact your Notes Administrator and ask him to create a full-text index.

Another way to see if a database is indexed is to open the Search Bar for the database. Choose any database view, and select **View, Search Bar** from the menu. The Search Bar appears above the View Pane (see Figure 7.2). It indicates whether the database has an index. You'll learn more about the Search Bar later in this lesson.

To create a full-text index for a database, follow these steps:

1. From the Full Text page of the Database Properties box, click **Create Index**. From the Search Bar in a database, click **More**, and then choose **Create Index**.

2. The Create Full-Text Index dialog box appears (see Figure 7.3). Select the options you want to apply to this index.

   Index Attached Files   Select this to be able to search all documents, including the attachments. Select **Raw Text Only** for a faster, but less comprehensive search (it searches just the ASCII text of the attachments). Choose **Binary Attachments** for a slower but more comprehensive search.

   Index Encrypted Fields   With this selected, Notes searches all words in fields including the encrypted fields.

   Index Sentence and Paragraph Breaks   Select to be able to search for words in the same sentence or paragraph.

Enable Case-Sensitive Searches   Selecting this option means that Notes differentiates between words based on the capitalization (case), so if you're searching for *Home*, the results won't include *HOME* or *home*.

Update Frequency   This option applies to server copies of databases, not to databases on workstations.

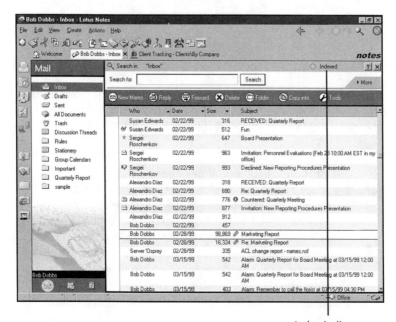

Index indicator

FIGURE 7.2   The Search Bar shows that the Mail database does have an index. "Not Indexed" displays when you need to create an index.

3. Click **OK**. Notes creates the index. When indexing is complete, the Database Properties and the Search Bar show that the database is indexed.

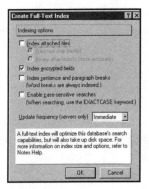

FIGURE 7.3   Be aware that each option you select will increase the size of the index and therefore the overall size of the database. However, the options do make the search more accurate.

Caution   A full-text index does take up disk space[md]about 20% the byte size of the database. Indexing a large database can therefore consume a measurable amount of disk space. In addition, Notes will only index documents that are 6MB or less in size (including attachments). Very large documents might therefore cause problems during indexing. In such a case, you should consult your Domino Administrator.

Search a Database

The best way to search a database is to search from a view. You open the database in an appropriate view and then click the **Search** icon to display the Search Bar. Enter the text you want to search for in the Search For text box (commonly called the "search box") and then click **Search**.

The results of the search display in the View Pane (see Figure 7.4). The documents are listed in order of relevance (the gray line in the left margin is darker at the top to indicate greater relevance).

Search box   Click to start search

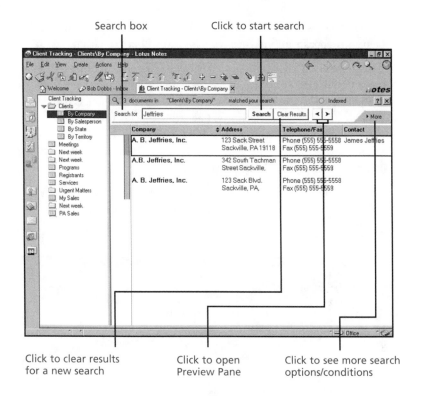

Click to clear results   Click to open   Click to see more search
for a new search   Preview Pane   options/conditions

FIGURE 7.4   The most relevant document (the one that exactly matches your search, or the document that contains the most occurrences of your search words) is at the top of the list. It has the search text in both the company name and the contact name.

Tip   The Welcome page also has a Search Bar from which you search the Database Catalog for text or open the Internet search engines, such as Excite, Lycos, or Yahoo! The Database Catalog is a database that contains information about the databases stored on the server. These same choices are available when you click the down arrow next to the Search icon.

If a document is in read or edit mode when you click the search icon, a dialog box appears to help you search for text within that document.

If you have a database view open, the Search Bar opens to help you search through the documents in the database (clicking the Search icon is an alternative to choosing **View, Search Bar** from the menu). Click the down arrow next to the Search icon (the arrow appears when you hold the mouse pointer over the icon) to view the Search menu. From this menu, which is context sensitive, you search for people or databases, do a Domain search, or open Internet search engines.

When you open one of the documents listed in the search results, every instance of the searched-for text is highlighted in the document (see Figure 7.5).

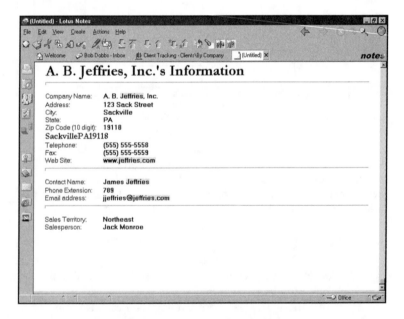

FIGURE 7.5   The search text was "Jeffries," so every mention of Jeffries is highlighted in the document.

When you no longer want to search for information, click the **Close** button (×) on the Search Bar, or click the Search icon.

Quick Search   You might not even have to engage
the Search Bar if the view you're searching is categorized or the first column is set in alphabetical order.
Just type a letter or word, and click **OK**. Notes goes
down the list of documents and stops at the first
instance of that letter or word. For example, in Help's
Index view, where the documents are categorized,
typing t stops at "Tab stops" on the list of categories.

Set Search Conditions and Options

Don't be disappointed if you don't get the results on your first try.
Sometimes, you are too specific and might not get what you want on the
first try. At other times, you are too general and get too many results to
sift through. Setting search conditions and options is a way of refining
your search to get better results.

Use Options

There are two options to use when searching. The first is Word Variants,
which expands the search to include variations from the root word (when
searching for "bowl" it also looks for "bowling," "bowls," "bowler," and
so on). The second is Fuzzy Search, which allows some room for misspellings (such as when you type "Philadlphia," but it still finds
"Philadelphia").

To activate either of these options when the Search Bar is open, click
More. The Search Bar expands (see Figure 7.6). Select **Use Word
Variants** or **Fuzzy Search** or both. Enter the text you are searching for in
the Search box and click **Search**.

FIGURE 7.6   When you expand the Search Bar, you see not only the
Options, but the Condition buttons.

Use Conditions

A condition sets criteria that must be met for a document to "match" the search. You use conditions in combination with your search text.

With the Search Bar displayed, click **More** to expand the Search Bar. Click the appropriate condition button to set the criteria for the search. Table 7.1 lists the buttons and describes what they do. When the condition is set, click **Search**.

Table 7.1   Search Condition Buttons

Button	Limits search to	Instructions
Date	Documents that were created or modified in relation to a specific date or time period	Choose **Date Created** or **Date Modified** from Search for Documents Whose field. Select how the date is to be related to the date value (is on, is before, and so on). Specify the number of days or date. Click **OK**.
Author	Documents that were created or modified (or not) by the specified author(s)	Choose **Contains** or **Does Not Contain** in the Search For Documents Whose Author field. Then, type in user names (separate names with commas), or click the Author icon and select one or more names from the Names dialog box. Click **OK**.

Button	Limits search to	Instructions
Field	Documents that contain a specified value in a particular field	Select the field from Search For Documents Whose Field). Choose how you want to evaluate the field from the list (contains, is on, is equal to, and so on). Specify the value for which you are searching. Click **OK**.
Form (by form used)	Documents that were created using one of the forms in the list	From Condition, select **By Form Used**. Select the form from the list. Click **OK**.
Form (by form)	Documents that contain specified values in the form.	From Condition, select **By Form**. In the blank form, enter values in all the fields you want to match in the search. Click **OK**.
Multiple Words	Documents that contain or don't contain specified words or phrases	In Search For, choose whether to search for any or all of the words or phrases you list. Then, in the text the words or which you want to search. Click **OK**.

The condition appears next to the search text (see Figure 7.7). It's possible to use more than one condition, although you should try searching using one condition first before further refining the search.

Condition token

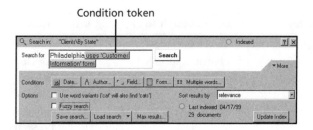

FIGURE 7.7 A condition token appears next to your search text after you define the condition. Double-click the token to open a dialog box and edit the condition. To delete the token, click it once, and then press Delete.

Refine Searches with Operators

An *operator* is a word or character that you type in the Search box to further define the search. For example, typing AND between two words in the search box means you want to find documents where both words appear. Table 7.2 lists the operators and their variations available for you to use.

Table 7.2   Search Operators

Operators and Variations	Description
And AND &	Finds documents that contain all the words or conditions combined with the operator. Example: Man AND Woman
* (asterisk)	A wildcard that represents any extension of letters, more than one character per asterisk (doesn't work with dates or numbers). Example: *ow, ho*, *ho*
CONTAINS Contains = (equal sign)	Specifies that the field before the operator must contain the text that follows the operator. Example: [title] = Favorite

Operators and Variations	Description
EXACTCASE Exactcase	Finds documents that contain words where the case matches exactly the example in the Search box. The database's case-sensitive option must be selected. Example: EXACTCASE Notes
Field FIELD [*fieldname*]	Finds documents in which the specified field contains the specified value, using the syntax *FIELD fieldname CONTAINS value*. Example: FIELD LName CONTAINS Dobbs
NOT Not !	Makes query negative. Examples: Man AND NOT Woman, Not [LName] CONTAINS Dobbs, FIELD LName CONTAINS NOT Dobbs
PARAGRAPH Paragraph	Finds documents in which words around PARAGRAPH are in the same paragraph and then ranks the documents by how close the words are. The database's indexing option must be on. Example: desk PARAGRAPH computer
Or OR | ACCRUE , (comma)	Finds documents that contain either of the conditions or words in combination with operator. ACCRUE works a little better when sorting results by relevance. Example: Man OR Mouse

continues

continued

Operators and Variations	Description
? (question mark)	A wildcard that represents any extension of letters—one question mark per character (doesn't work with dates or numbers). Example: ?ow, ho??
" " (quotes)	Place quotes around and, or, contains, and so on to have those words treated as words and not as operators.
SENTENCE Sentence	Finds documents in which words around SENTENCE are in the same sentence and then ranks the documents by how close the words are. The database's indexing option must be on. Example: desk SENTENCE computer
TERMWEIGHT Termweight	Gives weight to words in document when documents containing the words are found. Use any value between 0 and 65537, with higher number being most important in ranking. Example: TERMWEIGHT 50 manual OR TERMWEIGHT 75 automatic
= (equal to) < (less than) > (greater than) <= (less than or equal to) >= (greater than or equal to)	Numeric operators for use in searching for numbers or dates in number or date fields. Example: FIELD CreateDate > 1/1/1999

Display Search Results

Unless you dictate otherwise, search results display in order of relevance. To sort the resulting documents in a different order, click **More** on the Search Bar. From Sort Results By, select the option you want to use:

- **Relevance**   Sorts the resulting documents according to the number of matches in the document, with the document having the highest number appearing at the top of the list.

- **Last Modified**   Puts the resulting documents in date order by the date modified, with the latest being at the top of the list.

- **First Modified**   Puts the resulting documents in date order by the date modified, with the earliest being at the top of the list.

- **Keep Current Order (sortable)**   Leaves the documents in the order they appear in the view (only available if the current view provides column sorting).

- **Show All Documents (sortable)**   Displays all documents in the current view but marks the results as selected (can be sorted if column sorting is active in view).

Too many documents displayed in the results? Limit the number of resulting documents displayed by clicking **Maximum Results**, entering the number of documents you want to see as search results, and then clicking **OK**.

Save and Load Searches

If you perform the same search frequently, you can save the search criteria, so you don't need to enter all the conditions and options each time you search.

To save the search criteria, enter any necessary text in the Search box, select the options you need, set the conditions, and specify the display option you want. Then, click **Save Search**. Give the search a name (see Figure 7.8), and then click **OK**.

FIGURE 7.8   Enter a name to use when you want to call up this
search criteria again.

Later, when you want to use the search you created, you click **More** in the
Search Bar and then choose **Load Search**. Choose the name from the
drop-down menu, and click **Search**.

Save Your Search Results   If you have access privileges in the database to create a private folder, create
one to hold your search results. Choose **Edit, Select All**
to select all the documents that resulted from the
search. Drag the selected results to the new folder
icon.

Perform a Domain Search

A domain search enables you to search an entire Domino domain for documents, files, and attachments that match your search criteria. You cannot
perform a domain search unless the Domino Administrator has set up a
server for domain searching and you have access to the domain catalog
database where information on all the databases is stored.

To perform a simple domain search, follow these steps:

1. Click the down arrow next to the Search icon.

2. Choose **Domain Search**. The Domain Search form appears (see
   Figure 7.9).

3. Specify what you are searching for:

   Documents   Searches the titles and content of all Notes documents that are indexed. Click **More** and click the file system checkbox to search the file system.

Databases   Searches only database titles listed in the catalog (returns a list of databases).

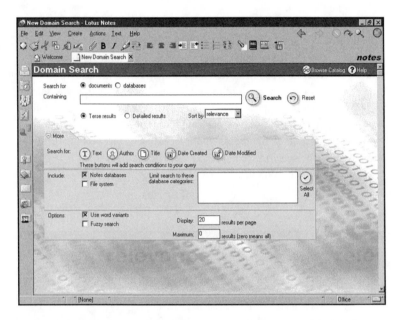

FIGURE 7.9   When you click More, you see buttons and fields that help you refine your search by setting conditions and options.

4. Enter the text you are seeking in the Search box (as you would when searching a view).

5. Select the type of results you want to receive:

   Terse   Displays only the relevance, the type (document or file system), the date of the document or file, and the title of the document or URL of the file.

   Detailed   Displays the title of the database and the author of the document in addition to all the information included with terse results. If searching the file system, Detailed also displays quite a bit of the document when the document is found in the file system.

6. From the Sort By drop-down list, choose how you want the results sorted: by relevance, by oldest, or by newest.

7. Click **Search**.

To perform a detailed search, follow Steps 1 through 6 in the preceding list. Then, click **More** to display more options. The **Text**, **Author**, **Title**, **Date Created**, and **Date Modified** buttons help refine the search for these specific items. Use any or all of these buttons. For each button you select, a new condition line appears (see Figure 7.10). Each condition line contains a logical operator (and, or, not, and so on), the type of item being searched for (based on the button you selected), text that sets the relationship to the value specified (contains, does not contain, is after, is before, and so on), and the value you enter.

Click this button to browse the databases listed in the catalog.

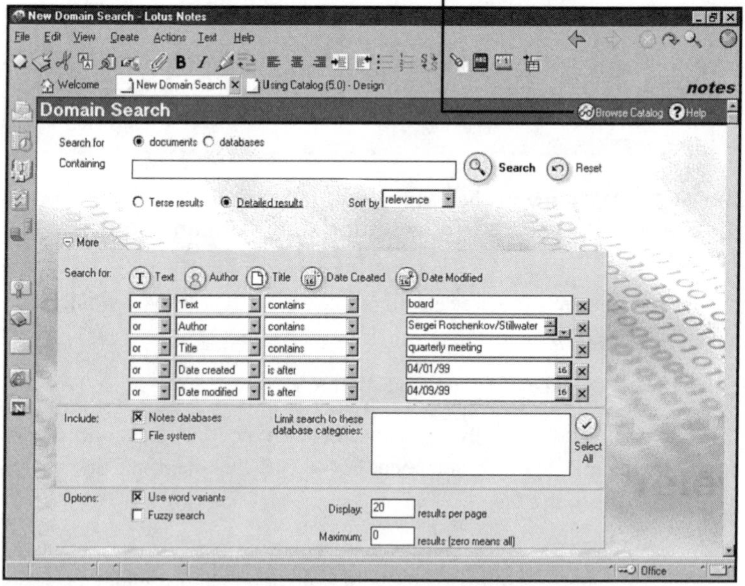

FIGURE 7.10—Each condition button adds a new line of condition statements. Click the × at the right end of the line to remove that condition statement.

In the Include section, choose to include **Notes Databases, File Systems,** or both. Enter categories to which you want to limit your search. Under options, determine whether to **Use Word Variants** in your search or perform a **Fuzzy Search.** You also specify how many **Results Per Page** you want to display and the **Maximum** number of results you want to show. Then, click **Search.**

Based on the type of results and order you specified, Notes lists as many entries as it can find. Only the number you specified is displayed on each page of results (when you search for databases instead of documents, all the results are returned on one page). A description of the number of results represented on the page as a portion of the total shows at the top of each result page. A repeat of what the query was appears on the next line. Previous and Next buttons also appear at the top and bottom of the page to enable you to go back or forward through the pages. To open one of the document or file system entries, click the link at the left of the entry. If the entries are for databases, click the database link icon to open the database.

In this lesson you learned how to index and search databases. In the next lesson you learn how to set mail and calendar preferences.

LESSON 8

Setting Mail and Calendar Preferences

In this lesson, you learn how to set your preferences for working with mail and the calendar. You also learn how to set the letterhead style for your mail.

Specifying Mail Preferences

Mail preferences enable you to determine how your mail works—who can read your mail, if mail should be encrypted automatically, whether all your outgoing mail is signed by you, and so on.

Complete the following steps to set your mail preferences:

1. Open your mail database.

2. Click the **Tools** button on the Action Bar and choose **Preferences**. The Preferences dialog box appears (see Figure 8.1). When the Mail page is active (the default) three tabbed pages appear below Mail: Basics, Letterhead, and Signature.

3. Click the **Basics** tab, if it's not already displayed. On this tab, the **Owner of This Mail File** (your name). To have Notes automatically check the spelling of your mail messages, enable **Automatic Spell Checking**.

4. Click the **Letterhead** tab. Select the default letterhead of your choice. A preview is provided at the bottom of the screen. When you change letterhead, memos created with your previous choice of letterhead do not change. New memos you create after selecting a letterhead here use the new letterhead. You can change letterhead as often as you like.

5. Click the **Signature** tab. Select **Automatically Append Signature to My Outgoing E-Mail Messages** if you want your signature added to all your mail memos. A signature can be a piece of text or an HTML file. Don't confuse this signature with electronic signatures which are an authentication feature as described in Appendix A. To create a text signature, choose **Text** and enter the signature text in the **Signature** box. To use an existing file as your signature, select **File** and enter the name of the file (or click **Browse** and select the file).

6. Click **OK**.

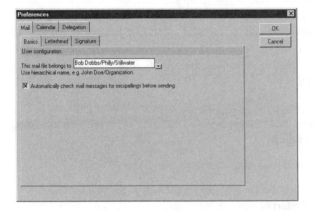

FIGURE **8.1**   The Preferences dialog box is divided into three sections—Mail, Calendar, and Delegation—which display as tabs on the first row of the Preferences box.

 Signatures that you create as text cannot be formatted, because the Signature feature of Notes does not allow that. However, if you attach an HTML file, formatting is preserved. If you want a scripted signature, create a signature in your word processing program and format it to your liking. Save it as an HTML file and attach it in the Signature file box.

HTML   Hypertext Markup Language is the coding used to format documents for the Web.

Setting Calendar Preferences

As you did with your mail, you set up how you want to use the features of the calendar using the calendar preferences. You learn more about using the calendar in the next lesson, but you can set calendar preferences even if you aren't yet familiar with the use of the calendar. For example, in the calendar preferences you set up your free time schedule and determine who can see your schedule. You specify when and how you want to be reminded of upcoming calendar events, set defaults for calendar entries, choose how time intervals display on your calendar, decide how to process meeting invitations, and specify who can view or manage your calendar.

Complete the following steps to set your calendar preferences (if you did not close the Preferences dialog box after choosing your mail preferences, skip to step 3):

1. Open your mail database.

2. Click the **Tools** button on the Action Bar and choose **Preferences**.

3. Click the **Calendar** tab.

4. Click the **Basics** tab to set the defaults for the calendar. From the drop-down list, select the type of calendar entry you want to automatically appear when you create a new calendar entry. Set the default length for appointments (in minutes) and meetings by specifying the number of minutes in the second box. In the Anniversaries box, enter the number of years you want an anniversary to be entered on your calendar. To check for conflicts when two events are set for the same time period, check **Enable for Appointments/Meetings.** In the **Advanced** section, indicate whether or not you want your Calendar entries to appear

in the All documents view of Mail and whether or not you want you Meeting invitations to appear in the Sent view of Mail. Finally, if you want to enter any personal categories for use in the calendar, type the category text in the **Personal Categories** text box.

5. Click the **Freetime** tab (see Figure 8.2), if it's not already displayed. Check the days you want to include in your free time schedule (the time you are available for meetings). For each day you checked, enter the hours of that day for which you are available for meetings.

6. (optional) Use the drop-down menu to determine who can request your free time information. Leaving this field blank means that everyone in your company directory (address book) can see when you have free time on your calendar. Viewing free time is not the same as viewing appointments or other information on your calendar, as you will learn in Lesson 9, "Using the Calendar."

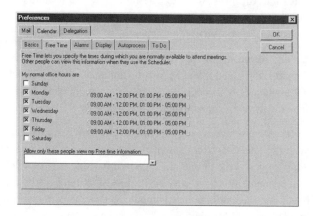

FIGURE 8.2 The Preferences dialog box with the Calendar Freetime tab selected. Here you indicate which days and times you are available.

7. Click the **Alarms** tab. Select **Enable Alarms** if you want Notes
   to alert you of upcoming events that you have entered in your
   calendar. When you select this field, the dialog box shows new
   fields, and a list of calendar entry types. Select the types of calendar entries about which you want to be reminded. Then enter
   the number of minutes or days in advance you want to receive
   the reminder. If you want to be alerted by a sound, select the
   Default Sound from the drop-down list (if your computer has
   sound capabilities).

8. Click the **Display** tab. To set the length of day you want to see
   in the calendar pages, indicate when you want the calendar day
   to start by selecting a time in the **Start displaying times at**
   field. Do the same for the ending time in the **Stop displaying
   times at** field. Select a number of minutes from the **Each time
   slot lasts** drop-down list to decide how far apart the times on
   your calendar should display as in 60-minute increments, 30-
   minute increments, and so forth.

9. Click the **Autoprocess** tab to determine how you want to process
   meeting requests. You must respond to all requests for meetings
   unless you select one of the following:

   Do not automatically process meeting invitations—This is the
   default setting, and if you keep it, no automatic processing of meeting invitations will occur. You receive meeting invitations in your
   Inbox, and you respond manually by accepting or declining.

   Automatically processing meeting invitations from all users—
   With this selected, Notes automatically accepts any meeting invitations for you if the time of the proposed meeting is free in your free
   time schedule. If you're busy at the time of the proposed meeting,
   Notes auto-declines the meeting, but places a memo in your Inbox
   titled "Declined Meeting Name" so you can accept later.

   **Automatically process meeting invitations from the following
   users**—The same rules apply as Automatically process meeting
   invitations from all users, except that this applies not to all users,
   but only to those you indicate. When you choose this option, a new
   field appears allowing you to select a person, people, or a group(s)
   from the Address Book.

Delegate meeting invitations to the following person—Forwards all meeting invitations to the person you specify. This is useful if someone else manages your calendar.

10. After you reply to a meeting invitation, the invitation remains in your Mail Inbox. To no longer see meeting invitations to which you replied, check **Remove Event Requests from my Inbox After I Respond to Them**. To prevent meeting replies from displaying in your Inbox, select **Don't show Meeting replies in my Inbox**.

11. Click the To Do tab. Deselect **Always show current To do's on today's calendar** if you don't want your To Do list to display in your calendar. You will still see To Do's in your To Do view.

12. Click **OK**.

Setting Delegation Preferences

The Delegation preferences are divided into two tabbed pages: Mail Delegation and Calendar Delegation. On these pages, you determine who can access your mail, see your calendar entries, and so forth. If the boxes remain blank, no one but you can do any of these. Putting someone's name in any one of the options gives that person permission to do that activity at any time. To select a name from the address book, click the down arrow next to the text box.

To set Delegation preferences, follow these steps (if the Preferences box is open, skip to step 3):

1. Open your mail database.

2. Click the **Tools** button on the Action Bar and choose **Preferences**.

3. Click the **Delegation** tab (see Figure 8.3). On this tab you specify who can read your mail and calendar; who can read and send mail on your behalf and read your calendar; who can read, send, and edit any document in your mail file; and who can delete mail and calendar entries.

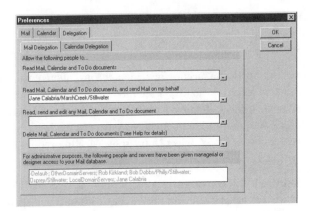

FIGURE 8.3   The Mail Delegation tab under Delegation in the Preferences dialog box is where you give access rights to your calendar and mail.

Click the drop-down arrow key in every field to determine

Who can **Read Mail**, **Calendar** and **To Do** documents using the drop-down menu in that field. People you include in this field can read all your mail messages except for encrypted messages, and all your calendar and To Do items except those marked private. By default the field is blank, and no one has this right.

Who can **Read Mail, Calendar and To Do documents and send Mail on my behalf** using the drop down menu in that field. People you include in this field can read all of your mail messages except for encrypted messages, all of your calendar and To Do items except those marked private. They can also send mail on your behalf, and when they do, mail messages will be marked By default the field is blank, and no one has this right. When others send mail on your behalf, they open your database and create a memo.

Who can **Read, send, and edit any Mail, Calendar and To Do document**. This is the same as the preceding selection, but with editor rights, so that they can edit your mail.

Who can **Delete Mail, Calendar and To Do documents** (*see Help for details). (The people you select to do this must already have been specified to read, send, and edit your Mail documents.) Here, designees also have the rights to delete documents. If they are listed in the Read Mail, Calendar, and To Do documents, and send Mail on my behalf fields, they can delete only messages that they create on your behalf. If they are also listed in the read send and edit any document field, they can delete any messages in your mail database.

5. Click **OK** to accept the settings and close the Preferences dialog box.

Opening Someone's Mail, Calendar, and To Do

For others to read mail, send mail, set appointments, and use the rights you have just given them, they need to open your mail database, or if you've been given rights, you need to open their mail database. To do so, choose **File**, **Database**, **Open**; switch to the mail server on which your mail is located; click the **Mail** folder; and select the database you want to open. If you have difficulty finding the mail database of another person, consult your Mail Administrator. Also, note that you do not need to give your password to someone else. When you assign these rights, those to whom you give access can use those rights without needing to know your password.

When you open another mail database, depending upon the access rights given you, you can see that person's Mail, Calendar, or To Do views.

When you give people access to your mail database, they can't read your encrypted mail sent to you, and you can't read encrypted messages they create on your behalf unless your user ID contains the encryption key used to encrypt the messages. Consult with your Administrator if you need to read each other's encrypted mail or if your designee needs to send encrypted mail on your behalf.

Using the Notes Minder

As long as you have your Notes client running, even minimized, you receive notification of any new mail. If you exit Notes, however, you have no idea that a new, and possibly urgent, memo has been delivered to your Mail database.

Notes has a utility that notifies you of new mail and any Calendar alarms even when you aren't running your Notes client. The utility is called the *Notes Minder*. When the Notes Minder is running, an envelope icon displays in the system tray of your Windows 95/Windows 98/Windows NT taskbar. The current status or number of new mail messages received pops up when your mouse point points to the icon. For example, it might read "Mail last checked at 4:45 PM." Double-clicking the icon launches Notes in your Mail file.

Clicking on the Notes Minder icon with the right mouse button pops up a menu (see Figure 8.4).

FIGURE 8.4   Right-clicking on the Notes Minder icon displays a pop-up menu.

Select a menu choice to do one of the following:

- **Open Notes** opens the Notes client and displays your Inbox.

- **Check Now** checks the status of your Mail file.

- **View Mail Summary** opens a dialog box that displays the unread messages in your Inbox. Double-clicking one of the messages in the Unread Mail Summary dialog box opens the Notes client and displays that message. To close the dialog box without viewing a mail message, click **OK**.

- **Properties** displays the Options for the Lotus Notes Minder dialog box (see Figure 5.8). In the Properties box, you set the types of notifications you want to receive (audible, visual, and/or missed alarms). You also specify how frequently you want the Notes Minder to check for incoming mail, or you can disable checking. Click **OK** to close the dialog box.

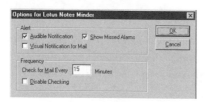

FIGURE 8.5   Specify whether you want to receive audible or visual notification when you get new mail, or both.

- **Enabled** has a check mark when Notes Minder is enabled. You click this menu selection to enable or disable the Notes Minder.
- **Exit** exits the Notes Minder.

Start Notes Minder initially by choosing **Programs, Lotus Applications, Notes Minder** from the Start menu (click Start on the Windows taskbar). Your Notes client does not have to be open.

Alternately, have the utility automatically start when you log on your computer by putting the executable file in the Start folder. To do this in Windows 98, choose **Settings, Taskbar & Start Menu** from the Start menu. Click the Start Menu Programs tab, and then choose **Add**. Click **Browse**, and locate the Notes Minder executable file (nminder.exe in the Notes folder). Select it, and choose **Open**. Click **Next**, and then double-click the StartUp folder in the Select Folder to Place Shortcut In list. Click **Finish**. To do this in Windows 95 or NT 4.0, check the Help files of these operating systems under "start up."

In this lesson, you learned how to set your preferences for both mail and the calendar, how to choose letterhead and how to use Notes Minder. In the next lesson, you learn how to use the calendar.

LESSON 9

Using the Calendar

In this lesson, you learn how to open and select calendar views, make entries in your calendar, check available time of others for meetings, respond to meeting invitations, and print the calendar.

Selecting Calendar Views

To open your calendar, click the Calendar bookmark or select **Calendar** from the Welcome Page, as shown in Figure 9.1. If you have your mail opened, you can click the calendar icon at the bottom of the Mail Navigator Pane, as shown in Figure 9.2.

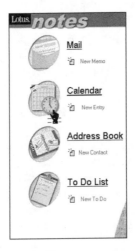

FIGURE 9.1   Access your Calendar from the Welcome Page.

—Calendar icon

FIGURE 9.2   Optionally open the calendar from your Mail Navigator Pane by clicking on the calendar icon.

The four calendar views that are available can be selected by clicking on the view name in the Calendar Navigator Pane (see Figure 9.3):

- **Calendar**—Displays appointments you make and meeting information for meetings you have accepted, in a one-day, two-day, one-week, two-week, or one-month format.

- **Meetings**—Lists meeting invitations and meetings you have accepted by date and meeting time.

- **Group Calendars**—Lists all group calendars that you have created.

- **Trash**—Stores all items in your Mail database (messages, calendar items, to do items) marked for deletion.

You can quickly go to a different date or change the format of the view by clicking on the Change View display buttons (see Figure 9.4).

Other ways to move around the calendar are

- To go to the current date, click the sun icon in the lower-right corner of the calendar.

- To go to a specific date, click the date on the date picker.

- To move ahead or back one month click the arrow icons located on the date picker.

- To move the calendar back or forward one page at a time, click the arrows located to the left (back) and right (forward) of the sun icon.

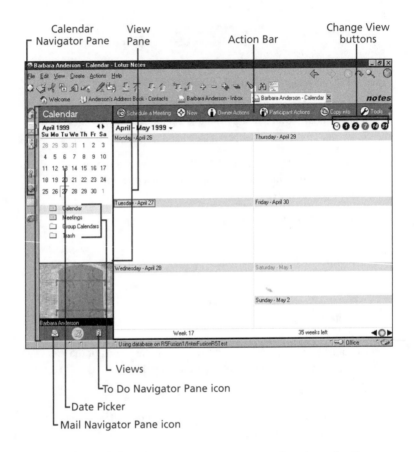

Views

To Do Navigator Pane icon

Date Picker

Mail Navigator Pane icon

FIGURE 9.3 The Calendar Navigator Pane contains views for the calendar.

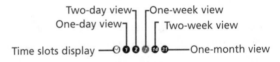

FIGURE 9.4 Change your view quickly and easily with the Change View buttons.

Understanding Calendar Entries

As explained in Lesson 8, "Setting Mail and Calendar Preferences," some calendar entries (Appointments, Meeting Invitations, and Events) affect your free time availability. Although others might not be able to view your *calendar*, they might be able to check your schedule to find out if you are available. Check with your Domino administrator if you have difficulty seeing the free time of others, or if others have difficulty seeing your free time. There are several types of calendar entries you can create:

- An **Appointment** is an entry in your calendar that does not include the process of inviting others in Notes. Appointments can have a start and end time, can be set to repeat, and can be marked private so that even those with access to your calendar cannot read the particulars about private appointments.

- **Meeting Invitations** are appointments in which you include and invite others from your organization. If those you invite are part of your Domino Mail system, Meeting Invitations are distributed to the participants' Inboxes. Meetings also appear on the calendars of invited participants when the participant has accepted the invitation. Like appointments, meetings have time values, have a beginning time and ending time within one calendar day, and can be set to repeat. You can send meeting invitations to people over the Internet and they will receive a text message, but not all of the formatting and graphics you see in the Notes form.

- **All Day Events** have a duration of at least one full day. Unlike appointments and invitations, you cannot specify a start time or end time. Events are typically used to schedule vacations, seminars, conventions, and the like.

- An **Anniversary** is an occasion that has no time value such as a birthday, working holiday, or payday. Anniversaries do not affect your free time. Anniversaries appear on your calendar only and can be set to repeat.

- **Reminders** are notes to yourself that display on your calendar on the time and date you assign to them. Reminders have a beginning time, but no time value (that is, no ending time). They display on your calendar only, and can be set to repeat. One common use is a reminder to make a phone call. Do not confuse Reminders with Alarms or To Do's.

Creating a Calendar Entry

The steps for creating an appointment, anniversary, reminder or event are similar. Here, we discuss creating those kinds of calendar entries. The steps for scheduling a meeting are found in Lesson 10, "Working with Meetings and Group Calendaring," under "Scheduling Meetings."

You can create a calendar entry at any time while in Lotus Notes, and you don't have to have the mail database open. To create a calendar entry, do one of the following:

> **From your Calendar Navigator Pane**—To create an **Appointment**, **Anniversary**, **Reminder**, or **Event**, click the **New** button on the Action Bar. To create a meeting, click the **Schedule a Meeting** button on the Action Bar.

> **From within the Calendar**—Double-click a date or time slot in the calendar displayed in the Calendar View Pane. Choose the Calendar Entry type from the Change Calendar Entry type list.

Depending on the type of calendar entry you create, the entry fields vary slightly. But each type of calendar entry, except meetings, have two tabbed pages: the Basic and the Options pages. Figure 9.5 shows the calendar event form.

Use your mouse cursor or the **Tab** key to move from field to field when creating a calendar entry. Remember that neither all the sections nor all the fields will be available to you. The following list describes the fields and their intended content on the **Basics** page of the calendar entry form:

> **Subject**—Type in several words that describe the calendar entry. These words will appear in the Calendar views and if sent to anyone else, in the Subject column in the Inbox.

> 🔟 **Begins / Ends (Date fields)**—Enter the start and end dates or click the date icon and select dates from the pop-up menu. Use the left and right arrows at the top of the pop-up calendar to move from month to month. Figure 9.6 shows the date pop-up calendar.

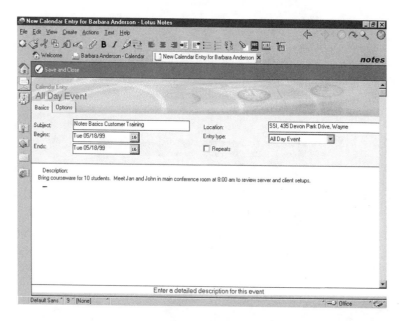

FIGURE 9.5 An All Day Event does not have a beginning or ending time but does have a beginning and ending date. Use this for scheduling vacation time and days you spend away from the office.

FIGURE 9.6 Using the pop-up calendar to select a date is a quick and easy way to enter dates.

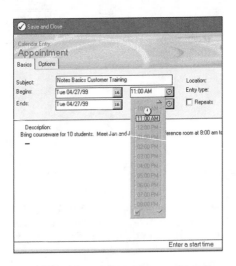**Begins / Ends (Time fields)**—Type in the start time and end time for the calendar entry. If you click the clock icon, you will see a time scale. Drag the indicators up or down the scale to set the time and duration of the appointment. Use the up and down triangles to see different parts of the scale (see Figure 9.7). Click the green check mark to accept the time setting.

FIGURE 9.7 Using the time scale to select a time is a quick method for filling in time and date fields.

Repeats—Place an **x** in the **Repeats** checkbox to set parameters for calendar entries that occur more than once, such as a weekly status meeting. The Repeat Options dialog box appears (see Figure 9.8). In the Repeat Rules dialog box select the **Repeat** interval from the drop-down list. Based on that choice, set the specifics of the frequency and intervals. Then, set the **Starting** date. Choose an ending date using the **continuing for** or **to** fields. Click **OK**.

The last field on this page is the **Description** field. Use this area to provide a more detailed description of the calendar entry. For example, you might want to supply an agenda for a proposed meeting. The Details field is a rich-text field, allowing you to apply text and paragraph formatting, as well as to insert file attachments and embed objects.

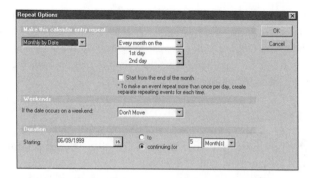

FIGURE 9.8 Fields in the Repeat Options dialog box change, depending on the type of repeat you select (monthly by date, weekly, and so forth).

The **Options** page contains additional settings for your calendar entry. These settings include the following:

Pencil In—Place an **x** in the checkbox to have the calendar entry appear on your calendar, but others will still see this time as available if they check your schedule.

Mark Private—This option is important if you have given other individuals access to *read* your calendar. Placing an **x** in the checkbox prevents the other calendar readers from seeing this appointment. Use this if you want to enter a confidential calendar entry such as a doctors visit. Others will see that your time is blocked, but will not have access to the appointment information.

 Going to the Beach? When you allow others to *read* your calendar, they can read all the specific details you put in your calendar, such as what your plans are for your day off. When you allow others to *check your schedule*, they can only see that you are available or that you are busy. They cannot see what you are doing during that time. Managing access to your calendars was covered in Lesson 8. You might want to revisit that lesson to set calendar preferences.

Notify Me—Place an **x** in the **Notify Me** checkbox to set the parameters for seeing and hearing a reminder for this calendar entry. In the Alarm Options dialog box, specify when you want the alarm to go off, the on-screen message, the sound to play, and whether you want an email notification to go to others.

Good morning!   Imagine yourself at home, snuggled up sleeping in your bed. The ringing of your phone shatters the still of the night. "Hello?" A digitized voice rasps, "This is your Lotus Notes notification. You have a meeting at 10:00 a.m. with the Production Team." *NOT!* Your computer must be on and you must have Lotus Notes open (even if minimized) or you must have Notes Minder running to see or hear calendar entry notifications.

Categorize—Select the category for this calendar entry document from the pull-down list. Personal Categories are defined in your Calendar Preferences (**Actions, Tools, Preferences**). Review Lesson 8 for more information about setting Calendar preferences.

Printing the Calendar

Having a calendar in Notes is really useful but for times that you are away from your computer, you can print out your calendar view, a list of calendar entries, or one or more calendar entries.

To print a Calendar view, do the following:

1. Choose **File**, **Print** from the menu.

2. Select your calendar **Print style** from the pull-down list (see Figure 9.9). (Click **Customize** to see more style options.)

3. Select the **From** and the **To** dates. Use the pop-up calendar icons to assist you with this task.

4. To print more than one copy, specify the number in the **Copies** field.

5. Click **Preview** to see what your printed output is going to look like or click **OK**.

FIGURE **9.9**   Set your calendar print options in the Print dialog box. There are many print formats available for calendars found in the Print Style dialog box.

Editing Calendar Entries

Our calendars aren't carved in stone—appointments get rescheduled, events are postponed, and meetings are called off. Notes supports your needs to modify calendar entries, move them to different dates, or delete them.

To modify a Calendar entry, edit the entry document by double-clicking the entry in Calendar view to open the document. You can alter any of the fields in the document, including **Entry Type**, to change the type of Calendar entry for the document. Save and close the document to have your changes take effect.

If you have a repeating entry, such as a weekly appointment, any changes you make to the original entry will affect the related repeats. For example, you try to change the start time for the appointment. The Change Repeating Entry dialog box appears (see Figure 9.10) and presents choices for how you want your changes to affect the related entries. You can choose to affect only the entry you have open, all the repeated entries related to this entry, only this and previous repeated entries, or only this and future repeated entries. Make your selection, and then choose **OK**.

You cannot change the days on which a repeating entry occurs, but you can delete future dates and re-enter the entry.

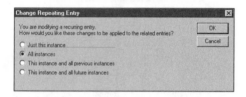

FIGURE 9.10   When modifying an entry that repeats, you must also specify how your alterations will affect the repeated entries.

 No Repeats   You can only set repeating entries when you create a calendar entry. You can't add repeating entries to an existing entry.

Although you can edit a Calendar entry and change the dates and times, it's often quicker to drag and drop the appointment to the new date or time. If the date to which you want to drag the entry is on the preceding or next page, drag the entry to the left or right arrow at the bottom right corner of the Calendar page, and hold it over the arrow until you see the current page. Then, drag the entry to its new position.

To scroll the times on a date, hold the entry over one of the scroll arrows on the date until the appropriate time appears. Needless to say, when you want to drag an entry to a new time, be sure the times show on the screen by clicking the Time Slot Display button at the top right of the Calendar screen.

If Notes asks whether you're sure you want to move the entry, click **Yes**.

When you need to delete a Calendar entry, open your Calendar, click the entry to select it (hold down **Shift** and click additional entries to select more than one), and then press **Delete**. Notes marks the entry or entries for deletion with a trash can. The entry or entries are then listed in the Trash folder. Pressing **F9**, clicking the Refresh, or closing the Mail

database will bring up a dialog box asking if you want to delete the
selected documents. Click **Yes** to delete them.

Converting Calendar Entries

Mail messages you receive might contain information about appointments
you need to make, events you need to attend, upcoming dates about which
you want to remind yourself, or other date-related information. You can
take that information directly from your mail message and convert it into
a Calendar entry.

Select or open the message, and click the **Copy Into** button on the Action
Bar. Select **New Calendar Entry**. A new entry document opens (see
Figure 9.11). The **Subject** of the new entry matches the Subject line of
the mail message. The body of the mail memo is added to the
Description of the entry, but a horizontal line appears above it along with
space for you to add any comments relating to the entry you're creating.
From that point, make any changes you need to the entry, and then save it.

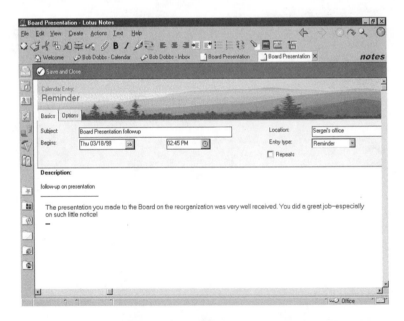

FIGURE 9.11 This reminder entry was based on an email that Bob
Dobbs received regarding a presentation he gave.

Calendar entries can likewise be used to generate mail memos. Select the entry in the Calendar view and then click **Copy Into** on the Action Bar. Choose **New Memo**. A new mail memo opens, and the Subject of the Calendar entry becomes the subject of the mail memo. You complete the memo and send it to the recipients you specify.

You can also create To Do tasks from Calendar entries, as discussed later in this lesson.

In this lesson, you learned how to switch calendar views, create and edit calendar entries and print calendars. In the next lesson, you learn how to create meetings and work with Group Calendaring.

LESSON 10

Working with Meetings and Group Calendaring

In this lesson you learn how to schedule and edit meetings, respond to meeting invitations, create group calendars, make entries in the group calendar, and view other calendars.

Scheduling Meetings

Lotus Notes is an ideal product for organizing group activities. Notes helps you to schedule meetings and invite participants, as well as to reserve rooms and resources for those meetings. In addition, Notes enables you to create a calendar for a specific group (or project) that is shared by those you define as the group.

After you define a need for a meeting, you need to inform all the people involved of the meeting time and place—and, of course, that their attendance is requested. Do this by creating a meeting invitation. The first time you create a meeting invitation, it will take you some time to learn to use all the meeting invitation features, including how to view the free time of others. After you create one or two meeting invitations, you find that this task is easy and quick. The steps to creating an invitation are the following:

- Create the invitation.

- Identify the invitees and others who you want to inform about this meeting.

- Check the free time of the invitees and (optionally) schedule your meeting time according to their availability.

- Determine how you want your invitees to respond to your meeting.

- Mail the meeting invitation.

As you can see, quite a few steps are involved in creating a meeting invitation. To begin, open your calendar and follow these steps:

1. With your Calendar open, click the **Schedule a Meeting** button on the Action Bar.

2. In the Meeting document (see Figure 10.1), enter a brief description for the meeting in the **Subject** field.

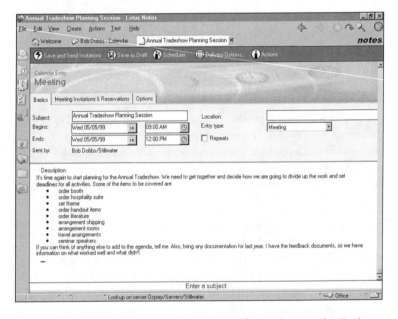

Figure 10.1   Enter the general meeting information on the Basics page.

3. Enter or select the **Begins** and **Ends** dates and times (click the button at the right end of the field to see a date or use the time picker).

4. For a meeting that will occur at regular intervals (such as a monthly meeting), select **Repeats** and enter your repeat options.

5. In the **Description** field, enter important facts about your meeting, such as its purpose, directions to the location of the meeting, and so forth. You can attach or embed files in this rich text field, such as supporting data for your meeting.

6. Click the **Meeting Invitations & Reservations** tab (see Figure 10.2). In the **Invite** field, enter the names of people you want to invite to the meeting (click the button at the right end of the field to select names from an Address Book).

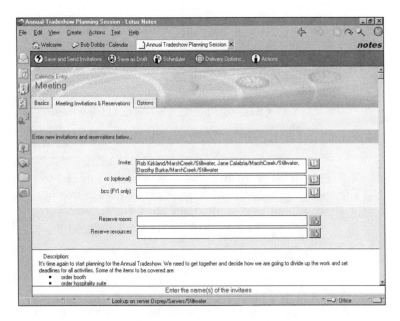

FIGURE **10.2**   Enter the names of the invitees on the Meeting Invitations & Reservations page.

7. (Optional) To provide a copy of the invitation to someone that informs him and keeps him updated about the meeting but doesn't *invite* him to the meeting, enter the person's name in the **cc** or **bcc** field. Use the **bcc** field only if you don't want other recipients to see the name of the person receiving an information-only copy of the invitation.

8. To check the availability of your invitees, click the **Scheduler** button on the Action Bar. Select **Check all schedules**.

9. The Free Time dialog box appears (see Figure 10.3). The time of each invitee is displayed by invitee. You can see the free time of each invitee (shown in white) by the names of the invitees, by the week, by who can attend, by who cannot attend, or by whose time wasn't found. If the schedule is **OK** for everyone, go to Step 10. If you see a conflict (**NOT OK** shows in red) in the schedule, do one of the following:

- Select a time from the **Recommended meeting times** field.

- Set a new date or time in the **Date** or **Time** field.

- In the **Free Time** field drop-down menu, select **All by Invitee** or **All by Week** and use the grid to specify a time free for all or most invitees.

- Click the **Change Invitee List** button to add or remove people.

Restricted or No Info schedules   These people have either changed their calendar preferences so that others cannot see their free time, or there is a problem with their calendar and they need to talk with the Notes Administrator.

10. When the Free Time dialog box indicates that the meeting time is OK (green) for everyone, click the **OK** button to close the box and continue with your meeting invitation. To schedule a resource, continue with step 11; otherwise, go to step 12.

11. (Optional) Click **Reserve Rooms** to book a room for the meeting. Click **Reserve Resources** to reserve resources, such as audiovisual equipment, for the meeting. Handling these reservations is covered more fully later in this lesson.

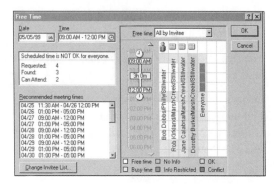

FIGURE 10.3   Here, a conflict displays in the schedule. Jane has no free time available on this day, and Dorothy's free time is not known at all.

12. On the **Options** page, check **Pencil In** to keep the time of this meeting available in your free time schedule. Select **Mark Private** to prevent people who have access to your Calendar from reading the invitation. To set up a notification for the upcoming meeting, click **Notify Me** and pick the appropriate Alarm Options. From the **Categorize** field, select an appropriate category for the meeting.

13. Click the **Delivery Options** button on the Action Bar to set any of the following options:

   • **I Do Not Want to Receive Replies from Participants** sends the invitation as a broadcast message that doesn't require a reply. Use this for large, general meetings where attendance is always required or there is such a large number of people invited that individual responses would be overwhelming.

   • **Prevent Counter-Proposing** stops the recipient from proposing a different time schedule for the meeting.

   • **Prevent Delegating** keeps the recipient from delegating attendance to another individual.

- **Sign** adds a digital signature to the invitation to guarantee that you are the person who sent it.

- **Encrypt** encrypts the invitation so only intended recipients can read it.

14. Save the invitation and send it to the invitees by clicking the **Save and Send Invitations** button on the Action Bar. Alternately, click **Save as Draft** on the Action Bar to save the invitation as a draft and send it at a later time.

Managing Meetings

After you have scheduled a meeting, you want to manage the meeting by checking on the status of responses to your meeting, rescheduling meetings when necessary, and possibly sending mail memos that relate to the meeting. All this management of the meeting can be done with the Notes Calendar and Notes Mail.

The Meetings view of your calendar displays a list of meeting invitations, both the ones you issued and those sent to you (see Figure 10.4). Use this view to quickly locate a meeting and open it. The meetings are listed in date order, oldest at the top.

Using Action buttons in this view, you can create new Meetings, take Owner actions on selected meetings, or take Participant actions on selected meetings. You can also copy meeting information into new memos, calendar entries, and To Do's.

To reschedule a meeting, follow these steps:

1. Open your Calendar and click the Meetings view. Select the meeting you want to change.

2. Click the **Owner Actions** button on the Action Bar, and select **Reschedule**.

3. The Reschedule Options dialog box opens (see Figure 10.5).

4. Modify the **Begins** and **Ends** dates or times (click **Check Schedules** to use the free time schedule to see when your invitees are available).

5. Click **OK**. Notices will be sent to the invitees, informing them
of the change of date or time. By checking **Include Additional
Comments on Notice** in the dialog box, you can add a short
explanation along with the notice.

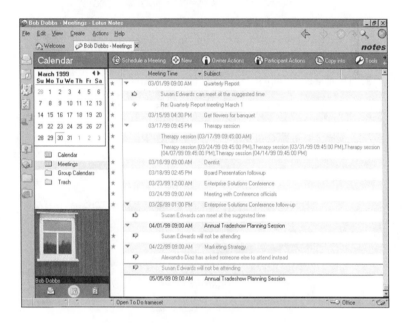

FIGURE 10.4 The Meetings view lists the meetings in date order,
oldest to newest, and also shows the responses from the invitees.

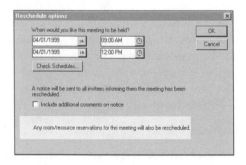

FIGURE 10.5 Room and Resources are automatically rescheduled
when you reschedule the meeting.

When you cancel a meeting, you need to notify all the participants that the meeting has been cancelled. The steps for canceling a meeting are as follows:

1. Select the meeting document in the Meetings view of the Calendar.

2. Click the **Owner Actions** button on the Action Bar, and select **Cancel**.

3. The Cancel Options dialog box appears (see Figure 10.6).

4. Click **OK** to close the dialog box, Notes automatically sends a cancellation notice to all the invitees for that meeting. If you selected **Delete Calendar Entry and All Responses**, Notes removes any documents related to the meeting. Again, you have the option to include a message along with the notice.

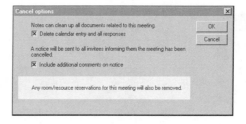

FIGURE 10.6   Notes automatically notifies all invitees of the cancellation and can clean up all related documents.

After you have received the responses to your meeting invitation, you should remove the names of invitees who won't be attending from the meeting document. You should then send a confirmation notice out to the remaining invitees to let them know the meeting is indeed on at the time and date specified. The notice will include the new list of participants for the meeting. To confirm a meeting, follow these steps:

1. Select the document from the Meetings view of the Calendar.

2. Click the **Owner Actions** button on the Action Bar, and select **Confirm.**

3. (Optional) Select **Include Additional Comments on Notice** in the dialog box, to give yourself the chance to add your own text to the notice.

4. Click **OK** to close the dialog box.

Although the Meetings view displays response documents to meeting invitations, it's not easy to determine if all the invitees have responded and accepted. To quickly review the status of the responses to your invitation, follow these steps:

1. Select the meeting in the Meetings view.

2. Click the **Owner Actions** button on the Action Bar, and select **View Participant Status**.

3. The Participant Status dialog box opens (see Figure 10.7), displaying the list of invitees, including optional or FYI invitees who were copied on the invitation. The dialog box displays the role of each person and the status of the invitation.

4. Click **Done** to close the dialog box.

FIGURE 10.7 You can sort the Participant status information by clicking the triangles next to the column headings to view by Name, Role, or Status.

As people respond to your meeting invitations, you receive memos in your Inbox accepting, declining, delegating, or proposing time changes for your meeting. To keep your Inbox clear of this traffic, click the **Tools** button in the Calendar and choose **Preferences**. In the Preferences dialog box, select the **Calendar** tab and then the **Autoprocess** tab. Enable the option **Prevent Meeting Replies from Appearing in My Inbox**.

If you want to send a memo to all meeting participants to update the agenda or to provide more details about the upcoming meeting, follow these steps:

1. Select the meeting in the Meetings view.

2. Click the **Owner Actions** button on the Action Bar, and choose **Send Memo to Participants**.

3. A new mail memo opens. The list of invitees appears in the **To** field, and optional invitees are in the **cc** or **bcc** field (depending on where you listed them in the meeting invitation).

4. The **Subject** field contains only the name of the meeting. The message area is blank, and you can create a message there as you would in any mail memo.

5. Click **Send** to send the memo to the invitees.

Making Room and Resource Reservations

Part of creating the meeting invitation is to specify and reserve a room and any equipment to be used for the meeting. As you learned earlier in this lesson, you can reserve a room or resource from the Meeting Invitations & Reservations page of a meeting invitation while you are creating an invitation or even after the meeting has been scheduled. You can also reserve a room or resource using the Scheduler button on the Action Bar after a meeting has been saved.

 To reserve rooms and resources, your organization must have rooms or resources in its Directory (Address Book). Check with your Notes Administrator if you don't see such resources in your Directory.

Rooms and resources can be reserved using one of two methods: Reserve them by their names (overhead projector or Ellis Room), or search for them by criteria (conference room that seats 10 people) or categories (conference rooms, audiovisual equipment).

 If you have difficulty or questions regarding room or resource reservations, consult with your Help Desk or your Notes Administrator. Our instructions assume that resources are included in your Directory and that Sites and Categories have been assigned.

To reserve a room or resource by name, follow these steps:

1. Open the meeting invitation and click the **Meeting Invitations & Reservations** tab.

2. (To reserve a room) Enter the name of the room you want to use in the **Reserve Rooms** field, or click the button at the right end of the field to select from a list of rooms.

3. (To reserve a resource) enter the name of the resource in the Resource field or select the name from the list that appears when you click the button for that field.

To search for a room by criteria (Site and/or seating capacity), follow these steps:

1. Open the meeting invitation.

2. Click the **Scheduler** button on the Action Bar, and choose **Find Room**(s).

3. Select a site in the drop-down menu of the **Site:** field. Sites are an optional service set up by the Notes Administrator. If no sites are available, this field can be left blank.

4. Enter the **# of attendees** field in that field. The number of attendees helps Notes to find a room based on its seating capacity. Don't leave this field blank.

5. Click the **Search** button.

6. Under **Search Results**, select the room you want to reserve, and click **OK**.

7. When you save the meeting entry, Notes sends a reservation request to your organization's Directory. This room is now "booked" and will not appear as an available resource during the time and date you have booked it.

To search for a resource, follow these steps:

1. Open the meeting invitation.

2. Click the **Scheduler** button on the Action Bar, and choose **Find Resource**(s).

3. Select a site in the drop-down menu of the **Site:** field. Sites are an optional service set up by the Notes Administrator. If no sites are available, this field can be left blank.

4. Click the Category button, and select a resource category from the list. Click **OK** to close this dialog box.

5. Click the **Search** button.

6. Under the **Search Results**, select the resource you want to reserve, and click **OK**.

7. When you save the meeting entry, Notes sends a reservation request to your organization's Directory. If this resource is automatically booked, it will not appear as an available resource during the time and date you have booked it. Your System Administrator controls the setting for resources and whether the free time of resources shows as booked. If you have any questions, consult with him.

Should you need to cancel a room or reservation (if you don't cancel the entire meeting), open the meeting invitation and click **Remove** next to the Rooms or Resources field. Save the invitation.

Responding to Meeting Invitations

You can accept or decline an invitation to a meeting. Unless prevented by the sender of the invitation, you can also propose a different meeting time that is more suitable for you or delegate the meeting to someone else.

When you receive the invitation in your Mail, you open the document. Click the **Respond** or **Respond with Comments** button on the Action Bar.

 No Respond Button? The sender does not expect an answer to the meeting invitation because the memo is a broadcast invitation. Click **Add to Calendar** to add the meeting to your Calendar. Click **Request Information** if you want to know more about the meeting.

Choose one of the following:

- **Accept** accepts the invitation. A memo of acceptance is sent, and an entry for the meeting appears on your Calendar.

- **Decline** rejects the invitation. A memo is sent noting that you decline the invitation.

- **Delegate** declines the invitation for you, but enables you to specify the person to whom you want the invitation sent. Notes then forwards the invitation to that person. This option might not be available if the owner of the invitation chose to prevent delegation.

- **Propose New Time** gives you the opportunity to propose an alternate meeting time that is more convenient for your schedule. You specify the new date or time and click **OK**. A decline memo goes to the invitation sender, but it displays the changes in schedule you propose. That proposal can also be accepted or declined. The Propose New Time option might not be available if the owner of the invitation chose to prevent new time proposals.

- **Tentatively Accept** accepts the meeting invitation, adds the meeting as an entry to your Calendar, but enables the **Pencil in** option on the Options page of the entry so the time still appears as free in your free time schedule.

Repeats If the meeting invitation is for a repeating meeting (does it have a **Repeating Info** tab?), your answer applies to each instance of the meeting. Check your schedule before you reply. Also, be aware you can't counter-propose for repeat meetings. You must first accept the invitation, then double-click the first instance in your Calendar of the meetings, click **Respond**, and choose **Propose New Time**.

If you chose **Respond with Comments**, add your comments to your answer. Click **Send** to send your response.

Are You Free? Don't assume that the owner of the invitation checked your free time before inviting you to the meeting. To be sure you have the time available, click the **Check Calendar** button on the Action Bar to see what you have scheduled for the day of the meeting before you respond to the invitation.

Rather than responding individually to each meeting invitation, Notes can automatically answer them for you. Click the **Tools** button on the Action Bar in the Calendar. Select **Preferences**. Click the **Calendar** tab and then the **Autoprocess** tab.

From the drop-down list, select one of the following options:

- **Do Not Automatically Process Meeting Invitations**—Under this option, the default, you respond manually to each invitation you receive.

- **Automatically Process Meeting Invitations from All Users—** This automatically accepts all invitations you receive.

- **Automatically Process Meeting Invitations from the Following Users**—Enter or select the names of the users whose meeting invitations you automatically will accept.

- **Delegate Meeting Invitations to the Following Person**—Enter or select the name of the user who will attend all your meetings for you.

Are you so popular that your meeting invitations are swamping your Inbox? The solution is to check **Remove Meeting Invitations from My Inbox After I Respond to Them** in the Autoprocess preferences.

Creating a New Group Calendar

A group calendar displays the free time schedules of a specified group of people. You quickly see who in the group is available or busy at a particular time. If you have access to their calendars, you can display them below the group calendar.

To open a group calendar, you open your Calendar and click the **Group Calendars** folder in the Navigation Pane (see Figure 10.8). Then, you double-click on the group calendar you want to view.

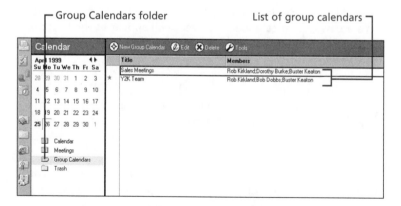

FIGURE **10.8**   From the list in your Group Calendars folder, double-click a group calendar to open it.

The group calendar displays the free time of all the members of the group(see Figure 10.9).

Click one of these
arrows to go back or
forward one week

Use scrollbar to move
quickly through dates

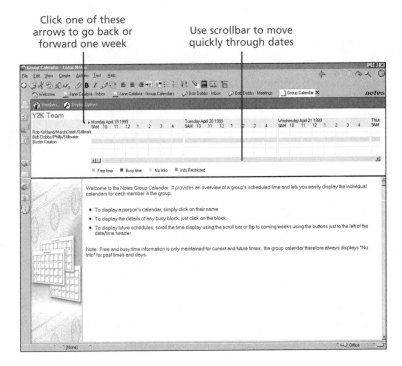

FIGURE 10.9   To display the details of any busy block, click it. If you have access to that calendar, the event will appear at the bottom of the screen; otherwise, you see instructions on how to use the group calendar.

Old Dates?   Group Calendars only display current and future dates. Older dates are marked as "No Info."

You determine the starting time of the group calendar and the total number of hours shown for each day. Click the **Display Options** button on the Action Bar. In the Options dialog box (see Figure 10.10), select a **Starting Time** and **Duration**. Then, click **OK**.

FIGURE **10.10**   In this dialog box, set the total number of hours showing for every day on the calendar and the time the days begin.

You're ready to create a group calendar for the people you work closely with in your department. You start by opening your Calendar and clicking on the **Group Calendars** folder. On the Action Bar, click the **New Group Calendar** button.

In the New Group Calendar dialog box (see Figure 10.11), enter the **Title** you want to use to distinguish this group calendar. In the **Members** box, enter the names of people or groups who will appear on the group calendar (click the button after the box to select names from the Directory). Choose **OK**.

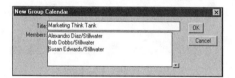

FIGURE **10.11**   Give the group calendar a title, and enter the names of the people or groups to be included.

Members of any group are changeable. To add or remove members from the group calendar, click the **Members** button on the Action Bar. In the Names dialog box (see Figure 10.12), click the name of any person or group you want to join the group and then click **Add** (you can check the margin next to each name and then click **Add** to add several people or groups at one time). To remove a person or group, click the name in the Added box and then choose **Remove**. Click **OK** to close the dialog box.

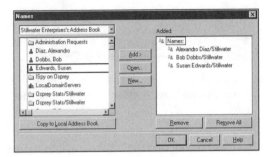

FIGURE 10.12   Add or remove names from the group calendar.

Provided the members of the group have given permission to have their calendars viewed by you (see Hour 7), clicking the person's name displays a view of his/her calendar (see Figure 10.13). If the person hasn't given you permission, you see a message saying "Unable to open user's mail database," and you must click **OK**.

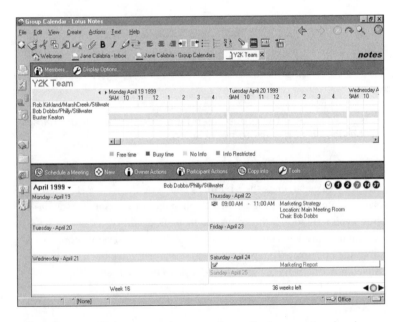

FIGURE 10.13   Click a person's name to see that person's calendar beneath the group calendar.

Whenever a time slot shows "busy," you click the time to display the calendar entry for that time slot (which appears only if you have permission to view the person's calendar).

Editing or Deleting a Group Calendar

From the Group Calendars folder, any selected group calendar can be edited or deleted.

Editing a group calendar involves changing the members or the title. You select the group calendar and click the **Edit** Action button. The New Group Calendar dialog box appears (refer to Figure 10.12), so you can add or remove members or modify the title of the group calendar. Make your changes, and click **OK**.

To delete a group calendar, select it in the Group Calendars folder and then click the **Delete** button on the Action Bar. A trash can marks the group calendar for deletion, and the group calendar document also displays in the Trash folder. Permanently remove the group calendar when you refresh your view, exit the mail database, or click **Empty Trash** on the Action Bar of the Trash folder. Confirm the deletion.

In this lesson you learned how to work with group calendaring and how to schedule manage and accept or decline meeting invitations. In the next lesson you learn how to work with To Do items.

LESSON 11
Working with To Do Items

In this lesson, you learn how to create items for your personal To Do list, how to keep track of your personal To Do list, and how to assign tasks to others by creating a Group To Do task.

Creating To Do Items

To help keep track of all the things you have to do, create a personal To Do item. Once created, a To Do item (optionally) displays in your calendar and is also found in your To Do view, found by clicking the To Do icon in your mail or calendar navigation pane (as shown in Figure 11.1). In previous versions of Lotus Notes, To Do items were called *tasks*, and we prefer the term *tasks*, so you might find we use these two terms interchangeably throughout this book.

To create a personal To Do entry, do the following:

1. Open your mail database or your calendar. Click the To Do view icon at the bottom of the Navigation pane (see Figure 11.1) to open the To Do view.

FIGURE 11.1 Three buttons at bottom of Navigation pane open the Mail, Calendar, or To Do view.

2. Click the **New To Do Item** button on the Action Bar. The New Personal To Do form appears, as shown in Figure 11.2.

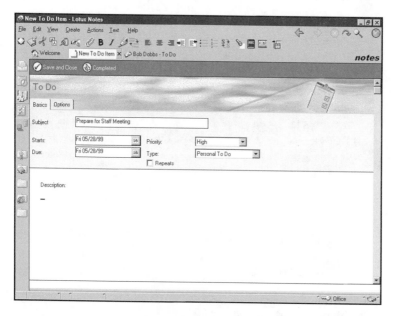

Figure 11.2 The To Do form consists of two pages of information: the Basics Page and the Options Page.

3. Enter a description for this To Do item in the **Subject** field.

4. To establish a start date for the task, enter the date in the **Starts** box or click the **Date** icon next to the box to select a date from the drop-down calendar.

5. Enter a date in the **Due** box to set a due date for the task or click the **Date** icon next to the box to select a date from the drop-down calendar.

6. To set a priority for the task, click **High**, **Medium**, **Low**, or **None** (the default is **Medium**). Setting this priority affects the order that To Do items appear in your To Do List. Those with a high priority will appear with an icon labeled "1" and will appear before any 2s, or medium priorities, and any 3s or low priorities. All no-priority tasks appear last on their respective dates in your To Do views.

7. **(Optional)** If you have a repetitive task, select **Repeats**. The Repeat Options dialog box appears (see Figure 11.3). Under Repeat, select the frequency of the repeat (such as **Monthly by Date**, then **Every other month on the**, and then the day). Under Continuing, specify when the repeating task ends by setting a time period or an ending date. To prevent the due date of the task from falling on a weekend, select an option under If the Date Occurs on a Weekend. Choose **OK** to close the dialog box. If you need to go back and change the Recurrence options later, click the **Settings** button. If you save a To Do item before you set Repeats, you cannot change it to a repeating To Do item, you must re-create it from scratch.

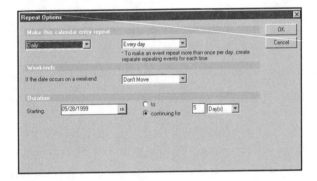

FIGURE 11.3   The Repeat Options dialog box is the same dialog box you see when you create a repeating calendar entry, such as a meeting.

8. **(Optional)** To receive a reminder when the task is coming due, click the **Options** tab and select **Notify Me**. The Alarm Options dialog box appears (Enter the number of **Minutes, Hours,** or **Days** either **Before** or **After** the due date you want to be alerted. Enter a message to display at that time. If you want a sound alarm, select **Play sound** and choose a sound in the drop-down list. To have a mail message sent, click **Send mail with entry title and description** and select recipients from the drop-down box that appears. When you are finished, choose **OK** to close the dialog box.

9. (**Optional**) click the **Options** tab and select **Mark Private** to not make your task available to others.

10. (**Optional**) Choose an appropriate Category such as **Holiday** or Vacation from the drop-down list or type your own category in the **Categorize** field.

11. Click the **Save and Close** button on the Action Bar to save the task. The task appears in your To Do view.

In addition to displaying in your To Do view, To Do items also appear in your calendar. You can change the default settings of Notes if you do not want To Do items to appear in your calendar. See Lesson 22, "Customizing Notes," for more information.

You also can assign To Do items to others. For example, if you and your staff plan to attend a convention, you can assign tasks to each member of your staff. To assign tasks to others, do the following:

1. Open the To Do view of your mail database. Click the **New To Do Item** button on the Action Bar. Choose **Group To Do**. The New Group To Do form appears, as shown in Figure 11.4.

2. Follow steps 3 through 12 of creating a Personal To Do document.

3. Click the **Participants** page. Select people for the Assign to: **cc** and **bcc** fields.

4. (**Optional**) Click the **Delivery Options** button on the Action Bar to set the following options:

    • Choose your **Delivery Report**, **Delivery Priority**, and **Return Receipt** options. These options are the same as the options you find when you send a Mail Memo.

    • Check **I do not want to review replies from participants** if you do not require the participants to respond to your assignment.

- Check **Prevent count-proposing** to prevent the recipient from sending the task back to you with a counter proposal.

- Check **Prevent delegating** if you do not want the recipient to assign this task to someone else.

- Choose to **Sign** and/or **Encrypt** to encrypt or attach an electronic signature to the memo.

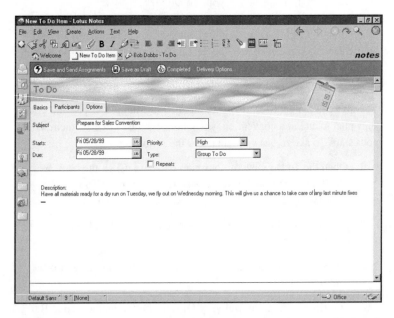

Figure 11.4   The New Group To Do form has three pages of information, with a page for selecting participants.

5. Click **Save and Send Assignments** on the Action Bar to send this notice, or choose **Save as Draft** to save it in your drafts view.

To Do or Not To Do?   Sometimes, it just seems as if there isn't enough time in a day and to make matters worse, Notes will place a To Do item that you assign to others, in *your* To Do view. Until you open the item, there isn't any way to identify this as a task you've assigned to someone else. We suggest you create a category called "assigned to others" or some such name and use this category when you assign tasks to other people. It will help you to keep your tasks separated from those you've delegated.

Responding to a To Do Item

When you are named as a participant on a To Do document, you receive a mail message in your Inbox. When you open the message, you find choices for responding to this To Do assignment on the Action Bar. Click the appropriate button on the Action Bar:

- **Respond**—Click here to **Accept** or **Decline** the task, **Delegate** the task to another person, or **Propose New Time** which allows you to change the due date. If you delegate the task, you must name a person to handle the task. However, you can request updates from the owner of the task (the person who created the To Do document). You can also receive updates if you decline the task. The last choice in this menu is **Completed**, which marks the task as completed and notifies the sender that you have completed the task.

- **Respond with Comments**—Contains the same choices as found in the Respond menu, but the return form includes a field for you to add comments when accepting, declining, delegating, proposing a new time, or completing the item.

- **Request Information**   Click here to ask for further information before accepting or declining the task. When you select this, you also have the opportunity to **Include comments on the reply message**.

When you select a response option, a mail message is generated and sent to the owner of the task. When the owner receives your response, he too has options which are available under the **Owner Actions** button on the Action Bar in the To Do view (the **Participant Actions** button in the view contains the same choices as the **Respond** button in the document). These include the following:

- Reschedule

- Cancel

- Confirm

- View Participant Status

- Send Memo to Participants

Converting Mail Messages to To Do Items

Convert mail messages to To Do items so that they appear in your To Do list. For example, converting a mail message from your manager that asks you to prepare your department's budget for next year to a task adds that message to your To Do list so that you won't forget to follow up. To convert a mail message to a task, do the following:

1. Select the document in the view pane or open the message.

2. Click the **Copy Into** button on the Action Bar. Select **New To Do**.

3. A new Group To Do opens. The subject of the mail message appears as the Title. The mail message becomes the Details. You can make any changes or additions you want to the information provided there.

4. If you want to assign the task to yourself, click the **OK** button on the Action Bar, or press the **Esc** key.

   To assign the task to anyone else, click **Group To Do** under Change To Do Type. Click **Save and Send To Do** on the Action Bar.

You also can create new tasks from Calendar entries. If you're creating an entry that also happens to be the deadline for a task, choose **Actions, Copy Into, New To Do** from the menu. Change any information in the new To Do document and then save and close it.

Existing tasks often generate new tasks, and you can create new tasks from an existing task document. With the existing task selected or open, choose **Actions, Copy Into, New To Do** from the menu. Complete the new To Do document, save it, and close it.

Viewing To Do Status

To keep track of the tasks you assign to yourself, tasks others assign to you, and tasks you assign to others, open the To Do view in the Mail database.

Three views are available for the To Do List: **By Due Date**, **By Category**, and **By Status**. The By Status view divides the tasks into **Overdue**, **Current**, **Future**, and **Complete**. Although you can change the status of an item, you can only **Mark Completed** or **Unmark Completed** by selecting it and clicking the button(s) on the Action Bar.

In this lesson, you learned how to assign tasks to yourself and to others, how to mark the tasks as completed, and how to view the tasks. In the next lesson, you will learn how to use the Address Books.

LESSON 12
Using the Address Books

In this lesson, you learn about the two address books found in Lotus Notes—the Public Address Book and the Personal Address Book—and how to use your Personal Address Book for creating Business Cards and Groups.

Defining the Address Books

Like Notes Mail, Notes Address Books are databases. You store your email addresses in Lotus Notes address books. In Lesson 5, "Managing Mail," you used the Public Address Book to add names to a Mail Memo. Lotus Notes has at least two address books available for your use—the Personal Address Book and the Company Address Book (sometimes referred to as the Domino Directory, or the Public Address Book; see Figure 12.1).

Your *Personal Address Book* has your name on it and is empty until you add people to it. In contrast, the Company Address Book, *Directory*, contains the addresses of employees in your company who use Lotus Notes Mail, and it has your company's name on it. Your Domino system administrator maintains this address book.

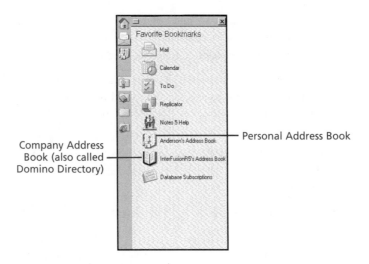

Company Address Book (also called Domino Directory)

Personal Address Book

FIGURE 12.1   The Address Book icons display in the Favorites Navigation Pane.

Using Your Personal Address Book

As is the case with your Mail database, the Personal Address Book is managed completely by you. In fact, you are the *Manager* (see Appendix A for a complete explanation of security and access rights) You are the only one who can read, modify, or delete entries. This database contains names, addresses, and other information on individuals and groups of people you communicate with—like a contact sheet or file of business cards. You don't need to add your fellow employees, because everyone in your company is already in the Public Address Book, so avoid duplicating entries that might already be found there. However, remote users (those who use Notes out of the office, at home, or on their laptops) might need to add people from the Public Address Book to their Personal Address Book because they may have access to only one address book when they're not connected to the Domino server. For more information on remote users, see Lessons 20, "Setting Up for Mobile Use," and 21, "Using Notes Remotely."

To open your Personal Address Book, click the Personal Address Book database icon in the Favorites Navigation Pane. The Personal Address Book Navigation Pane displays the following views:

- **Contacts**   The people you have in your Personal Address Book are listed with their telephone numbers and company information. (If you are new to Lotus Notes Mail, your address book is probably empty.)

- **Contacts By Category**   The same people that are listed in your Business Card view, but now they are sorted into categories that you create.

- **Groups**   Lists the groups of people you created as mailing distribution lists.

Creating Contacts

The information you store about a person—name, title, company, address, phone, fax, email address, and so on—is kept in a Contact document, such as the one shown in Figure 12.2.

To create a Contact document for a new person, click the **New Contact** hotspot on your Welcome Page, or open your Address Book and click the **Add Contact** button on the Action Bar. and follow these steps:

1. Starting on the **Basics** page, use the **Tab** key or the mouse to move from field to field. Type the information into each applicable field such as first name, middle name, last name, and so forth.

2. Click on the small triangles to the right of the **Title** and **Suffix** fields to bring up a list of keywords. You will also have keyword choices in the **Company** field in the **Business** section.

3. Fill in the phone numbers in the appropriate phone number fields, or click the Phones icon to bring up the **Phones** dialog box. In this box, you can change the names of the Phone Labels, for example, you might want to have two company phone numbers or two home phone numbers and here, you can change the labels to reflect that (see Figure 12.3).

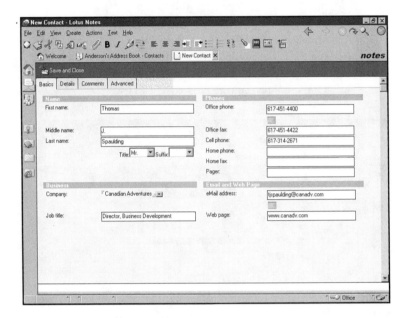

FIGURE 12.2   Tabbed pages separate the sections of a Business Card document.

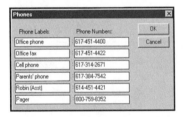

FIGURE 12.3   These phone number labels have been customized.

4. Click the icon below **eMail address** to bring up the Mail Address Assistant (see Figure 12.4) and follow these steps:

Mail Address Assistant—Select the type of mail system that person uses (Fax, Internet Mail, Lotus cc:Mail, Lotus Notes, X 400 Mail, or Other). If you aren't sure which mail system to choose, consult your Domino system administrator. Click **OK**.

A second Mail Address Assistant dialog box is displayed. Fill in the name and the email address, or username and domain, of that user (see Figure 12.5). Consult your Domino system administrator if you're not sure how to enter the address, especially for Internet and Fax addresses. When you are finished, click **OK**.

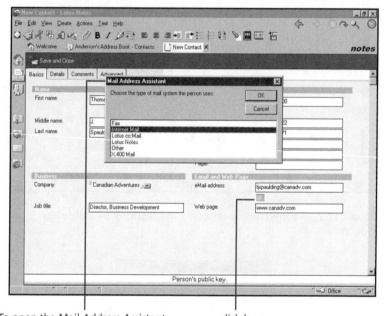

To open the Mail Address Assistant...   ...click here

FIGURE 12.4   Choose the person's mail system from the Mail Assistant dialog box.

FIGURE 12.5   The second Mail Address Assistant dialog box is for creating Internet mail addresses.

What's a Domain? A *domain* is a group of servers listed in one Public Address Book. If you don't know the domain name, see your Notes administrator. For more information on Internet Mail addressing, see Lesson 6, "Using Mail Tools."

5. If this contact has a Web page, use the Web page field to record the address. Once you've saved this contact, you can visit that Web page directly from the Personal Address Book by selecting the contact, clicking the **Tools** button on the Action Bar, and selecting **Visit Web Page.**

6. Continue to the next tabbed page, **Details.** In the Business Address field, click the address icon to display a business address dialog box, as shown in Figure 12.6. Do the same for the Home address field. Fill in all fields for which you have information that is relevant to you.

FIGURE **12.6** The Business Address Assistant is similar to the Home Address Assistant.

7. Click the **Comments** page. Here, a rich text field allows you to keep any kind of formatted text information, attach files, and so forth. You can even paste a photograph onto this page.

8. Click the **Advanced page.** In the **Categories** field, you can categorize your contact so that it will show in the appropriate category when using the view **Contacts by Category.** If you want a contact to display under more than one category, separate categories with commas. Be consistent and watch your spelling, or

you'll end up with several similar categories—Friends, Friend, Fiend—which makes it harder to find people.

9. Click the **Save and Close** button on the Action Bar to save this information in your address book.

 The form and information found for contacts in your Personal Address Book differs from the information you find on an individual in the Company Address Book. For example, the Company Address Book does not have a field for a Web address or birthday. You might want to record this information on a fellow co-worker, because lots of people have personal Web pages these days. In this case, instead of creating a new contact in your address book, copy that person from the Company Address Book into your Personal Address Book. Once it's added to your Personal Address Book, complete the information you want to keep. Remember, you don't need to copy the Company Address Book into your Personal Address Book for the mere purpose of being able to send email to a fellow employee. However, if a person's name or address changes in the Company Address Book, you will have erroneous information in your Personal Address Book. If you are a mobile Notes users, please be certain to complete Lessons 19 through 21 so you have a full understanding of address books and replication.

 Adding a Person from a Mail Message   When you receive a mail message from a person who is not listed in your Personal Address Book, you can add that person. Open or select the mail message and then click the, **Tools** button on the Action Bar and select **Add Sender to Address Book**.

Creating Mailing Lists

If you want to send a mail message to more than one person, you can type each person's name, separated by a comma, or you can create a *mailing list*. To create a mailing list, follow these steps:

1. Select **Groups** from the Personal Address Book Navigation Pane.

2. Click the **Add Mailing List** button on the Action Bar.

3. The Basics section of the Group document is displayed as in Figure 12.7. Type a short, descriptive name for your group in the **Group Name** field.

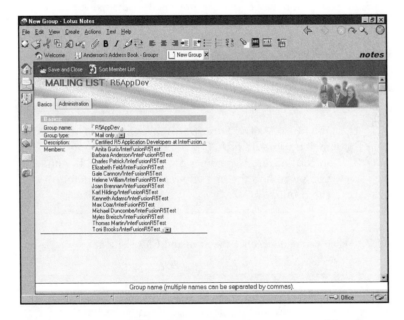

FIGURE **12.7**   Mailing Lists can save time when you are addressing mail.

4. Click the small triangle to the right of the **Group Type** field and select one of the following:

   • **Multipurpose**   Enables you to use this list for mail and purposes other than mail.

- **Access Control List Only**   Only used to specify security levels in Access Control Lists. This is used by the Domino system administrator and not relevant to the Personal Address Book.

- **Mail Only**   Used to define mailing lists. This is the selection you choose for groups. When you choose this option, the Group document becomes a Mailing List document.

- **Deny List Only**   Only used by the Domino system administrator. This is used by the Domino system administrator and not relevant to the Personal Address Book.

5. Type a short description of the group in the Description field. Although this is not a mandatory field, it might remind you why you created this group.

6. Click the down arrow next to the field and select the names from your Personal Address Book.

Too Much Mail?   Lotus Notes saves a copy of your mail by default. Including yourself in a group results in your having two copies of a mail message, the one you saved and the one you received as a member of the group.

7. When you're done, click the **Save and Close** button.

Creating Groups from Mail   If you have a mail message open that includes a list of recipients, you can create a group for that list. Open the message and choose **Actions, Add Recipients, to new Group in Address Book** from the menu. A new group document opens with the Members field filled in with the names in the list. Complete the other fields and save the document.

After you create the group, you can use it when you address memos. Simply type the name of the group in the To field (Quick address completes the name as you type), and Notes sends your email to all the people in the group. If a person drops out of the group or a new person is added, you can edit the group document by selecting it from the Groups view and clicking the **Edit Group** button on the Action Bar. By using the group name when addressing your mail, you can save a lot of typing.

 Quick Memo to Group   To quickly address a memo to a group, open the group view, highlight the group and click **Write Memo**.

Some groups need to exist only for the length of a project on which you're working. When you need to remove a group from your Personal Address Book, select it from the **Groups** view and click the **Delete Group** button on the Action Bar.

In this lesson, you learned about the address books and how to use your Personal Address Book for creating contacts and groups. In the next lesson, you learn how to navigate the Web using Lotus Notes.

LESSON 13
Navigating the Web

In this lesson you learn how to browse Web pages with Notes, save Web pages, set up agents, and use subscriptions.

Setting Browsing Preferences

Lotus Notes offers you the ability to surf the Internet, the Web and your company intranet using Notes as your browser or other browsers, such as Netscape Navigator or Microsoft Explorer. There are advantages to using Notes as your Web browser, however, and the main one is that you can store copies of Web pages in a Notes *database* for viewing when you aren't connected.

There are two ways that Notes can be set up to browse the Web using Notes:

- Notes can retrieve the pages directly. In this setup, the Web pages retrieved by Notes are stored locally, and only you can view them.

- An InterNotes server can retrieve the Web pages (an InterNotes server is a Domino server that performs Web browsing services). In this setup, the retrieved Web pages are stored on the server, and any user with access to that server can view the pages.

You need to consult your Domino Administrator to find out what way your organization is set up to retrieve pages.

When you want to retrieve Web pages directly from the Notes client, you must have either a direct or a proxy connection to the Internet. A direct connection uses TCP/IP (Transmission Control Protocol/Internet Protocol) and a dial-up modem or leased line. TCP/IP is a network protocol that is used for the Internet (a *network protocol* defines how computers on a network communicate with one another). A proxy connection uses TCP/IP and a proxy server that connects to the Internet for you (instead of going directly to an Internet service provider, or ISP, to connect). Check with your Domino Administrator to find out what type of connection you have.

Each of your location documents contains a setting for your Web browser preference. You might use a different method of connecting when you are in the office (such as a proxy server) than you would when working at home and disconnected from the office network (such as a modem connection directly to an ISP). Therefore, you need to specify for the current location which Web browser you want to use. You only need to do that once for each location you use.

To retrieve pages directly, and specify Notes as your Web browser, follow these steps:

1. Choose **File, Mobile, Edit Current Location** from the menu to open the Location document (or click the **Location** button on the Status bar and choose **Edit Current**).

2. When the Location document opens, click the **Internet Browser** tab (see Figure 13.1).

3. From the Internet Browser list, select **Notes** as your browser.

4. Select **From Notes Workstation** from the Retrieve/Open Pages list.

5. After consulting with your Domino Administrator, you should know whether you use a proxy server to connect to the Internet. If you do, click the **Basics** tab, and in the Proxy field enter the name or IP (Internet Protocol) address for that server (each computer on the Internet has a unique address that is the IP address). The Domino Administrator should supply that information for you.

6. Click the **Save and Close** button on the Action Bar.

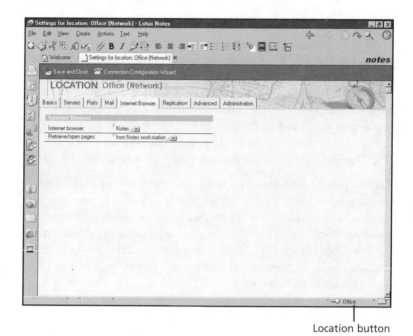

Location button

FIGURE **13.1**   Choose the Web browser you want to use for this Location from the Internet browser list.

To make Notes your default browser for all locations, choose **File, Preferences, User Preferences** from the menu. From the Additional Options list, select **Make Notes the Default Web Browser on My System**. Then, click **OK**.

To browse the Internet using an InterNotes server, choose **File, Mobile, Edit Current Location** from the menu to open the Location document. Click the **Internet Browser** tab. From the Internet Browser list, select **Notes** as your browser. Select **From InterNotes Server** from the Retrieve/Open Pages list.

Then, click the **Servers** tab. Specify the name of the InterNotes server you'll be using (ask your Domino Administrator) in the InterNotes Server field. Click **Save and Close** when you are finished.

To use Microsoft Internet Explorer, Netscape Navigator, or another Web browser, you must have that program installed on your computer. Confirm this and choose **File, Mobile, Edit Current Location** to open your current Location document. Select the **Internet Browser** tab. In the **Internet Browser** field, choose the browser you want to use—**Netscape Navigator, Microsoft Internet Explorer,** or **Other** (for **Other,** you must specify the path for the browser). Click the **Save and Close** button. If you have Microsoft Internet Explorer on your system when you install Notes for the first time, the Notes Install program imports the existing Internet Explorer proxy settings into the Notes Location document. Any changes you make to proxy settings in Internet Explorer do not take effect in Notes.

Surfing

The Personal Web Navigator is one of the bookmarks on your Databases page. You use this database to browse Web pages. To open this database, or to open a Web page, click the **Open URL** icon in the upper-right corner of your screen (or press **Ctrl+L**). The Address box opens, as shown in Figure 13.2. Enter the URL (Uniform Resource Locator), or address, of the Web page you want to visit, or click the down arrow at the right end of the field and select an address you visited previously. It isn't necessary to enter the complete address because Notes assumes the http:// part of the URL. Just start the address with the www when you enter it, such as www.mcp.com.

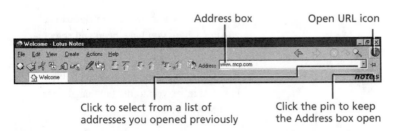

Address box   Open URL icon

Click to select from a list of   Click the pin to keep
addresses you opened previously   the Address box open

FIGURE 13.2   Open Web pages by entering the URL in the Address box, just as you do in many browsers.

To have Notes automatically create hotspots from URLs that appear in rich text fields of Notes documents, choose **File, Preferences, User Preferences** from the menu. On the Basics page, select **Make Internet URLs (http:// ...) into Hotspots** from the Additional Options list. When the hotspots appear in the documents, you click them, and Notes opens the URL. To detect text as a URL in the rich text field, however, it must begin with http://. Also, you must close and reopen a document you're editing or creating for the URL to become a hotspot.

Use the Navigation buttons in the upper-right corner of your screen to navigate among open pages (see Figure 13.3). Table 13.1 explains their uses.

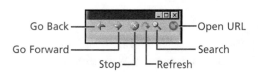

Go Back ——— ——— Open URL
Go Forward ——— ——— Search
Stop ——— ———Refresh

FIGURE **13.3**   Navigate though Web pages using these buttons.

Table 13.1   Navigation Buttons for Web Pages

Name	Description
Go Back	Takes you to the previous page you had open when you click once.
Go Back List	Click the down arrow next to Back to see a list of where you have been and select a page from that list to revisit.
Go Forward	After you have gone backward, clicking Forward takes you to the next page after the one you're on.

Name	Description
Go Forward List	Click the down arrow next to Forward to see a list of all the pages you've visited and select one to reopen.
Stop	Stops loading the page you requested from the Internet.
Refresh	Reloads a Web page directly from the Internet.
Search	Click to search a view, find a database, or search the Internet.
Search List	Click the down arrow next to Search to search for people or databases or to start an Internet search engine such as Lycos or Yahoo!
Open URL	Click to open the Address box, in which you enter a URL you want to visit.

Searching for Information

Finding information on the Web can seem overwhelming, but there are several Internet search engines that exist to help you. Click the Search List navigation button to see a list of engines you can use to search, such as Excite, Lycos, Search.com, and Yahoo! When the site opens, follow the instructions on that page to search for the information you want.

You might prefer a search site that is not included in your list and that you can add that to the list of search sites. Go to your favorite search site by entering the URL in the URL locator and pressing **ENTER**. Click the task button for the open search site, drag it over the Internet Search Sites folder (located in the More Bookmarks bookmark), and release the mouse button.

Storing Retrieved Pages

When you use Notes to retrieve Web pages directly, the pages are stored in the Personal Web Navigator database on your local drive. If you use an InterNotes server to retrieve Web pages, the pages are stored in the Server Web Navigator database located on that server. An InterNotes server is shared by many users, so the Server Web Navigator database will also contain pages that have been visited by other users.

 Notes will not automatically store pages if you are using Notes with Internet Explorer and you've selected **Manually Store Pages for Disconnected Use** under the Size options in the Internet Options document. In that case, open the page and then choose **Actions, Keep Page** from the menu to manually store the page in the Personal Web Navigator database.

For the pages that are stored, you need to specify how often they should be updated. From the menu, choose **File, Mobile, Edit Current Location**. When the Location document opens, select the **Advanced** tab, and then click the **Web Retriever** tab (see Figure 13.4).

Select an option from Update Cache:

* **Never**—Select this option if you never want to update your stored Web pages. This is the default setting.

* **Once Per Session**—Choose this option to update stored Web pages once per Notes session.

* **Every Time**—Select to update stored Web pages each time you open one. This is especially important when you need up-to-date information every time you open a page (such as with stock prices).

Click the **Save and Close** button on the Action Bar to save your choices.

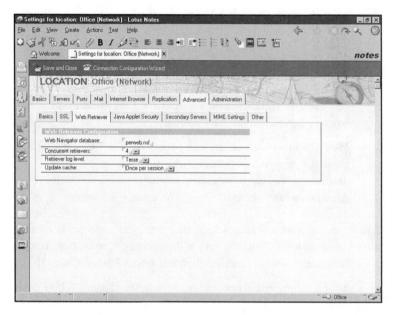

FIGURE **13.4**   Messages about Web retrieval are stored in your
Notes log, where information on daily activities in Notes is kept. In
Retriever Log Level, select **None** to have no messages sent (the
default) about Web retrieval, **Terse** to send minimal messages, or
Verbose to send all messages.

How many parts of a Web page do you want to
retrieve at once? Do you want to retrieve the text,
images, and video all at the same time? You can set
Notes to retrieve more than one at a time by choosing
File, Mobile, Edit Current Location from the menu,
clicking the **Advanced** tab, selecting the **Web
Retriever** tab, and then selecting a number in the
Concurrent Retrievers field (15 is the default).
However, the more retrievals you have working at the
same time, the more computer memory you use, and
the slower your computer will be in downloading
pages.

Using Personal Web Navigator Agents

There are two agents that automate a couple of important tasks for you:

- **Page Minder** keeps an eye on particular Web pages and notifies you when the contents of the page change. Page Minder only runs when your Notes workstation is running.

- **Web Ahead** retrieves all the Web pages that have URL links on a particular page and saves them to the Personal Web Navigator database, so you can browse them at your convenience. Web Ahead only runs when your Notes workstation is running

Before you set your preferences for these agents, you must enable agents to run on your computer. You only have to do this once. Choose **File**, **Tools**, **User Preferences**. Check **Enable Scheduled Local Agents**. Click **OK**

To set your preferences and options for the Web Ahead agent, follow these steps:

1. Open any Web page, and choose **Actions, Internet Options** from the menu

2. Select the **Web Ahead** tab (see Figure 13.5).

3. In the Preload Web Pages field, enter the number of levels of pages you want to save (when you click a link and open another page, that's level 1; when you click a link on that page and open a third page, that's level 2).

4. Click the **Enable Web Ahead** button.

5. Click the **Save and Close** button.

The Web Ahead agent automatically runs every 30 minutes once you set it to run. After it successfully runs on a page placed in the Web Ahead folder, Notes removes the page from that folder. You can also drag and drop pages into the folder. To run the Web Ahead agent for a Web page follow these steps:

1. Open the Web page and then choose **Actions, Copy to Folder** from the menu.

2. Choose **WebBot**, **Web Ahead Folder** and click OK.

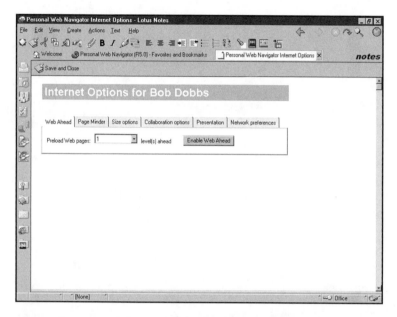

FIGURE **13.5** If you haven't already done it, a notice appears when you click Enable Web Ahead to remind you to enable scheduled local agents in User Preferences.

The Page Minder watches a Web page and notifies you whenever that page modified. To run Page Minder, follow these steps:

1. Open any Web page and choose **Actions, Internet Options** from the menu.

2. Click the **Page Minder** tab (see Figure 13.6).

3. Complete the following fields and click **Enable Page Minder**:

    • **Search for Updates Every**—Sets the frequency (**Hour, 4 Hours, Day**, or **Week**) that the agent checks to see if there are changes to the page content.

    • **When Updates Are Found**—Specifies how you are to be alerted when pages change. Select **Send a Summary** to get a message saying the page changed or **Send the Actual Page** to get the updated page. The updated page or summary is sent to you in your mail.

• **Send To**—Specifies the name of the person to alert about changes in the page. Be sure your own name appears there if you want to be notified. Click **Address** to select people from an Address Book.

4. Click **Save and Close** to save your choices.

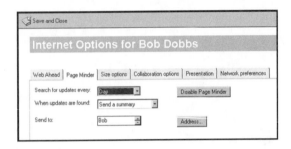

FIGURE 13.6   Specify the settings to have Page Minder remind you of changes to Web pages.

When you're ready to run the Page Minder agent on a Web page, open the page and choose **Actions, Copy to Folder**. Select **WebBot, Page Minder Folder**. Then, click **OK**.

Eventually, you'll want to stop getting reminders about a page. You do that by deleting the page from the Personal Web Navigator or Server Web Navigator databases. To delete a page, follow these steps:

1. Select either **Personal Web Navigator** or **Server Web Navigator** (if you have made a replica copy). Click **Open**.

2. In the Navigation Pane of the database, select **WebBots, Page Minder**.

3. Select the Web page, and then click the **Delete** button. (If you want to keep the page, but remove it from the folder only, choose **Actions, Remove from folder** on the menu.)

4. Close the database and confirm the deletion of the page.

·Viewing Pages Offline

To browse when you are disconnected from the Internet, you need to change your Location document (or switch to a Location that is disconnected, such as Island). Choose **File, Mobile, Edit Current Location** from the menu to open the Location document. Select the **Internet Browser** tab. From the Retrieve/Open Pages field, choose **No Retrievals**. Then, click the **Save and Close** button on the Action Bar.

Quick Edit!   Quickly edit a location document by clicking the location in the status bar and choosing **Edit Current** from the pop-up menu.

With **No Retrievals** selected, Notes will only retrieve pages from the Personal Web Navigator or Server Web Navigator database. Notes won't retrieve pages from the Web. You will have to reconnect and change the setting in the Location document before you can retrieve new or updated pages.

If you switch to the Island (disconnected) location, you should use this setup so you can continue viewing Web pages you've stored.

To browse pages stored in the Server Web Navigator database while disconnected, you'll have to make a replica of the database (see Lesson 19 to learn about replication). Do that just before you disconnect to ensure you have the most up-to-date copy of the database.

Forwarding and Mailing Pages

Forwarding the Web page sends the body of the Web page to the recipient (be sure you also include the URL). That way, the recipient can immediately see why the page caught your attention, making it more likely that the person will visit the page. However, to ensure that the person can access all the features of the page, you should forward the *URL* instead of the page.

To forward a page, open the Web page and choose **Actions, Forward** from the menu. Then select **Forward Copy of Page**. In the Mail Memo, enter or select the names of the recipients in the To field. Type any necessary comments, and then click **Send**.

The page you forward might not look exactly as you saw it on the Web if you specified **Notes with Internet Explorer** as your browser and you forward a copy of a page to a user who uses Notes as his browser. The contents of the page are converted from HTML to rich text, so some differences might occur. Also, when using Notes with Internet Explorer, you are able to forward URLs using the FILE protocol, which you can't do in Notes.

To forward a URL, start from the open Web page and choose **Actions, Forward** from the menu. You then select **Forward Bookmark to Page**. You enter the names of the recipients in the To field (see Figure 13.7) or select them from the Address Book. Type any comments you want to accompany the URL, and then click **Send**.

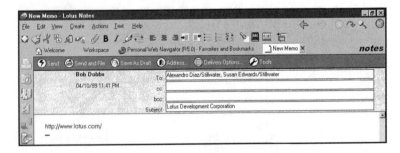

FIGURE **13.7**   This Mail Memo forwards the URL of the Lotus Web page to two recipients. When the memo is received, the recipient can click the URL to open the Web page.

Performing Housekeeping

Storing all the Web pages you visit could result in a very large database file. At some time, you'll have to remove some of those files. One way to do this is to use the Housekeeping agents to automatically delete stored Web pages. When enabled, this agent runs daily. To enable Housekeeping, follow these steps:

1. Open the Personal Web Navigator

2. Choose Actions, Internet Options.

3. Click the **Size Options** tab (see Figure 13.8), and select one of these options:

   - **Reduce Full Pages to Links If Not Read Within**—Select this option to have Notes delete the contents of the Web page but save the URL so you can still open the page on the Web. Then specify the number of days that the Web page should be in the database before deletion.

   - **Remove Pages from Database If Not Read In**—Choose this option to have Notes delete the entire Web page. Then specify the number of days that the Web page should be in the database before deletion.

   - **Disable**—Select this option to disable the agent that automatically deletes stored Web pages.

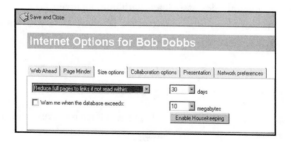

FIGURE **13.8**   Set your housekeeping options to reduce the size of Web pages that haven't been read recently or to delete those pages.

4. **(Optional)** If you want to be warned when the database gets to a certain size, select **Warn Me When the Database Exceeds** and then specify a size in megabytes.

5. Click **Enable Housekeeping.** The **Choose Server to Run On** dialog box appears. Select **Local** and click **OK.**

Like Page Minder and Web Ahead, you must enable scheduled local agents. If you've done this once, you need not do it again. If you've not enabled scheduled agents, choose **File, Preferences, User Preferences,** and place a check mark next to **Enable scheduled local agents.**

Instead of relying on an agent to delete your Web pages, you can perform this task manually. You open the Personal Web Navigator or Server Web Navigator databases on Local and do one of the following:

- Select **Other, House Cleaning** in the Navigation Pane to display a list of documents sorted in ascending order by document size (click the column header to sort the list in another order). Select the documents you want to remove, and then click **Delete** on the Action Bar. Notes deletes the selected documents (and confirms this when you exit the database).

- Select **Other, File Archive** if you want to delete documents based on file size. Notes displays a list of files that are sorted by file size. Select the documents you want to remove, and then click **Delete** on the Action Bar. Notes deletes the selected documents and any files associated with that document, such as graphics or video files. Confirm the deletion when you exit the database.

Create Subscriptions

When you subscribe to a Domino database, Notes retrieves information and updates on a regular basis to keep you informed of current events. As long as the database supports subscriptions (whether it is located within your company or on the Web) and you have subscriptions enabled in your database, you can subscribe and stay informed.

To enable subscriptions, choose **File**, **Preferences**, **User Preferences**. Click the **Basics** icon and check the **Check subscriptions** box in the **Startup Options**.

Complete the following steps to subscribe to a database:

1. Open the database to which you want to subscribe.

2. Choose **Create, Subscription** from the menu.

3. Click on **Basics**.

4. Enter a Subscription Name.

5. Indicate your preferences for retrieving information from the database by completing the form. The preferences are different for different types of databases (see Figure 13.9).

6. Click **OK**.

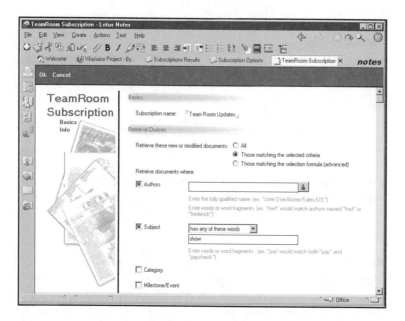

FIGURE **13.9**   This subscription checks for documents that contain the word *show*. Click the Address Book icon to enter names of Authors and have the subscription search for documents by author name.

How do you see your subscriptions? Click the **Favorite Bookmarks** folder and then select **Database Subscriptions**. When you first open the Database Subscriptions (see Figure 13.10), a list of the databases to which you subscribe appears in the left pane and the results of the expanded subscription display in the right pane.

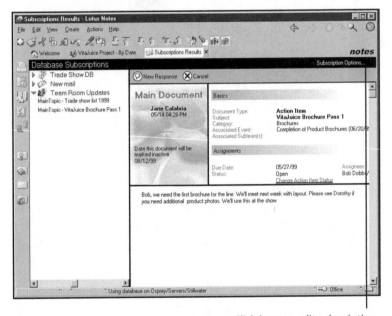

Click here to edit subscription

FIGURE 13.10   Here, three database subscriptions appear in the left pane. Documents meeting subscription criteria appear in the right pane. Click **Subscription Options** to edit or delete the subscription.

To edit or delete a subscription, click **Subscription Options** in the **Database Subscriptions View** (see Figure 13.10). A list of enabled subscriptions appears (see Figure 13.11). To disable a subscription, select it and click the **Enabled/Disabled** button on the Action Bar. The database moves to the Disabled list.

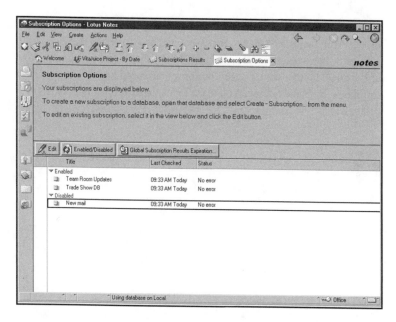

FIGURE 13.11   If you disable the wrong subscription, select it and click the **Enabled/Disabled** button to enable it again.

To edit a subscription, click the **Edit** button on the Action Bar. The subscription page appears where you change your selections.

> Our technical editor and Notes guru, John Palmer, wants us to remind you that Subscriptions can also be added to the Welcome Page. This is an example of information push technology where information comes to you, instead of you looking for it. You learn how to customize the Welcome Page in Lesson 22, "Customizing Notes."

To control how long subscriptions results are kept before they are discarded, click the **Global Subscription Results Expiration** button on the Action Bar. Enter the number of days you want to keep the subscription results, or choose **Keep results forever**. Click **OK**.

In this lesson you learned how to use the Personal Web Navigator to browse Web pages, how pages are saved, and how to set up the Web Navigator to save additional pages and check other pages for updates. You also learned how to search pages, perform housekeeping, and create subscriptions. In the next lesson you learn to manage documents in Notes databases.

LESSON 14
Managing Documents

In this lesson, you learn how to refresh views, edit documents, and view unread documents. You also learn how to find and replace text in a document and in a database.

Refreshing Views

It is not uncommon for Notes users to have several databases open at one time; the mail database is usually one of them. Over time (minutes, hours) new documents are added to databases that do not appear in the View pane unless you occasionally update, or refresh, the view. Refreshing the view forces Notes to present a current, accurate listing of documents that have been added to the database since you opened the view. This is a similar process to refreshing a Web page.

Notes tells you when new messages have been added to your mail database by placing a Refresh icon on your View pane. If the icon appears, click it, press **F9,** or click the Refresh icon found on the Navigation Bar (see Figure 14.1) to refresh the view. If no Refresh icon appears in your View pane, it is not necessary to refresh the view.

Refresh icon

Refresh navigation
button

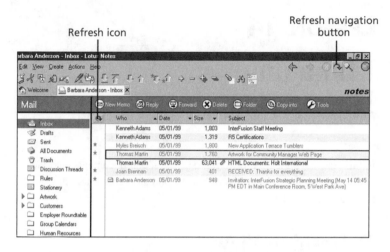

FIGURE 14.1   When you see the Refresh icon in your View pane,
click it to refresh your view.

Editing Documents

To edit a document, select the document and choose **Actions**, **Edit** from
the menu. You also can press **Ctrl+E** to place the document in edit mode
or double-click the document while reading it. Depending on the database, you might also be presented with an **Edit Document** button in the
Action Bar.

 Depending on the database in which you are working,
it is possible that you do not have editing rights to a
document. If you need to but are unable to edit a
document, contact your Domino system administrator.

When you finish editing a document, press the **Esc** key, or click the **X** in
the Task Button. Depending on the database in which you are working,
the Close Window dialog box or a Lotus Notes dialog box appears, asking
if you want to save your changes (select **Yes**, **No**, or **Cancel**). If you
are editing a Mail Memo, you might see other choices as described in
Table 14.1.

TABLE 14.1   Options for the Close Window Dialog Box

Option	Action
Send and Save a copy	Applicable to Mail Memos and mail in databases. Saves a copy of the memo in your Sent folder and sends the memo to those listed as the recipients.
Send Only	Sends a memo to the recipients and saves no copy.
Save Only	Saves a copy in your drafts folder; does not send the document.
Discard Changes	Same effect as Cancel. No versions are saved, and nothing is mailed.

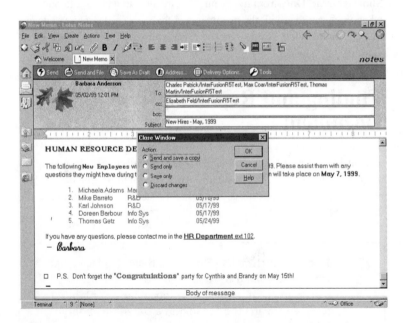

FIGURE 14.2   Pressing Esc or closing a Mail Memo window while editing or creating a memo brings up the Close Window dialog box.

Editing Sent & Received Messages Because it does not serve any purpose, you probably will not be modifying mail that has already been sent or new mail that you receive. If you want to copy all the text from one message into a new memo, calendar, or to do document, select the document in the view and then use the **Copy Into** button on the Action Bar. Remember, too, that you can forward messages, sending a message you've received on to another person.

Viewing Unread Documents

To view only documents or messages you have *not* read, choose **View**, **Show**, **Unread Only** from the menu. This menu command is a toggle—when you want to see all the documents in the view (including read documents), choose **View**, **Show**, **Unread Only** again and remove the check mark next to **Unread Only.**

Finding and Replacing Text in a Document

You can easily find words or phrases within a Notes document or mail message. You can find text, or you can find and replace text (depending on your access level to that document) After you find text, you can replace it quickly and effortlessly by using the same Find and Replace dialog box.

Find or Search? Use Find or Find and Replace when you are searching for text within a document. To search an entire database for documents containing text, see "Searching for Text in a Database" later in this lesson.

To find or replace specific text in a document, follow these steps:

1. If you are Finding only, the document must be open. If you want to Find and Replace, the document must be in edit mode. Choose **Edit**, **Find/Replace** from the menu. The **Find Text in Document** dialog box is displayed as pictured in Figure 14.3.

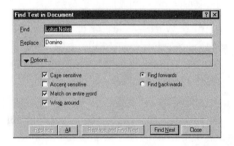

FIGURE 14.3 You can find or replace words or phrases anywhere in a document.

 I Can't Replace the Text! Whether or not you can replace text in a document depends on two things: First, you must be in edit mode and, second, you must have sufficient access rights to edit that document. If you are working in your mail database, you are the manager of the database and can, therefore, replace whatever you want. If you're working in a database other than mail, it is possible that you do not have rights to edit documents, particularly if you didn't create the documents. For more information on Notes and Domino security, see Appendix A, "Understanding Security and Access Rights."

2. In the Find text box, enter the text you want to find. The entry can consist of up to 99 characters and spaces.

3. (**Optional**) In the Replace text box, enter the text you want to substitute for the found text.

4. (**Optional**) Click the twistie to the left of Options. Choose any of the following options:

Case sensitive—Searches for the character string that matches the case exactly, as with names of programs or people.

Accent sensitive—Tells Notes to include diacritical accent marks (such as those used in foreign languages).

Match on Entire Word—Finds the character string you entered only when a space precedes and follows the word. For example, if you enter *the* and do not choose Whole Word, Notes finds such words as *their*, *there*, and *other*.

Wrap around—Searches the entire document regardless of your cursor position at the time you start the search. If not selected, Notes will search from the cursor position forward or backwards, depending on the selection of **Find forwards** or **Find backwards.**

5. Click the **Find Next** button to find the next occurrence of the word in the text. Choose the **Find Previous** button to find the previous occurrence of the word. If it finds a match, Notes highlights the word in the text and leaves the Find and Replace dialog box open.

6. (**Optional**) Click the **Replace** button to replace the highlighted text that Notes found with the text you typed in the Replace text box. Or, if you're sure you want to replace all occurrences, click the **All** button to replace them all automatically.

7. (**Optional**) Click **Find Next** or **Find Previous** to skip this occurrence and find the next occurrence of the specified text. You can click **Replace and Find Next** to replace the found text and jump to the next occurrence.

8. **Click** Close to close the dialog box.

Shortcut   Press **Ctrl+G** to find the word or phrase again without opening the Find and Replace dialog box. Notes remembers what you entered in the Find and Replace dialog box the last time, and it finds that text again.

Searching for Text in a Database

Another way to find information in a document is Quick search, which is a great way to find information in a view, such as your Mail Inbox view.

To use Quick search, open the view you want to search and begin typing the word you want to find. Notes searches the first sorted column of the view for the documents that match in the database, not the entire document contents.

Another kind of search available in Notes is a full-text search, in which you use the *Search Builder*. This type of search looks through the contents of the documents in a database, without having to open documents. To perform a full-text search, the database must first be indexed and contain a full-text index. A full-text index is a special file created by Notes that creates an index to the contents of documents. If a database has been full-text indexed, it is indicated so on the Search Bar. To view the Search Bar, choose **View**, **Search Bar** on the menu. With full-text-indexed databases, you can do the following:

- Create search formulas to find documents

- Save search formulas to reuse later

To use the Search Builder, follow these steps:

1. In database view, choose **View**, **Search Bar**. The Search Bar appears above the view pane.

2. Enter a word or phrase in the **Search for** text box.

3. Click the **Search** button. A list of all the documents that contain the word or phrase in the view pane (see Figure 14.4).

4. Click the **Clear Results** button to start a new search and display all the documents in the database.

If your database is not indexed, create a full-text index by clicking the More button on the Search Bar. Click the Create Index button that appears on the expanded more page. Accept the defaults for creating the index and click OK. To learn more about full text indexing and the choices found in the Full Text Index dialog box, search Lotus Notes Help for *create index.*

You also can set search criteria when you use the Search Bar. To do so, click the **More** button at the right end of the Search Bar. The pop-up menu shown in Figure 14.4 appears.

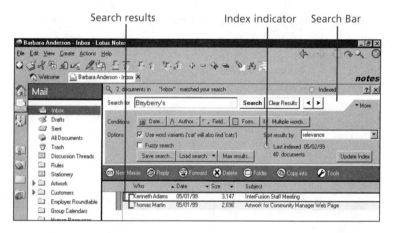

FIGURE 14.4   Notes lists the documents that contain the search text.

- **Conditions**—Search by date, author, field, form, or word combinations. In the multiple word dialog box you can find ALL or ANY word occurrences. If you want to find all words listed (documents that contain the word *blue* and *red*), choose ALL. If you want to find either of the words listed (documents that contain the word *blue* or the word *red*), choose ANY. The **Fill Out Example** button assists you search for words by giving you a sample of the form to fill out.

* **Use Word Variants**—Includes variants, such as plurals, in the search. For example, if you enter the word *network*, Notes finds *networks*, *networking*, and so on.

* **Sort Results by**—You can choose how you want the documents presented to you in the view.

* **Sort by Relevance**—Lists the documents with the most occurrences of the word first.

* **Save Search**—Displays the Save Search dialog box in which you can name the search so that you can use it again. After you save a search you can reload it by clicking on the **Load Search** button. The search will automatically be carried out.

* **Delete Saved Search**—(An option found in the Load Search button.) Displays the Delete Saved Search dialog box from which you select saved searches and delete those you no longer use.

In this lesson, you learned how to refresh views, edit documents, and view unread documents. You also learned how to find and replace text in a document and how to search a database using the Search Bar. In the next lesson, you learn how to edit and format text and fields.

LESSON 15

Editing and Formatting Text and Fields

In this lesson, you learn about text fields; how to select, move, and copy text; how to format text and paragraphs; how to set page breaks; and how to use the permanent pen.

Selecting Text

Before you can copy, move, delete, or format text in a document, you must select it. The quickest and easiest method of selecting text in a document is to click and drag the mouse cursor across the text you want to select. When text is selected, it appears in reverse video, as shown in Figure 15.1.

If you selected too much text or you didn't mean to select text at all, click the mouse anywhere in the document to deselect the text. Alternatively, you can press the right or left arrow on the keyboard.

Shortcuts Double-click any single word to select just that one word. Position your cursor in the left margin of a rich text field, click once to select a line of text and click twice to select a paragraph.

Click here

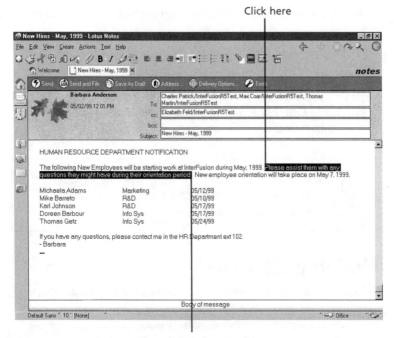

Then drag to here and
release the mouse button

FIGURE 15.1 Click and drag the mouse to quickly select text.

Moving and Copying Text

You can move text from one part of the document to another part of the
same document or from one document to another. You also can copy text
between documents or within the same document. Follow these steps to
copy or move text:

1. Select the text you want to move or copy.

2. Choose **Edit**, **Cut** if you want to move the text, or choose **Edit**,
   Copy if you want to make a duplicate of the text. The text is
   copied or moved to the Windows Clipboard.

3. Reposition the cursor where you want to place the text (it can be in the same document or in another document).

If you want to place the cut or copied text in another document, use the Window menu to switch back to the database or to another open document.

4. Choose **Edit**, **Paste**, and the copied or cut text appears at the insertion point.

 Shortcut   If you prefer to work from the keyboard, press **Ctrl+X** to cut text, **Ctrl+C** to copy text, and **Ctrl+V** to paste text.

Undoing Changes

Undoing a change such as formatting, or cutting text cancels the effects you just applied and returns the document to its previous state. For example, if you cut some text and you didn't mean to, you can undo that action. The text is returned to its original location. To undo changes, choose **Edit**, **Undo** or press **Ctrl+Z**.

You must choose to Undo an action before you perform another. Because Notes can remember only one action at a time, each new action replaces the last one.

 Can't Undo   Not all changes and edits can be undone. If the Undo command is dimmed, you cannot undo your previous command.

Types of Fields

Notes forms contain several types of fields. Some are automatically filled in and others are fields in which you enter information. Notes fields in which you enter data are easily identified because they are the white boxes—usually to the right or below the static text that describes the field—where you type in information as you have seen in the heading of the Mail Memo form.

The following list describes the common field types you find in Notes database forms. Not all forms contain all of these elements.

- **Text Fields**—Fields in which you can enter words and sentences, usually titles or topics. You cannot format text in a text field.

- **Rich Text Fields**—Fields in which you can enter text, import text, import graphics such as .PCX or .TIFF files, and attach files. The body of the Mail Memo is a document. You can apply both text and paragraph formatting in rich text fields.

- **Keyword Fields**—Fields in which you select choices from a list. The Company field in the Business Card is a keyword field. Depending on the database design, you might be able to enter or even add your own keywords.

- **Date/Time Fields**—Very often, these fields are automatically filled by Notes, using your computer's clock. Most time fields display hour and minute, while most date fields display month, date, and year.

- **Number Fields**—Fields that can contain only numbers, such as currency or quantities.

To enter information into a field, click inside of the field and begin typing. To move from field to field on a form, press the **Tab** key.

Fields within the mail database are rarely fixed-length fields, which means they grow in size as you type information into them. In some cases, a database designer can make a field fixed-length to keep the integrity of the data consistent. For example, he might design the area code field to accept only three characters.

For the most part, information that you place in Notes fields can be copied, moved, or deleted as you would in any word processor. However, as stated above, the ability to format text and paragraphs in a field is reserved for rich text fields.

How Can You Tell?   If you see the font size and type displayed on the left side of the status bar at the bottom of your screen, you are in a rich text field. Put your cursor in the **To** field of a New Mail Memo. Nothing displayed. Now move your cursor down to the body of the message. See? There it is, just like Figure 15.2.

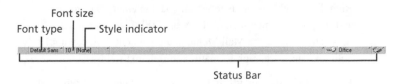

Font size
Font type   Style indicator
Default Sans   10   [None]   Office

Status Bar

FIGURE 15.2   The body of the Mail Memo is a rich text field with a default font of Helv 10.

Formatting Text

You can change character formatting in any rich text field to make your documents more interesting or attractive, or to emphasize important text. As pictured in Figure 15.3, character formatting includes working with the following characteristics:

- **Font**—Apply a typeface to text in the document. For example, you can make a title stand out by applying a different typeface to it. You are limited to the fonts available in your operating system.

- **Size**—Apply a size to the text increases or decreases the size of the printed or displayed text. Typically, larger text (say, 24-point size) commands more attention, and smaller text (10-point, for example) is reserved for details.

- **Style**—Apply special text formatting—plain, bold, italic, underline, strikethrough, subscript, superscript, shadow, emboss, or extrude—to add emphasis and clarity to your document.

- **Color**—Apply color to text to further define the text in your document.

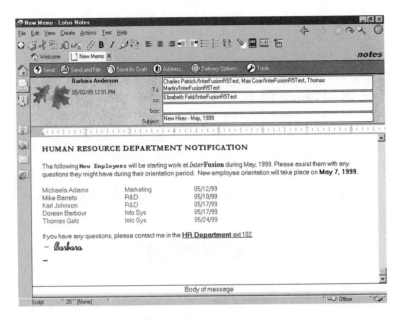

FIGURE 15.3   Character formatting makes your documents more attractive.

Font/Typeface—A font is a set of characters in one style and size. Times New Roman, Courier, and Helv are common fonts and Helv10 is a different font than Helv12.

Point—A measurement of type; there are 72 points in an inch. Body text is generally 10- or 12-point, and headlines or titles are usually 14-, 18-, or 24-point.

Select your text before you apply formatting. There are several methods of applying text formatting after you have selected it:

- **Status Bar**—Click directly on the font name and font size and select your new choices from the pop-up lists.

- **Menu**—Press **Alt+T** on your keyboard to open the **Text** menu bar. Select your character formatting from the pulldown menu.

- **Keyboard Hotkeys**—**Ctrl+B** for Bold, **Ctrl+I** for Italic, **Ctrl+U** for underlining, **F2** to increase the font size, **Shift+F2** to decrease the font size. *Hint: Hotkeys are listed in the Text pull-down menu.*

- **Text Properties Box**—Press **Ctrl+K** or select **Text, Text Properties** from the menu bar. Font properties are changed in the first tab as seen in Figure 15.4.

- **SmartIcons**—Bold and Italic SmartIcons are available by default.

- **Right Click**—Choose the most common types of text formatting from the shortcut menu.

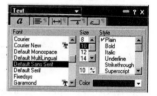

FIGURE 15.4   When you are done formatting your text, close the Properties Box by clicking on the X in the upper-right corner.

    Highlight the Good Points   To add some extra emphasis to existing text, add some color to the line. Choose **Text, Highlighter** from the menu and then select your color: yellow, blue, or pink. As you drag your mouse cursor over text, it is highlighted in the color you choose. Don't forget to turn it off when you are done by choosing **Text, Highlighter** and deselecting the highlighter.

Formatting Paragraphs

Apply paragraph formatting for the same reasons as you apply text formatting—that is, to add emphasis and clarity to your documents. As pictured in Figure 15.5, paragraph formatting includes working with the following characteristics:

Alignment—Move the paragraph to the left margin or right margin, center it between the left and right margins, fully justify it to both the left and right margins, or continue it past the right margin without word wrapping.

Margins—Set ruler measurements for your left and right margin. You can also indent or outdent the first line of a paragraph or the entire paragraph.

Tab Stops—Set ruler measurements for tab placement. Choices include left tabs, right tabs, centered tabs, and decimal place tabs.

Line Spacing—Set the amount of space you want between lines of text in your document. Choices include

- **Interline**—Determines the space between the lines of text within a paragraph.

- **Above**—Determines extra space added above a paragraph.

- **Below**—Determines extra space added below a paragraph.

- **Single, 1 1/2, or Double**—Sets the spacing for the selected paragraph.

Lists—Extremely helpful for adding emphasis to documents, each item on the list is preceded by sequential numbers, small black dots, check boxes, square boxes, or circles.

Select your paragraph before you apply formatting. There are several methods of applying paragraph formatting after you have selected it:

- **Menu**—Press **Alt+T** on your keyboard to open the **Text** menu bar. Select your individual paragraph formatting from the pulldown menu.

- **Keyboard Hotkeys**—**F8** for Indent, **Shift+F8** for Outdent. *Hint: Hotkeys are listed in the Text pulldown menu.*

- **Text Properties Box**—Press **Ctrl+K** or select **Text, Text Properties** from the menu bar. Paragraph properties are changed in the second and third tab as seen in Figure 15.6.

- **SmartIcons**—Alignment, Indent, Outdent, and List SmartIcons are available by default.

- **Right Click**—Choose the most common types of paragraph formatting from the shortcut menu.

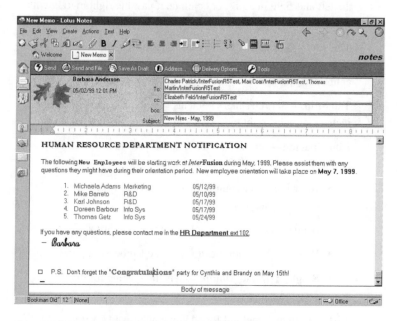

FIGURE 15.5   Very effective documents are created when you combine both character and paragraph formatting.

FIGURE 15.6   The Text Properties box remains open while you format text and paragraphs. It can be moved by dragging the title bar.

Paragraph   In Notes, a paragraph is defined as a line with a hard paragraph return (which you create by pressing **Enter**) at the end of it. A paragraph can contain several sentences, several words, or one word or letter, or it can even be a blank line. To see your paragraphs as you type, choose **View, Show, Hidden Characters**.

 If you find you use the same formatting over and over (same font, same size, and so forth) you are a candidate for using styles. Search for *styles* in the Help database and learn how to save and reuse your formatting preferences.

Using Page Breaks

Notes automatically breaks pages for you, but you might not always like where the page break falls. You can insert page breaks to organize the pages in your document to suit yourself.

 Can't See Breaks?   If you cannot see the page breaks that Notes creates, choose **View, Show, Page Breaks**.

To insert a page break, follow these steps:

1. Position the insertion point where you want a page break.

2. Choose **Create, Page Break**. Notes displays a thin black line across the page to show the page break.

The Permanent Pen

The permanent pen enables you to add text in a different color or font than the default font settings so that it stands out from the rest of the document. This is especially useful for collaborative projects because each user can work in a different color permanent pen; everyone can see who contributed to the document by the color of the text. This feature is easier to use because text formatting occurs while you type, as opposed to you typing and then going back to format your text. Permanent pen only works in a rich text field such as the body of a message. The default permanent pen is bold red text.

I Didn't Say That   When a message or document is forwarded to you from another person, you can edit your copy of the original message. However, because it is not appropriate to modify the sender's text without her knowledge, use permanent pen to add your own comments before forwarding it on to anyone else.

 To turn on the permanent pen, choose **Text, Permanent Pen, Use Permanent** or click the **Permanent Pen** SmartIcon. "Permanent Pen enabled" displays in the status bar at the bottom of your screen. Then, type the text you want to appear in the permanent pen style. To stop using the permanent pen and begin using normal text again, click the **Permanent Pen** SmartIcon again, or remove the check mark next to **Use Permanent Pen** in the menu.

Rub It Out   Strikethrough text is used to mark text that you want to edit out (for example: ~~Exchange~~ Notes). To accomplish this with the permanent pen, first select the words you want to strike through. Then use the hotkey combination **Shift+Backspace** to mark the text.

To change the look of the permanent pen from the default bold, red text, type some text and apply the formatting to that text. Then, select the text and choose **Text, Permanent Pen, Set Permanent Pen Style**. In setting the permanent pen formatting, you can set the font, and the font color, size and style. In this lesson, you learned about rich text fields; how to select, move, and copy text; how to apply character and paragraph formatting; how to set custom page breaks; and how to use the permanent pen. In the next lesson you learn how to create links, tables, and sections.

LESSON 16
Enhancing Documents

In this lesson, you learn how to create document, database, and view links, as well as tables and sections.

Creating Document, Database, Anchor, and View Links

Links are pointers to other documents, views, or Lotus Notes databases. If you want to send a mail message and refer to a page in the Help database, you can create a document link in your mail message. When the recipient receives your mail, he can click the **Document Link** icon and see the page to which you are referring.

Links work the same way that hypertext works in the Help database, displaying underlined text that you click to open other documents, or by displaying an icon that represents the link. There are four types of Lotus Notes links that you can create and include in your mail messages or Lotus Notes documents (see Table 16.1).

Table 16.1 Types of Links

This Icon	Named	Does This
	Anchor Link	Connects to a *specific location* in the same document, or in a different document.

This Icon	Named	Does This
	Document Link	Connects to another Lotus Notes document. It can be a mail message or a document within an entirely different database. Double-clicking a document link results in the linked document appearing on the screen.
	View Link	Connects to another database view (other than the default view).
	Database Link	Connects to another database opened at its default view.

It's important to understand that links only work when they are linked to documents, views, and databases to which others have access. If you link to a document that has been deleted or to a database not available to or accessible by the person to whom you are sending the link, it simply won't work.

Creating Document Links

The examples in this lesson create links from a Mail Memo to the Help database. Be sure to use the server copy of the Help database, not a local copy. If you have access to discussion databases or other types of Lotus Notes databases, try these exercises using those databases instead of the Help and mail databases.

To create a document link, follow these steps:

1. Begin a mail message by filling in the header (address, subject line, and so on) information.

2. In the body field of your message, type a sentence telling the recipient what information is in the document that's linked to your Mail Memo (this is a courtesy, not a requirement). You might type something such as **I'm learning how to create a document link. If you want to learn too, click here.**

3. Press the **spacebar** (or to create an arrow **-->** press spacebar, dash, dash, greater than sign) at the end of your sentence. Open the Favorites Navigator Pane using the Button Bar to access other databases without exiting this mail message.

4. Click the **Help** database icon to open the database. Do a quick search for links. Click on the twistie to expand the using in documents section Double-click to open the Using **links, buttons, hotspots, and sections in documents** document.

5. With the Help document open, choose **Edit, Copy as Link, Document Link** from the menu.

6. You created your document link. The next step is to paste it into your mail message. Click on the New Memo task button to return to your memo.

7. Place your cursor at the end of your sentence, remembering to leave the blank space. Choose **Edit, Paste** to insert the Document Link icon into your mail message (see Figure 16.1).

8. Send your mail message. Press **Esc** to close the Help database, or click the **X** in the Notes Help task button.

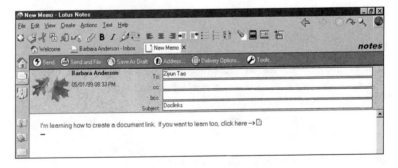

FIGURE 16.1 A document link is inserted at the position of your cursor when you create the link.

You can see the results of your document link by looking at the copy of the mail message you just sent. Open the Sent view of your mailbox and double-click the copy of the mail message you just created. If you want to display the name of the linked document, point at the document link icon and hold your mouse pointer there without clicking. A small hand appears, pointing at the link icon.

If you want to see the linked document, click the **Document Link** icon.

 A Weak Link? Remember, the success of links depends on the proper rights, or access, to a document or database. Be careful using document links with mail messages. For example, no one has access to your Inbox but you. You won't have success sending a document link to "Bob" so that he can see the message in your Inbox that you received from "Mary." Bob can't access your mailbox. In this case, you must forward Mary's message to Bob.

Lotus Notes automatically creates document links when you use the reply option of Mail. Look in your Inbox and locate a mail message you've received as a reply. It's easy to identify replies when you use the Discussion Thread view because the replies are indented. You can generally find them in your Inbox too because the subject line usually starts with **Re:**. Double-click to open a reply. You see a document link located at the end of the subject line. Lotus Notes automatically placed that document link; it points to the message to which this message is replying. Click the document link, and you can see the original message. This is an extremely helpful Mail tool, enabling you to easily work your way back through the path of mail messages.

 One quick way to see the linked document without clicking on the document link icon is to choose **View, Document Link Preview** from the menu. The linked document appears in a Preview pane at the bottom of the screen.

A database link connects to the default view of another database. To create a database link, choose **Edit**, **Copy as Link**, **Database Link** from the menu while the database is opened.

Creating View Links

A view link works similar to document links and database links. To create a view link, follow the previous steps, but open the view to which you want to link when you copy your view link. Choose **Edit**, **Copy as Link**, **View Link** as your menu commands.

Creating Pop-Ups

A *text pop-up hotspot* displays pop-up text. This is handy when you send information to several people, and only parts of that information are needed by some of those people. For example, if you're including terms that won't be understood by all the recipients, you can put the definitions in text pop-ups. Those recipients who need the definitions can click a word and additional text appears with the explanation of the term, as seen in Figure 16.2.

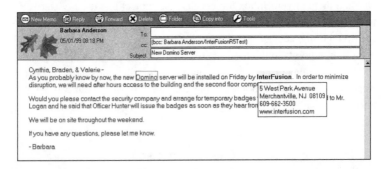

FIGURE **16.2** A text pop-up hotspot is used to provide instructions, additional information, or directions.

A text pop-up can be created only in a rich text field, such as the body of your mail message. To create this kind of hotspot, follow these steps:

1. Begin a mail message by filling in the header information.

2. In the body of the mail message, type your message. Determine which word(s) you want to become the text hotspot word (Figure 16.3 uses *Domino*).

3. Highlight that word by selecting it with your mouse. Choose **Create**, **Hotspot**, **Text Pop-Up** from the menu.

4. The HotSpot Pop-up Properties box appears, as shown in Figure 16.3.

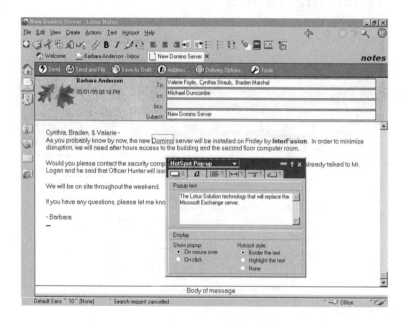

FIGURE 16.3 Additional help is available by clicking on the question mark in the upper-right corner of the HotSpot Pop-up Properties box.

5. In the Popup Text box, fill in the text you want to pop up when this hotspot is clicked. When you have finished typing the text, click the check mark.

6. Choose whether you want the pop-up to appear when the user holds the mouse over your text (**On mouse over**) or clicks on the pop-up (**On Click**).

7. Determine your hotspot appearance by selecting one of the Hotspot Style radio buttons.

8. Close the Properties box. Finish and send your message.

You can see the effects of your pop-up by looking at the copy of your message in Sent mail.

Inserting Tables

Tables offer an excellent way to organize data, and you can easily add tables to your mail messages. Figure 16.4 shows a mail message with a table inserted.

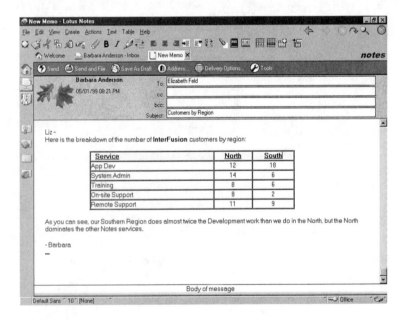

FIGURE 16.4 Tables inserted into mail messages can be read by other Notes users.

To insert a table in your mail message, follow these steps:

1. Create a new memo.

2. Position your cursor in the body field where you want the table to appear.

3. Choose **Create**, **Table** or click the **Create Table** SmartIcon. The Create Table dialog box appears (see Figure 16.5).

4. Enter the number of Rows and Columns you want in your table. Check Fixed Width if you do not want the table to adjust to the width of the screen. Once you create a fixed width table, you set the column widths in the Table Properties box.

5. Select the table type:

   Basic table—Add formatting options (colors, borders and so forth) in the Table Properties box after you have created the table.

   Tabbed table—Each row is presented as a different tabbed page. Add labels for the tabs in the Table Properties box after you have created the table.

   Animated table—Creates a table which displays a different row every two seconds. Intervals can be set in the Table Properties box after you have created the table.

   Programmed table—Creates a table that presents a different row based on the value of a field. This is an advanced table in which you must create a field and so forth and this table is beyond the scope of this book.

6. Click **OK**.

You can edit; insert columns and rows; and add borders, colors, and shading to tables. If you right-click an element of the table, the properties box appears from which you can select properties for tables, rows, columns, or text. You can also edit a table by placing your cursor in the table and clicking the Table Properties SmartIcon on the SmartIcon Toolbar. To learn more about editing and formatting tables, search the Help database for *table*. You also learn more about table creation in *Sams Teach Yourself Lotus Notes R5 in 24 Hours*. Figure 16.6 shows an example of two types of tables: standard and tabbed.

Figure 16.5   When you create a table, indicate the Table Type in the Create Table dialog box.

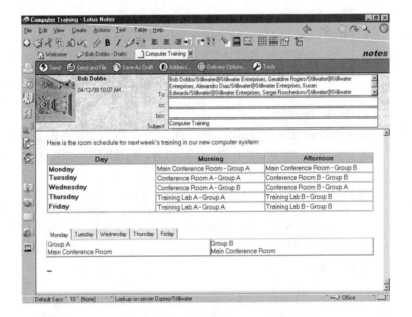

Figure 16.6   Here, information appears first in the form of a basic table, then as a tabbed table. Each row (in this case each day of the week) becomes a page in the tabbed table.

Creating Sections

Sections are helpful in making large documents more manageable. You can gather all the information on one topic into a section. Sections collapse into one-line paragraphs or expand to display all the text in the section, so a reader doesn't have to read sections that aren't of any interest. Figure 16.7 shows a document with both expanded and collapsed sections.

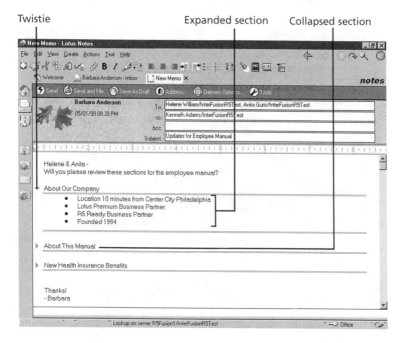

FIGURE 16.7 Twisties are indicators that the document contains collapsed sections.

When you gather text into a section, a small triangle appears to the left of the section head. To expand a section, click this triangle (called a *twistie*). Clicking again on the twistie collapses the section. To expand all the sections in a document, choose **View**, **Expand All Sections** from the menu. To collapse all sections, choose **View**, **Collapse All Sections** from the menu.

To create a section in your message, follow these steps:

1. Create a new mail message. Type several paragraphs in the body field.

2. Select the paragraph or paragraphs you want to make into a section.

3. Choose **Create**, **Section** from the menu.

The first 128 characters of the paragraph become the section title. If you want to change it, follow these steps:

1. Click the section title.

2. Choose **Section**, **Section Properties** from the menu (see Figure 16.8).

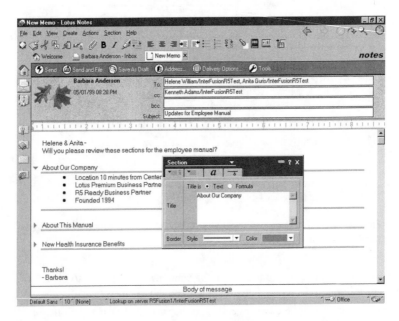

FIGURE 16.8   Set the option to create a section title (visible even when the section is collapsed) in the Section properties box.

3. Click the **Title** tab.

4. Select **Text**, and then replace the text in the Title box with the section title you want. Don't use carriage returns, hotspots, or buttons in section titles.

5. Under Section Border, choose a **Border Style** from the list box and a **Border Color** from the list box.

6. If you want to hide the title of the section when it expands, click the **Expand/Collapse** tab, and check **Hide Title When Expanded** (see Figure 16.9).

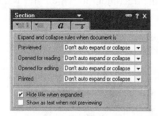

FIGURE **16.9**   The Section Properties box with the Expand/Collapse tab selected is where you set expand and collapse options for each section.

If you want to format the section title, select it and choose **Section, Section Properties**. Click the Font tab; select the font, size, style, and color you want for the section title.

You can copy and move sections as you would any other text or paragraphs with cut, copy and paste commands. For more information on rearranging text, see Lesson 15, "Editing and Formatting Text and Fields." When you want to remove a section but still want to keep all the text in the section, select the section and choose **Section, Remove Section** from the menu. If you want to remove the section and all its text, however, choose **Edit, Clear** or press the **Delete** key.

Creating Link Messages

Link Messages are used to send a document link to mail correspondents. By using the Link Message feature of Notes, you also use a special mail template that fills the entire mail message in for you except for the To, cc, and bcc fields. For example, a new policy is created in your HR Policy database, and you want to bring that to the attention of a Mail Memo recipient. Create a Link Message, and send that message to your co-worker.

To create a Link Message, follow these steps:

1. Open or select the document to which you want to create a link for your mail correspondents. The document does not need to be in your Mail database. It can be a Web page, a Notes document, or a Notes database or view.

2. Choose **Create, Special, Link Message** from the menu. A Link Message document opens (see Figure 6.12).

3. Enter the name(s) of the recipient(s) in the **To** field and change the Subject if necessary. Use the action buttons to add **Delivery Options**, and **Send** the message as you would any other mail message.

FIGURE 6.10   The Link Message automatically creates the message for you, and you only have to add the names of the recipients.

When your recipient gets the Link Message in the mail, she opens it and clicks the link icon to open the document you wanted to share with her.

Access Required Your recipient must have access to the database, Notes server, and/or Internet location that contains the document for which you sent the link. If not, she won't be able to open it. Remember, not everyone has access to your Mail database, so you are better off replying with history or forwarding mail messages instead of using Link Messages with mail documents.

In this lesson, you learned how to create links, tables, and sections. In the next lesson, you learn how to create attachments.

LESSON 17

Working with Attachments

In this lesson, you learn how to create, manage, detach, and launch file attachments.

Understanding Attachments

There might be times when you want to send a file to someone through email. That file might be a Domino database, a spreadsheet, a word processing document, a compressed file, a graphics file, or a scanned photograph of your grandchildren—almost any type of file. In Lotus Notes, you can attach an entire file within the rich text field, or body, of your mail message and send it. The file you attach is a copy, so your original remains intact on your computer.

The user who receives your mail can detach your file and save it. If the recipient has the same application program in which the file was created, she can launch the application, opening the file in its native application.

Attachments can be placed only in rich text fields, and the body of the mail message (where you type your message) is the only rich text field in the Mail Message form.

 Not Just for Mail   Although you tend to use attachments most often when working with your mail database, you can attach a file to any database document that has a rich text, or body, field. For example, in a personnel database there might be an attachment in a person's document that is a scanned picture—the person's portrait.

Creating Attachments

To attach a file to a Lotus Notes mail message, do the following:

1. Create the mail message. Make sure your insertion point (cursor) is in the message body at the exact point at which you want the attachment to appear.

2. Choose **File**, **Attach** or click the **File Attach** SmartIcon. The Create Attachments dialog box appears, as shown in Figure 17.1.

FIGURE 17.1   The Create Attachment(s) dialog box allows you to search your file system for an attachment.

3. In the Create Attachments dialog box, enter the name of the file you want to attach in the **File Name** box and then specify its location by choosing the correct drive and directory, or folder. Or, specify the location first and then select the filename from the list.

4. The **Compress** box is enabled by default. Leave this box checked.

5. Click the **Create** button. The attached file appears as an icon within the body of your mail message.

Compressed Files   Compressed files transfer faster than those that are not compressed. It might take a little longer to attach the file to your message, however, because Notes compresses the file during the attachment process. A compressed file also takes up less disk space on the server. However, don't expect the compression to have any value when traveling through the Internet, except to save space on your own machine if you save the message. If you want to send compressed files via the Internet, use a compression program such as WinZip.

The appearance of the icon depends on the type of file it represents and whether or not you have the original software that this file was created in installed on your PC. If you are attaching a Lotus 1-2-3 file, you see a Lotus 1-2-3 icon in your mail message. If the file is a Microsoft Word file, you see a Microsoft Word icon in your mail message. If you don't have native software installed for that file, you see a generic document icon.

When you receive mail that has an attachment, a paper clip icon appears next to the mail message in your Inbox (see Figure 17.2).

| Bob Dobbs | 10/16/98 | 24,185 🖉 First Quarter budget |

FIGURE 17.2   A paper clip icon in the Inbox indicates the document has an attachment.

Viewing Attachments

When you receive an attached file, you can view the attachment even if you don't have the application in which it was created. Open the mail message, double-click the attachment icon, and click the **View** button in the Properties box (see Figure 17.3). You might not be able to see the file exactly as it was originally formatted (it might display in straight text), but the Viewer provides a menu that lets you see the file in different ways depending on the type of file. For example, you can display a spreadsheet file with or without gridlines. After you finish looking at the file, press **Esc** to leave the view.

FIGURE **17.3**   The Attachment Properties box provides details about the file and enables you to launch, view, or detach the attachment.

Can't View or Launch an Attachment?   There are three possible reasons for failing to view or launch an attachment. First, the Attachment viewer must be installed on your PC in order to view the attachment. If it is not, consult with your Notes Administrator. Second, the file you are trying to view must be one supported by Lotus Notes. Many types of files are supported by Lotus Notes; for a complete list, consult the **Help** database and from the **Index** view, do a quick search for **attachments**, then click **types** of, and select **Using file attachments in documents.** Lastly, if you're trying to *launch* the attachment, you must have access to the application that was used to create the file.

The Properties box also gives you information about the attached file: its name, the size of the file, and the date and time it was last modified.

Detaching Files

To store the attached file on your hard disk or a network drive, detach the file. Then, at your convenience, open the file in the appropriate application. To detach a file, do the following:

1. Double-click the attached file icon.

2. Click the **Detach** button on the Properties box.

3. In the Save Attachment dialog box (see Figure 17.4), specify the filename you want to give the detached file and the drive and directory (or folder) in which you want to store it.

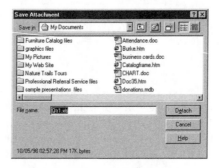

FIGURE 17.4   The Save Attachment dialog box.

4. Click the **Detach** button in the Save Attachment dialog box; close the Properties box.

To detach more than one file, right-click the body of the document and choose **Attachments**, **Detach All** from the pop-up menu. The Save Attachments to dialog box appears, as shown in Figure 17.5. Specify the drive and directory, or folder, in which you want to save the files. Click **OK**.

FIGURE **17.5**   The Save Attachments to dialog box.

Launching Files

If you want to look at an attached file in the application in which it was created, launch the application from within mail. To launch an attachment, double-click the attachment icon and then click the **Launch** button on the Properties box. You can then view the document and make changes. You can save it or print it from the application. You can close the application when you finish with the file. Lotus Notes and your mail message remain open the entire time you are working in the other applications.

 Out for Launch   If you can't launch the attachment, you probably don't have that application installed on your computer. You can still use the View option, as described in the beginning of this lesson, to see the unformatted contents of the attachment.

Printing the Attachment

Printing the attachment is not a problem when you have the application program installed on your computer. You can print it from that program. You can still print the attachment if you don't have the application program, however, by completing the following steps:

1. Double-click the attachment icon to open the file.

2. Click the **View** button on the Properties box.

3. Choose **File**, **Print**. The File Print dialog box appears (see Figure 17.6).

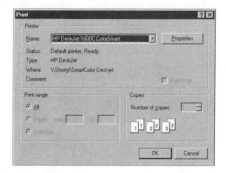

FIGURE 17.6   The File Print dialog box.

4. **(Optional)** The default setting in the File Print dialog box is to print all of the document. If you want to print only a portion of the attachment, highlight that segment before you choose **File, Print**. Then, after you open the File Print dialog box, choose **Selection** under Print Range.

5. Click **OK** to print the document.

Unexpected results, such as code lines or unusual characters, might occur when you print from the viewer. Whenever possible, therefore, it is better to print from the native application.

If you decide to make changes to a file you launched and save it again, you should use the Save As command to give it a name you will remember. At the same time, you specify a location on your computer where you want to store the file. Also, saving changes this way does not affect the original attachment sent to you.

If you receive an attachment that you want to make changes to and then return, detach the file. Open it in its original application, make your changes, save the file, and create a new mail message, attaching the modified file to return to the sender. Send the file back with a slightly modified filename, maybe with an **R** at the end of the filename so the recipient knows that you have made revisions and doesn't overwrite his original with your revised file.

In this lesson, you learned how to create, launch, detach, and print attachments. In the next lesson, you learn about working with a discussion group and communicating via a discussion database. You also learn how to work in a collaborative database environment.

LESSON 18

Joining a Discussion or TeamRoom Group

In this lesson, you'll learn to read a discussion and TeamRoom database, create documents, and receive automatic notification of changes in the databases.

Joining the Group

A discussion database is shared among those in your workgroup and is usually focused on one topic, such as an advertising campaign, a new product line, or some other special interest. Think of a discussion database as a meeting place where you can share your ideas on the subject at hand (see Figure 18.1). A discussion database is based on a discussion template and always follows a certain format:

- **Main Documents**—Documents based on a category or keyword. For example, your company has a discussion database built for introducing new product ideas. To propose widgets as a new product idea, create a new, main document containing your thoughts on widgets.

- **Response Documents**—Documents created to respond to a main document. For example, Mary knows that widgets were a big item in the '70s, and marketing trends show that items from the '70s are making a comeback. Mary creates a response document, responding to the main document "widgets." In her response document, Mary shares information about products from the '70s as they relate to widgets.

- **Response to Response**—Documents created to respond to an existing response document. For example, John knows that the total widget sales in the '70s exceeded $4 million. He responds to Mary's response document with a response-to-response document, sharing that information.

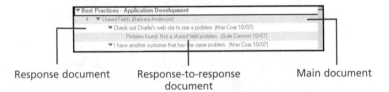

Response document   Response-to-response   Main document
                                   document

FIGURE **18.1** In this view, you see the main document, and listed beneath it are the responses and the responses to those responses.

You must know the difference between these types of documents, even though the forms used to create the documents might look very similar. The purpose for these different types of documents is to determine where they sit within a view. A main document is not indented; a response document is indented under the main document to which it is responding; and a response-to-response document is indented under the document to which it is responding. In a discussion database view, a discussion thread is always displayed, as follows:

Main document

Response document (indented)

Response-to-response document (indented under response)

Even though discussion databases can be developed for different kinds of discussions and forms can look different between databases, the common denominator is that all discussion databases follow the discussion thread outline, as shown in the previous paragraph. A sample of a discussion thread view can be found in your mail database.

Generation Gap?   A *parent* document can be a main, response, or response-to-response document. When you create a response document to an existing main document, the main document becomes the parent document. When you create a response-to-response document to an existing response document, the response document becomes the parent. When you create a response-to-response document to an existing response-to-response document, the first response-to-response document is the parent. You could think of it this way: a document becomes a *parent* document when it has *document children*. All the response and response-to-response documents under a main topic are considered the *descendents* of the main topic document. Threaded discussions show a new *generation* at each indentation level.

Viewing the Discussion Database

A discussion database can provide different views as determined by the designer of the database. Figure 18.2 shows a discussion database in which documents are viewed by category. You can expand or collapse the categories to see or hide the main, response, and response-to-response documents by clicking the Expand/Collapse SmartIcons on the toolbar.

Do the Twist!   Click the twisties to quickly expand or collapse categories. If a document has children, a twistie is displayed to the right of the parent document; the number of responses is also listed to the right. Click the document twistie to see children documents and possibly other twisties.

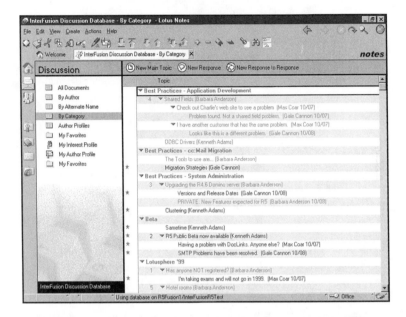

FIGURE **18.2**   A typical discussion database contains a Navigation
Pane, several views and buttons on the Action Bar.

The default discussion database (yours might look different) contains the
following views:

- **All Documents**—Displays all documents contained in the database that are viewed in a discussion thread format.

- **By Author**—Sorts and categorizes documents by author.

- **By Alternate Name**—Sorts and categorizes documents by the
  alternate name used by the author. An alternate name might be a
  second language name or a nickname, depending on how your
  organization uses it.

- **My Interest Profile**—Displays your Interest Profile document
  in edit mode.

- **By Category**—Sorts and categorizes documents by topic, or
  category.

- **Author Profiles**—Enables you to see information about the users of the discussion database. **My Author Profile** displays your Author Profile document in edit mode.

- **My Favorites**—Is a folder where you can place copies of documents.

Reading Documents

Select the main, response, or response-to-response document you want to read from the view, and double-click it to open it. When you finish reading, click the **Cancel** button on the Action Bar or press **Esc** to return to the view.

If you open a response or response-to-response document, you can easily view the parent document by clicking the **Parent Preview** button on the Action Bar. You can also accomplish this task by dragging the thick line (the Preview Pane border) from the bottom of the document to open the Preview Pane. Alternatively, you can click **Doclink**, which is displayed in the heading of the response or response-to-response document.

Creating a Main Document

You can join a discussion group by responding to a main, response, or response-to-response document or by creating your own main document. To create a new main document, follow these steps:

1. In the discussion database, click the **New Main Topic** button on the Action Bar. The New Topic form appears (see Figure 18.3).

No New Main Topic Button?   The designers of your discussion database might have customized the action buttons to your company's needs. Instead of "New Main Topic," your button might say something such as "New Product."

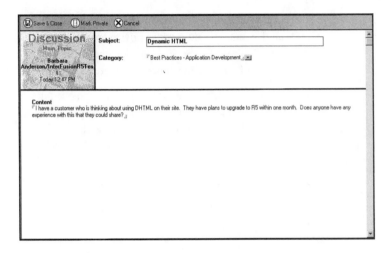

Figure 18.3   You can also create a New Main Topic from the menu. Choose **Create, Main Topic.**

2. Select a category for your main document from the keyword list provided. Depending on the design of your database, you might be able to type in your own category, or you might be required to select from a predefined list.

3. Enter a document title. Remember that the document title appears in the database views. It is similar to the Subject line of a Mail Memo and should define the purpose of your document. In a new product ideas database, your document title should briefly define your new product idea, such as "hula hoops." In a discussion database that covers corporate policies, your document title might be something such as "I disagree."

4. Enter your message content. The message content field is likely to be a rich text field, much like the body of a Mail Memo. If it is a rich text field, you can include graphics, text formatting, and paragraph formatting.

5. Use the **Mark Private** button on the Action Bar if you don't want anyone to see this document except for you. You might use this if you are in the process of creating a document but are not ready share it with others. Use this function in the way you would save your Mail Memo as a draft.

You can see your private documents in your database views, but no one else can. Documents you mark as private appear in the view with the word "Private" preceding the document title. You can see an example of a Private document in Figure 18.2.

When you are ready to share the document with others, open it, click the Edit Document button on the Action Bar, finish editing, and click the **Mark Public** button on the Action Bar. Save the document, and it appears in the views of all people who have reader access to the database.

6. When you have completed your document, click the **Save & Close** button on the Action Bar.

Creating Response Documents

You can create a response document only as a reply to a main document. Response-to-response documents are typically created as replies to response documents. To create either a response or response-to-response document, first identify the parent document by selecting it in the View Pane or by opening it.

From the Action Bar, choose either the **Response** or **Response-to-Response** button. Complete the Document Title and Message Contents field as seen in Figure 18.4. If you are not ready to share this document with others, choose **Mark Private** from the Action Bar. When you are done, select **Save & Close** from the Action Bar. Your document appears in the View Pane in its appropriate indentation.

 What Did He Say?   To view the parent document while creating your response document, drag the heavy line (the Preview Pane border) from the bottom of the document to open the Preview Pane at the bottom of the screen. Alternatively, choose **View, Parent Preview** from the menu

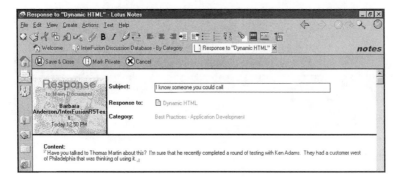

FIGURE 18.4   The message content of the response document is a rich text field.

Setting up an Interest Profile

An **Interest Profile** enables you to be notified via email when new documents are created in the discussion database that meet certain criteria. A link to create an Interest Profile displays in the Navigation Pane and is called **my Interest Profile**. Click this to set up your Interest document (See Figure 18.5). After you create and save your Profile, you can edit it by clicking the **My Interest Profile** link. There are three settings that you can modify in the Interest Profile:

> **Authors**—Use the pull-down list to select an author name from the Company Address Book or from your Personal Address Book. You will be notified any time that the person you selected from the list creates a new main, response, or response-to-response document. You can choose more than one author.

> **Categories**—Use the pull-down list to select categories that exist in this discussion database. You will be notified any time that main, response, or response-to-response documents are created with the categories you selected.

> **Subjects**—Separate each new subject by putting it on a new line. You will be notified any time main, response, or response-to-response documents are created with one of these words in the Subject line.

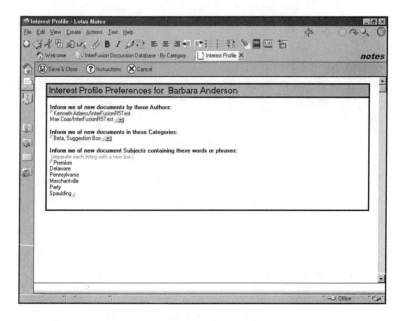

FIGURE **18.5**   Modify My Interest Profile by clicking it in the Navigation Pane.

You don't need to open My Interest Profile to add new topics. Any time you have a main topic or response open or selected in the view, choose **Actions, Add Topic/Thread to Interest Profile** from the menu. A dialog box confirms that the topic was added to your Interest Profile and that you will be notified if any documents appear on this subject. Click **OK** to close the dialog box.

Creating an Author Profile

An Author Profile contains information about you. Where the discussion database is shared by a larger organization in which participants might not all know one another, the Author Profile gives you a personality. In addition, the Author Profile is a useful tool in determining the qualifications of participants. For example, informing others that you have a background in hazardous waste removal might add credence to your proposal to remove all garbage disposals from the lunchrooms. The Author Profile also provides information that helps people contact you outside the discussion database. You can even add a picture of yourself.

To create or edit an Author Profile, click **My Author Profile** in the Navigation Pane of the discussion database. In the Author Profile (see Figure 18.6), enter your email address, phone number, role in the discussion database, goals, and any additional relevant information. If you have a picture of yourself saved as a graphic file, click the **Import Photo Here** field and choose **Create, Picture**. Select the picture file, and click **Import**. This makes your picture available to Notes users. To have your picture seen by Web users, click the **Attach Photo Here** field and attach your photo file there. Click **Save & Close** when you complete your Author Profile.

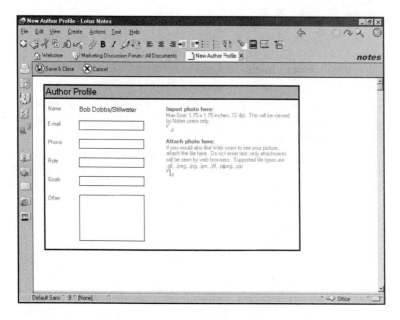

FIGURE 18.6   The Author Profile contains information to help others contact you and know something about your goals and role.

To see the author profiles of other users, open the Author Profile view.

Participating in a TeamRoom Discussion

Like the discussion database template, the TeamRoom template displays documents in hierarchical order (main, response, response-to-response) but also provides additional views, such as Chronological, By Subteam, By Milestone/Event, and even a Calendar view.

It's not typical that you, the Lotus Notes client and end user, would create a TeamRoom database, but it is certainly possible. Here, we assume that the TeamRoom project has been started for you, and we introduce you to some of the forms found in the TeamRoom database.

As we said earlier, TeamRoom is like a discussion database on steroids. Whereas a discussion databases enables you to introduce a topic and see the discussion thread as others respond to it, TeamRoom offers more automation and workflow processes. It starts with a Team Leader who identifies the need and purpose for the project and acts as a manager of the team, essentially managing the contents and participants. Then, the Team Facilitator (not necessarily a different person) is responsible for the actual maintenance of the database and performs such tasks as adding new members, identifying teams and subteams, teaching people how to use the database, and so forth. Finally, team members (like you and us) participate in the TeamRoom through discussions (main topics, response documents), tracking and performing tasks and actions assigned to us or created by us. We also generate reports and milestones, and we work with the team toward common goals set by the Team Leader or Facilitator.

It's difficult to show you a step-by-step process in the TeamRoom environment, or at least to show you one in which you can actually participate at work, because the TeamRoom is essentially customized as it is created. Because Discussion Databases are older and more widely used, we're pretty confident that you can gain access to a discussion database at home or on the Web. TeamRoom is new, and there's a chance you won't be able to access a TeamRoom database. Here, we show you some of the views and forms that are standard in the TeamRoom database. Ask your Domino Administrator if your firm is using a TeamRoom database that you can access, or better yet, if you identify a need for the TeamRoom database, ask your Administrator to work with you in designing a TeamRoom database for your department or company.

Figure 18.7 shows the Navigation Pane of a typical TeamRoom database. Note that views are categorized by Team Documents, Personal Documents, Project Information, Documents Assigned to Me, and Documents I Created. Within each category, you find additional views, such as By Date, By Category, By Milestone/Event, Active Team/Subteam Status, and so forth.

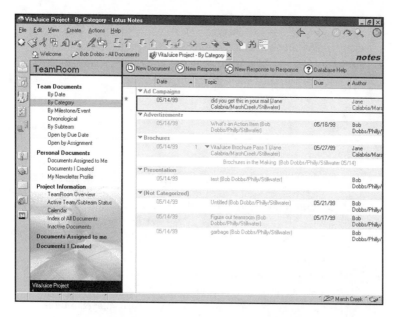

FIGURE 18.7   Available default views in TeamRoom include By Date, By Assignment, By Milestone/Event, and Documents Assigned to Me.

Typically, a TeamRoom contribution begins with the Main Document (see Figure 18.8). There are an unlimited number of documents that can be defined and provided in a TeamRoom database, but by default, four documents are displayed. By clicking New Document on the Action Bar, you select what type of document to create. The default document types are the following:

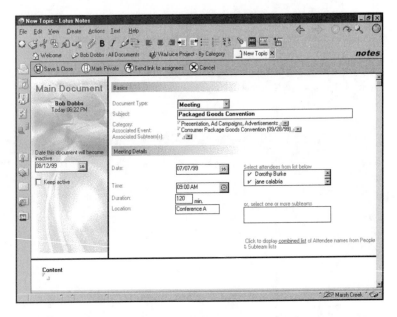

FIGURE 18.8   Set a meeting and invite others using the document type Meeting.

- **Discussion**—Use this to create a new Main Topic. Here, you can enter names of people you want to review the document and set a review date, and when people review the document, they click a hotspot that says "Mark Reviewed by Me" (displayed only in edit mode).

- **Action Item**—This is the same as a Main Topic form but is used to assign tasks to others. Using this form, you assign action items to other TeamRoom members with or without a due date. Everyone on the assigned list has Editor access to the document until the hotspot "Mark Complete" (displayed only in edit mode) has been clicked by someone.

- **Meeting**—Use this to schedule meetings, but note that the meeting does not appear on your personal calendar unless you click the button called "Add to My Calendar". Note that Domino's group scheduling feature is not a part of the TeamRoom database. You can set meetings, but you cannot access Free Time from this database.

- **Reference**—Use this as you would use the Discussion form, but do not use it when you are soliciting responses.

Hopefully, this section helps you to understand the purpose of the TeamRoom database. TeamRoom is a fairly new concept, and in our estimation is a great improvement over the discussion database; however, we feel there are still a few holes in the TeamRoom capabilities. For example, when you propose a meeting in TeamRoom, you don't have the benefit of checking Free Time of others or even checking your own calendar without switching over to your Calendar view.

In this lesson, you learned how to read and add documents to a discussion database, and you were introduced to a TeamRoom database. You also learned how to receive a mail notification of changes to a database and how to set Interest and Author Profiles. In the next lesson, you learn about replication.

LESSON 19

Understanding Replication

In this lesson, you'll learn about replication, how to create a new Mail replica, and how to copy from the Public Address Book.

How Replication Works

Domino servers store many databases, and when you are in the office connected to the Domino network, you can open databases on the server directly from your workstation. Most of the databases that you access, including your mail database, are stored on your home server. Often, companies have multiple Domino servers, and you need to access databases on several Domino servers in your company.

 Home Server   The term used for the Domino server on which your mail database resides. If you can access several Domino servers at work, the one containing your mail database is the one referred to as your *home* server.

When you are not in the office, however, you need to access the server via a modem. If you have a lot of work to do in a database (such as reading and replying to mail), remaining on the phone line can be costly. You'll also find that working via modem is much slower than being on the network in the office. When this situation occurs, you'll want to replicate databases.

Replication is the process of "synchronizing" the same databases on different computers. It is actually a special copying process. Replication does not overwrite the entire database as copying a database would.

Instead, it updates only the documents you modified, and it does the same thing for everyone else who replicates the database. As people call in to replicate a database, they receive the most recent copy of the documents in the database on their own computers. The server receives their changes, and the server sends them any updates that have occurred since they last replicated. Eventually, the modifications circulate to everyone using the database.

When you are ready to replicate a database, you place a telephone call from your computer (using your modem) to the server in your office. After the two computers "shake hands" and recognize each other, your computer begins sending updates you made to the database replicas. Then your computer receives any modifications made to the database since you last replicated. The replication process is illustrated in Figure 19.1.

Now look at replication with regard to your Mail database. To receive your mail, you call in to the server from home (or from the road) and replicate your Mail database After you disconnect from the server, you read your mail, reply to some messages, delete some messages, and file some messages in folders. During this time, Mary Jones creates a new mail message for you, which is waiting on the server replica of your mail database. When you finish reading and replying to mail, you call in to the server and replicate mail again. During this replication period, the changes you made while disconnected (new replies, deletions, and so forth) are sent to the server copy of your mail database, and Mary's new message is sent to your replica of the database.

Each database has a unique *replica ID* that identifies it as a genuine replica and not just a copy of the database (see Figure 19.2). If the database on your computer does not have the same ID as the one on the server, replication won't occur.

Before replicating, the server also checks to see when the replica copy of the database on your computer was last modified. If that date is more recent than the date the database was last successfully replicated, the database replicates. The server also looks at the modification and replication dates on the server replica. If that replica was modified since the last replication, replication occurs. Domino maintains a replication history of each database you replicate (see Figure 19.3).

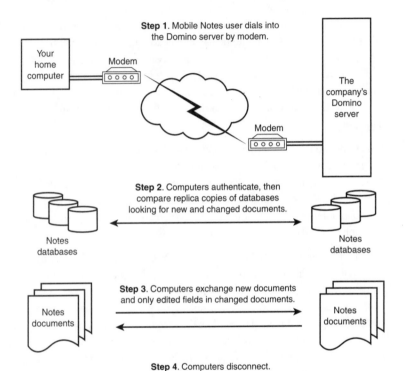

Step 1. Mobile Notes user dials into the Domino server by modem.

Your home computer

Modem

The company's Domino server

Modem

Step 2. Computers authenticate, then compare replica copies of databases looking for new and changed documents.

Notes databases

Notes databases

Step 3. Computers exchange new documents and only edited fields in changed documents.

Notes documents

Notes documents

Step 4. Computers disconnect.

FIGURE 19.1   Every time yo replicate, changes made to the database since your last replication are sent to your replica copy.

FIGURE 19.2   The Database Properties box displays the Replica ID on the Info tab.

FIGURE **19.3** The Replication History displays in the dialog box and can be sorted by Date (shown) or by Server name.

When the database replicates, it updates only those document fields that have been changed since the last replication and adds any new documents. Each document has its own *unique Notes identification number* assigned to it when it is first saved (see Figure 19.4). Part of that number is a document-level sequence number that increases each time you modify the document. If the number is higher for a particular document than the database on the server, it is replicated to the server. Any documents that you deleted or that were deleted from the server replica leave a *deletion stub*, and that is replicated so the document is deleted from other replicas of the database unless **Do not send deletions** was checked in the replication settings.

FIGURE **19.4** The Document Properties box displays the unique Notes identification number on the Document IDs page.

When replication is complete, you hang up. You now have an updated copy of the database on your PC.

Setting Replication Preferences

You can control the replication process by specifying what type of files you want to receive, how old the files can be, and the priority of the database replication. All this is controlled under Replication Settings. There are three ways you can open the Replication Settings dialog box for the database you have open or selected:

- Choose **File**, **Replication**, **Settings** from the menu.

- Right-click the bookmark and select **Replication**, **Settings** from the shortcut menu.

- Click the **Replication Settings** button on the Database Properties box.

The Replication Settings dialog box (see Figure 19.5) has four pages of settings—Space Savers, Send, Other, and Advanced. You click the appropriate icon to change pages.

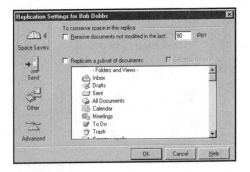

FIGURE **19.5**   The Replication Settings dialog box (Space Savers page) for a mail database contains options for removing old documents.

The purpose of the options on the Space Savers page is to limit the amount of space the replica takes up on your hard disk. The Send page includes options about what types of items you want to send when replicating with the server. On the Other page, you can disable replication temporarily and specify the priority of the replication. The Advanced page has options to control how you replicate with a specified server (which is important if you replicate with more than one). Table 19.1 quickly summarizes the important features of the dialog box that you might need to use.

Table 19.1 Important Replication Settings Options

When You Need To	Set This Option (On this Page)	Description
Delete documents on your replica without deleting them on the server copy	Do not send deletions made in this replica to other replicas (Send page)	Normally, when you delete a document in your replica, a deletion stub is repli cated to the server, which replicates it to all the replica copies, so your deletions affect everyone else's replica.
Eliminate documents created before a certain date	Only replicate incoming documents saved or modified after(Other page)	Specify the begin- ning date.
Limit the number large attachments or memos you receive	Receive summary and 40KB of rich text only (Space Savers page)	Only receive the beginning of the mail memo (To, From Subject) and no more than 40KB of the message.
Remove old documents	Remove documents not modified in the last days (Space Savers page)	Enter how old (in days) a document is when it's dropped from your replica.

When You Need To	Set This Option (On this Page)	Description
Receive only part	Replicate a subset of documents (Space Savers page)	Check this item and then select the views and folders you want to replicate of the database (hold down Ctrl to click more than one).
Stop replication	Temporarily disable replication (Other page)	If you are stopping replication because of a problem with the database, call your system administrator for assistance.

Creating a New Mail Replica

People who use their computers outside the office and away from the network are referred to as *mobile users*. If you're one of these mobile users, it's a good idea to replicate the important databases you need to your laptop *before* you take the laptop out of the office. This will save you time on the telephone lines. Of course, the most important of the databases you want to replicate is your mail database. Before you begin, confirm with your system administrator that you need to make a new Mail database replica. There could be a copy on your laptop that doesn't have an icon associated with it and therefore doesn't show in your workspace. To find out if a replica is on your computer, right-click the bookmark for your mail file and choose **Open Replica**. If **local** appears in the list of replicas, you already have the replica on your laptop. Notes is smart enough to place local replica information on the bookmark when you have opened the server copy if the local replica exists.

Making a new replica is a one-step process. Later in this lesson, the section "Using the Replicator Page" shows you how to update this replica (or replicate) on an ongoing basis. It's very important to make a new replica of a database only once:

1. Select or open your mail database, and then choose **File, Replication, New Replica** from the menu (or right-click the bookmark, and choose **Replication, New Replica** from the menu).

2. The **New Replica** dialog box appears (see Figure 19.6).

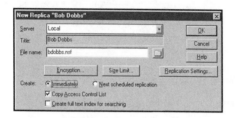

FIGURE 19.6   The **New Replica** dialog box permits you to create a full text index at the time you create a new replica.

3. Make sure the Server displayed is **Local**. Notes automatically fills in the Title and the File Name.

4. Under Create, click **Immediately**.

5. Remove the check mark from **Copy Access Control List**.

6. Click **OK**.

After this, any time you want to replicate (update) your mail, use the Replicator page, as shown later in this lesson.

Replicating the Address Book

You have two Address Books. Your Personal Address Book, which has your name on it, contains all your personal contacts. It resides on your hard disk. The Public Address Book is the one with the organization's name on it, and it contains all the names of the people in your organization. When you are connected to the network in the office, you have access to this Address Book, which resides on the server.

Because the Public Address Book resides on the server, you can't access it remotely until you call in to the server. This could cause problems for you in addressing mail or selecting names of people in the organization for database selections. Although you can select people in the Public Address Book and copy and paste them into your Personal Address Book, it would be far easier to have a copy of the Public Address Book that you can replicate. Depending on the size of your company, however, the Public Address Book can be a large database. You don't really need everything in that Address Book, you need people's names and addresses. Therefore, when you replicate the Public Address Book, you only want to replicate the *Minimal Address Book*.

To replicate the Minimal Address Book:

1. Select or open the Public Address Book, and then choose **File, Replication, New Replica** from the menu.

2. The **New Replica** dialog box appears (refer to Figure 19.6).

3. Make sure the Server displayed is **Local**. Notes automatically fills in the Title and the File Name. Change the File Name to something other than names.nsf. You already have a file of that name on your hard disk: It's your personal Address Book. We usually add the first initial of the company to the beginning of the filename. Changing the filename won't make any difference to the replication because replication depends on the Replica ID and not the name.

4. Under Create, click **Immediately**.

5. Click **Replication Settings**. In the Replication Settings dialog box (see Figure 19.7), make one of the following choices from the **Include** drop-down list:

   Minimal Address Book—Replicates the minimum information required to send unencrypted mail.

   Minimal Address Book, Encryption—Replicates the minimum information required to send encrypted or unencrypted mail.

Minimal Address Book, Person Info—Replicates the minimum information required to send unencrypted mail but also includes all the personal information from the Person documents.

Minimal Address Book, Person Info, Encryption—Replicates the minimum information required to send encrypted or unencrypted mail but also includes all the personal information from the Person documents.

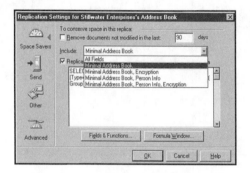

FIGURE **19.7**   The Replication Settings dialog box for the Public Address Book include options for replicating a Minimal Address Book.

6. Click **OK**. Then click **OK** again to start replicating.

Using the Replicator Page

The Replicator page is one of the selections found in the Favorites bookmarks. It provides a central location to handle all your replication needs. By using the features available on the Replicator page (see Figure 19.8), you can set options to control which databases replicate, with which servers you are replicating, and whether you want to receive full or truncated (shortened) documents when you replicate.

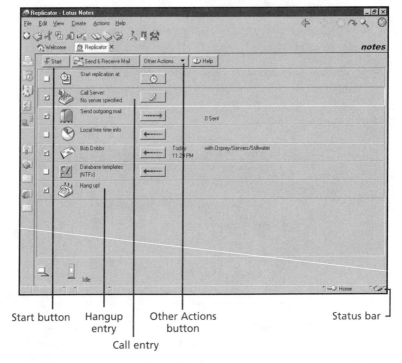

Start button   Hangup | Other Actions   Status bar
                entry | button
                        Call entry

Figure 19.8   The Replicator page contains Call and Hangup entries
if the current location uses direct dial to a Notes server.

There are several rows, or entries, on the Replicator page:

- **Start Replication at**—Sets a schedule for replication. Most
  mobile users don't schedule their replications because that
  requires having the PC and Notes running during the scheduled
  time. Click the action button on the entry row to set the schedule
  (see Figure 19.9).

  Set the replication schedule in the Location document on the
  Replication tab.

- **Send outgoing mail**—Sends all pending messages from your
  Outgoing Mail database.

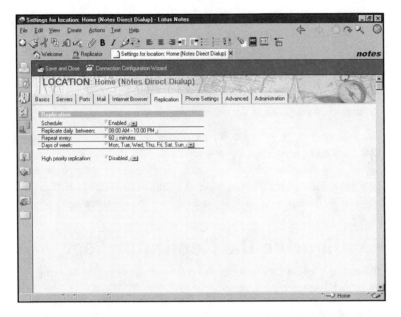

FIGURE 19.9   The Replication tab of the Location document. When a replication schedule is Enabled, choose times, days and repeat options.

- **Databases**—For each local database replica that you have, there is a database entry on the Replicator page.

- **Database templates**—Templates are used to create new databases and to refresh the designs of any template-based databases you have. You probably will not need to replicate your templates with the server. (You need to do this only to update your templates.)

- **Call and Hangup**—In addition to the automatic entry rows created for your databases, you can create call and hangup entries for automatic dialing from mobile locations to servers. These entries automatically appear if you specified that you used Notes remotely when you configured your Notes installation.

On each of the entry rows, there is an action button. Use these buttons to specify replication options relating to that entry row, such as whether to send or receive documents for that database, or in the case of a call entry, to specify the server and phone number to call.

Each entry row also has a checkbox. To include an entry in the replication, click the checkbox (a check mark appears). When you click the **Start** button on the Action Bar, Lotus Notes performs the functions of each checked entry row in the order of the rows.

The status bar at the bottom of the page shows information about the current replication, letting you know when Lotus Notes is attempting to call a server, what database is being replicated, the progress of the replication, how many minutes are left, and when the replication is finished. After replication, the status bar displays statistics for individual entries.

Configuring the Replicator Page

Except for a few of the fixed entries on the Replicator page, you can move and delete entries to suit your needs.

To delete entries, do the following:

1. Click the entry you want to delete. This selects the entry.

2. Press the **Delete** key.

3. When asked if you want to delete the entry, select **Yes**.

Be careful when deleting database entries. The settings for the databases on the Replicator page can be customized by location. If you remove a database from the Replicator page, however, it is removed from all locations. Instead of deleting the entry, remove the check mark to deselect it from the replication process.

Lotus Notes replicates the databases in the order they appear on the Replicator page. To move an entry, do the following:

1. Click the entry and hold down the mouse button.

2. Drag the entry to the position where you want it.

3. Release the mouse button.

The order of the databases and the databases that are checked for replication can be different for each location. From Home, you'll want the Outgoing Mail and your mail database high on the list. From the Office location, you don't need to replicate your mail until you're ready to take your computer out of the office, so your mail database might not be checked for replication. To set up the page differently for each location, select the location first by clicking the **Location** button on the status bar, then rearrange the entries, and check the ones you need at that location. For more information on Location documents, see Lesson 20, "Setting Up for Mobile Use."

In this lesson, you learned about replication, making a new Mail replica, and replicating the Public Address Book. You also learned to work with the Replicator page. In the next lesson, you learn how to set up for mobile use.

LESSON 20
Setting Up for Mobile Use

In this lesson, you'll learn how to create a connection document and a location document and how to configure your modem and ports for working away from the office on Notes.

What You Need to Go Remote

To work remotely from home, a hotel room, or a location outside of the office in which you are not connected to your local area network, you need the following:

- A computer with Lotus Notes 5.0 or Notes Mail installed

- A modem connected to your PC

- A phone line for your modem

You also need the following information, which you can obtain from your Lotus Notes Administrator:

- The name of your Domino server

- The phone number of the Domino server

- A copy of your certified Notes User ID (if you don't already have it)

With this information, you can configure your modem, create necessary Connection and Location documents, and replicate mail as described throughout this lesson.

Creating Location Documents

Notes always needs to know where you are when you are working, and the information it needs comes from a Location document. The Location document tells Notes details such as how to connect you to the network, where to find your mail database, how to dial the phone, and what port to use.

Seven location documents automatically appear during the installation process: Home (Network Dialup), Home (Notes Direct Dialup), Internet, Island (Disconnected), Office Network, Travel (Network Dialup), and Travel (Notes Direct Dialup). You'll find them in your Personal Address Book in the Locations view (click the **Settings** icon at the bottom of the Navigation Pane if the Locations view isn't listed). You can customize the Locations to suit your needs or create your own Location documents.

Typically, the Office location is the one you use when you are in the office, connected to the LAN (Local Area Network) via a network port. The Home locations are set up for remote connection via modem, as are the Travel locations. There are two Home and two Travel locations; you select the appropriate one for the way you dial to the server—either directly (Notes direct dialup) or via dialup networking (Network Dialup). In the Travel location documents, you might want to specify your area code so that Notes dials 1 and the area code of your home server. The Home and Travel documents assume you are using a local replica of your mail database.

To customize the Home (Notes Direct Dialup) Location document, for example, follow these instructions:

1. If you have your Personal Address Book open to the Settings Navigation Pane, select the **Locations** view, and then double-click **Home (Notes Direct Dialup)** to open the location document. If not, click the **Location** button on the status bar (the name of the current location is displayed there). Select **Edit Current** if Home (Notes Direct Dialup) is the current location; otherwise, select **Home (Notes Direct Dialup)**, then click the **Location** button again, and choose **Edit Current**.

2. You'll see the Home (Notes Direct Dialup) Location document
   with the **Basics** tab selected (see Figure 20.1). Notes Direct
   Dialup is already selected as the Location Type and Home
   (Notes Direct Dialup) as the Location Name. Enter an **Internet
   Mail Address** if you want. Indicate (**Yes** or **No**) if you want to
   be prompted for the date, time, or phone when you use this location. You can display alternate names (such as nicknames or
   names in other languages if your company uses them) by changing the Default Display Name type.

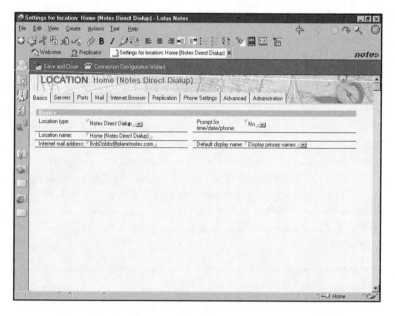

FIGURE 20.1   If you need help with fields on the Location document, hold your cursor over the field for pop-up help. If the cursor
turns into a hand, click and hold the left mouse button to see an
expanded explanation for the field. Of course you can always press
F1 for context-sensitive help.

3. On the **Servers** tab, enter the name of your home server in the **Home/Mail Server** field. Your home server is the server you connect to at work that stores your mail database. Type its full name (for example, Osprey/Stillwater is the name of the server Osprey in the organization Stillwater).

4. If you use a Passthru server, specify the name of that server in the **Passthru Server** field. Specify the Domino Directory Server and Catalog/Domain Search Server also, if your company uses them.

> **Passthru Server** Some companies have many Domino servers. The Notes Administrator might determine that one of those servers will act as the traffic controller for incoming calls, referred to as a *Passthru* server because your call must pass through that server to reach the server where your mail is stored. Ask your Notes Administrator if you're going to be dialing in to a Passthru server. You need the Passthru server name and telephone number, as well as the server name that contains your mail database.

5. The enabled ports should already be listed on the Ports tab with the COM port for your modem being checked.

6. On the **Mail** tab, complete the following:

    • **Mail File Location**—Choose **Local** to use a local replica of your Mail file. (**On Server** means you connect directly to the server to use your mail.)

    • **Mail File**—Enter the path and filename of your Mail file (usually `Mail\name`).

7. On the Internet Browser tab, specify the **Internet Browser** you use (Notes, Notes with Internet Explorer, Netscape Navigator, Microsoft Internet Explorer, or Other).

8. On the **Replication** tab, leave **Schedule** set to **Disabled** unless you plan to leave your workstation running and want replication to occur automatically at the times you set. In that case, choose Enabled. Then specify the time during the day that you want replication to occur, how often you want to connect for replication, and on what days of the week you want the schedule to run.

9. On the Phone Settings tab, enter any necessary **Prefix for Outside Line** you need to dial first to connect to a phone line outside your office, home, or hotel (such as 8 or 9 or the disconnect code for call waiting). Fill in the **Area Code At This Location** so Notes can tell whether it needs to dial 1 and the area code to reach the server. If you plan to use a calling card, enter the access number and card number. Use commas to create pauses.

10. The Advanced tab has settings for your time zone and daylight saving time.

The remaining fields on this form contain either default information or don't apply to Mail options. Click the **Save and Close** button on the Action Bar to save the file and close the document.

 There's no need to edit your **Travel** location document for the current phone and time information when traveling outside your normal area code/time zone. Just mark the location document to prompt for time/date/phone on the **Basics** tab of the Travel location document, and you'll be prompted for the information whenever you switch to that location

Creating a Connection Document

To access a Domino server, you need a Server Connection document, which contains information about your server: the name of your server, the phone number to dial for your server, and the type of connection you are making (such as Notes Direct Dialup).

If you want to dial directly in to a Domino server, rather than using a passthru server, we recommend you create your Connection document by running the Connection Wizard. Place your location document in edit mode and click the **Connection Configuration Wizard** button on the Action Bar. Follow the wizard's instructions, supplying information about your connection as you go.

If you want to dial a service provider first and then connect to Notes server, follow these steps:

1. Open your Personal Address Book, and click the **Settings** icon at the bottom of the Navigation Pane.

2. Select the Connections view. Open the connection document you will use for the service provider (such as home), and click **Edit Connection** on the Action Bar.

3. Specify **Network Dialup** as the Connection type (you'll probably need some help from your System Administrator in setting this up).

4. In the **Use LAN port** field, select the port you'll use when you connect to the network.

5. On the **Network DialUp Networking** tab, make a selection in the **Choose a Service Type** field (Apple Talk Remote Access, Microsoft Dial-Up Networking, or Macintosh PPP).

6. Click **Edit Configuration** to enter the connection name, login name, password, phone number, area code, country code (if necessary), and the dial-back phone number.

7. Click **OK** to save your changes (see Figure 20.2).

If your Domino server is accessed by other means, you need create a custom connection document. We suggest you talk with your Notes Administrator for assistance in creating a custom connection document.

If you are going to call in to more than one server, you need a Server Connection document for each one. The exception is the use of a *Passthru* server as previously discussed in the "Creating Location Documents" section of this lesson.

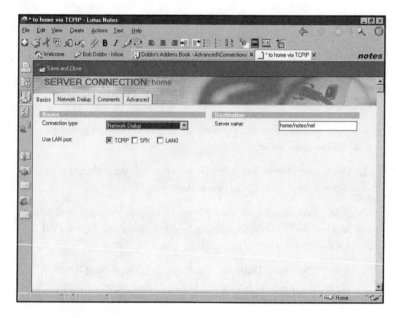

FIGURE 20.2   The Server Connection document contains information about how you connect to a server and which servers you connect to.

 Alphabet Soup? If this lesson is sounding like alphabet soup to you, you might be better off having your Notes Administrator configure this connection for you or send you a field-by-field instruction for each connection document you need before you hit the road!

Configuring Ports and Modems

After you complete the server information in the connection document, you need to specify a modem type and the port your modem uses, as follows:

Ports   Computers have several outlets into which you can plug cables or peripherals, which are called ports. Each port has a name. When working remotely, ports are called COM ports and are distinguished by number (COM1, COM2, and so forth). Only one device, such as your modem, can be assigned to each COM port. When working on a network, Lotus Notes identifies ports by their network protocols (TCPIP, SPX, LAN0, Banyan Vines).

1. Choose **File**, **Preferences, User Preferences** from the menu.

2. In the User Preferences dialog box, click the **Ports** icon (see Figure 20.3).

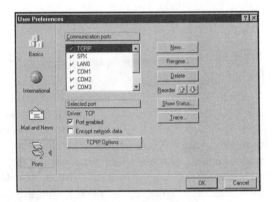

FIGURE 20.3   The **User Preferences** dialog box with the **Ports** page displayed indicates which ports are enabled.

3. From the **Communications Ports** list, pick the port your modem uses, such as COM1 or COM2.

4. Check **Port Enabled**.

5. Click the **Options** button (the name of the port is on the button). The **Additional Setup** dialog box appears (see Figure 20.4).

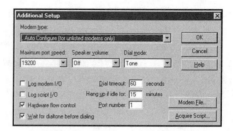

FIGURE 20.4   Choose a modem type, speaker options, and port speed in the **Additional Setup** dialog box

6. Specify the Modem Type you have (use the Autoconfigure or Generic All-Speed Modem type if you don't know), and enter any settings you need for your modem (such as maximum port speed).

7. Click **OK** to exit the dialog box.

8. Click **OK** to exit User Preferences.

 Don't Know Which Port or Modem?—If you're using Windows 95 or 98, click the **Start** button on the Windows taskbar, and choose **Settings, Control Panel** from the menu. Double-click the **Modems** icon to open the **Modem Properties** box. The brand and model number of the modem display in the list. Select the modem from the list (if it isn't already selected) and choose **Properties**. Look in **Port** to see the port the modem is using. The **Maximum Speed** also appears in this dialog box. If you're running Windows NT to see the port number, open **Modems**.

Our last piece of advice for setting up for mobile use is to plan to take this book with you when you leave. The book size lends itself well to fitting in your laptop case, and you'll have a wealth of information with you on the road.

In this lesson, you learned to configure Notes to work outside the office by creating Connection and Location documents and by specifying the port and modem you'll be using. In the next lesson, you learn about using Notes when you're working outside the office.

LESSON 21
Using Notes Remotely

In this lesson, you'll learn how to work with Notes when you aren't in the office—by replicating mail, creating replicas of databases, managing file sizes, and encrypting local databases.

Understanding Notes Mobile Users

A *mobile* user is one who works in Notes while disconnected from the Notes network. You become a mobile user when you are working at a desktop computer from home or by using a laptop computer from a client site, a regional office, home, or hotel. As a mobile user, you connect to the Notes network via a modem instead of a LAN or WAN.

You don't want to read and reply to mail while connected to the server over a modem. Working while connected via a modem is time-consuming and possibly expensive, particularly if you are calling long distance. Therefore, mobile users generally replicate their mail databases to their laptops or desktops at home. You can work in your local replica, saving phone time for the replication process. You can access your data quickly, make and store all new documents and updates, and send everything back to the server in one short phone call.

 Depending on your company's Domino capabilities, it's possible to access your mail or other database with a Web browser with no need to install the Notes client on your laptop. Check with your Notes Administrator to find out if your company has these capabilities. Also, read Appendix A, "Understanding Security and Access Rights," under the section "Web Access to Mail" before you contact your Administrator.

Creating Replicas Remotely

You need to work on a database that's stored on the server at the office, but you're working away from the office. You need a copy of the database on your own computer that can be replicated with the original on the server. Your first step is to set up your computer to work remotely (see Lesson 20, "Setting Up for Mobile Use"). The next step is to create replicas of any databases you need to work offsite (including your mail database) if you weren't able to replicate them while you were connected in the office (see Lesson 19, "Understanding Replication").

 Dial-Up Networking The instructions for calling in and creating a new replica from the server do not apply to you if you use Dial-Up Networking instead of dialing in directly to your Domino server. You should use the instructions in Lesson 19 under the section "Creating a New Mail Replica" to create your new replicas.

To start the process of creating a new replica, you need to call the server:

1. Choose **File, Mobile, Call Server** from the menu. The Call Server dialog box appears (see Figure 21.1).

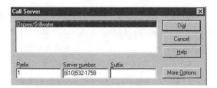

FIGURE 21.1 If you call in to more than one server, all servers are listed in the Call Server dialog box, and you select the one you want to call.

2. Pick the name of the server you want to call (if you have more than one).

3. Click **Dial**. The status bar indicates when you are connected.

The first time you connect, you need to make the replica copy of the database. After that, you use the Replicator Page (see Lesson 19) to replicate modifications and new documents with the server. It's very important to make a new replica of a database only once:

1. Choose **File**, **Database**, **Open** from the menu. When the Open Database dialog box appears (see Figure 21.2), select the name of the server where the original database is from the Server drop-down list.

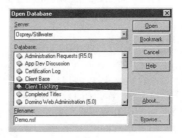

FIGURE 21.2   The Open Database dialog box

2. From the Database list, select the database you want and then click **Open**.

3. When the database opens, choose **File**, **Replication**, **New Replica**.

In the New Replica dialog box (see Figure 21.3), make sure the Server displayed is **Local**. Notes automatically fills in the **Title** and the **File Name**.

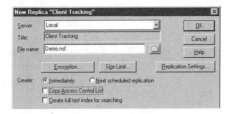

FIGURE 21.3   The New Replica dialog box.

4. Under Create, click **Immediately.**

5. Click **OK.**

Repeat the set of instructions above for each database for which you need a new replica. When your call is complete, you need to disconnect from the server.

1. Choose **File, Mobile, Hang Up** from the menu.

2. When a dialog box appears with your modem port highlighted, click **Hang Up.**

Using Outgoing Mail

When you installed Lotus Notes on your remote computer or laptop, you specified that you would be using a remote connection. As part of the installation process, Notes then created a replica *stub* (or place holder) of your mail database; the first time you attempt to open the database, Notes initializes the database by calling the server and making the full replica. If you have been using Notes from the office and only recently decided to go mobile, you have to make a replica of your mail database (as you did in Lesson 19) before you leave the office. Otherwise, use the instructions in the previous section, but specify your mail as the database you want to replicate (it's in the \mail folder on the server).

When you work with a replica of the mail database, outgoing mail is stored temporarily in the Outgoing Mailbox database. When you replicate or send mail to the server, the outgoing mail is sent, and the Outgoing Mailbox database mailbox is emptied. Incoming mail is automatically deposited in your Inbox.

To see the mail that is waiting to be sent, open the Outgoing Mail bookmark. You can view a list of the messages awaiting delivery, but you can't read the mail message from the Outgoing Mail database.

Getting Your Memo Back   When you're connected to a LAN or WAN, you can't snatch your mail back after you've sent it. Deleting the Mail Memo from your mail database won't stop its delivery. When you work remotely, however, you can stop the mail before it gets to the server. If you haven't replicated or sent mail yet, the mail is still in the Outgoing Mail database. Open the database, select the mail message, and click the **Delete Message** button on the Action Bar. You'll also have to delete your copy of it in your mail database.

Replicating Mail

Access the Replicator Page by clicking the Replicator bookmark. The Replicator Page provides a central location to handle all your replication needs. By using the features available on the Replicator Page, you can set options to control replication of your mail and any other databases you might use. Lotus Notes automatically creates a **Send Outgoing Mail entry** on the Replicator Page, as shown in Figure 21.4. For information on how to configure your Replicator Page, see Lesson 19, "Understanding Replication."

For each local database replica you have, you also see a database entry on the Replicator Page. You can replicate these databases at the same time you replicate your mail. Click the checkbox (a check mark appears) at the beginning of the database entry row you want to include in the next replication.

In addition to your mail, your outgoing mail, and the database entries for all your replicated databases, the Replicator Page has a call entry and a hang-up entry that dial the server and hang up when replication is completed. All you have to do is click **Start**.

The status bar at the bottom of the page shows information about the current replication, letting you know when Lotus Notes is attempting to call a server, what database is being replicated, the progress of the replication, how many minutes are left, and when the replication finishes. After replication, the status bar displays statistics for individual entries.

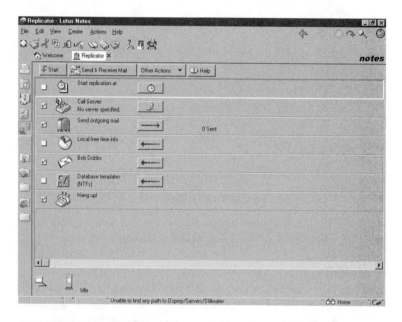

FIGURE 21.4   The Replicator Page.

Using Send/Receive Mail

Before you leave the office to go on the road, make sure of the following:

- Your location and connection documents are set up.

- Your replicas are created, and you've added any necessary entries to the Replicator Page.

- You have a phone cord, extra battery packs, and a power adapter.

- You have the phone number for your Notes administrator. (Please don't tell him we suggested you travel with his cell phone number, home phone number, and beeper number!☺)

- You have a copy of the help database on your computer.

To send and receive mail while working remotely, follow these steps:

1. Plug one end of the phone cord into your modem's port and the other into a phone jack on the wall or on the back of a phone.

2. Click the **Location** button on the status bar, and choose your current location if it's not already selected.

3. Click the **Replicator** bookmark. Then choose one of the following methods:

   • Choose **Actions, Send and Receive Mail**.

   • Click the **Send & Receive Mail** button on the Action Bar.

   • Click the **Other Actions** button on the Action Bar and choose **Send Outgoing Mail** (to send mail only).

Notes initializes the modem, and the call goes out to your server. Your new mail is replicated to the server, and the server replicates any new mail to your computer. After replication is complete, your computer hangs up. If you want to stop the mail from being sent or the replication process, click **Stop**. As soon as you return to the office, remember to switch your location back to one for connection to the network.

 My Other Databases Didn't Replicate! Sending and receiving mail does not replicate your other databases—only your mail database. You must click the **Start** button on the Replicator Page to replicate other databases. To replicate some, but not all, select the database(s) and click the **Other Actions** button on the Action Bar, and choose **Replicate selected database**.

Managing File Size

To keep your mail database at a manageable size, delete old mail frequently. On occasion, you should *compact* your databases to get rid of the empty spaces left by the deleted documents. You can compact any of the local replicas you have by doing the following:

1. Right-click on your Mail bookmark, and choose **Database, Properties**.

   When the Database Properties box appears, click the **Info** tab (see Figure 21.5).

FIGURE **21.5** The Info page of the Database Properties box.

2. Click the **% Used** button.

3. If the percentage is under 90, click the **Compact** button. If not, you don't have to compact the database.

Encrypting Local Databases

Security is an issue in every company, and should your laptop become lost or stolen, the information stored in your Notes databases is no longer secure. To help ensure that information on your laptop is available to only you, encrypt the local copies of databases on your laptop.

 Encryption can slow you down! Encrypted databases can take a long time to open. Use encryption only if you have a real security issue.

To encrypt a local copy of a database, follow these steps:

1. Right-click the database bookmark, and choose **Database Properties**.

2. On the Basics tab, click the **Encryption** button.

3. From the **Locally Encrypt This Database Using** drop-down list (see Figure 21.6), select **Medium** encryption. Select **Strong** encryption only if your system administrator instructs you to do so.

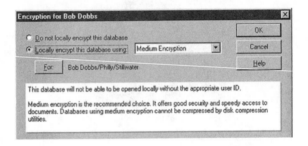

FIGURE 21.6   Choose to locally encrypt databases in the Encryption dialog box.

4. Click **OK**.

Working Offline

Although it's horrible to contemplate, there are times when you won't be able to connect to the server—via a LAN, a WAN, or a modem. For example, you might be traveling by plane or train or staying in an older hotel/motel with hard-wired phones. In these cases, you need to work *offline*. We suggest you change your User Preferences to prompt you for a location each time you start Notes, this will help you to remember to select the appropriate location. Change your location to **Island (Disconnected)** so your computer does not attempt to connect to the server if you accidentally try to open one of the databases only found on the server.

Remember to change your location when you reach a site where you can connect to the server.

In this lesson, you learned how to work remotely with Notes. In the next lesson, you learn how to customize Notes to work efficiently for you.

LESSON 22
Customizing Notes

In this lesson, you learn how to customize the way you work in Notes through the use of user preferences. You also learn about customizing SmartIcons.

Setting User Preferences

You can change a number of settings that affect your workspace and how you work in Notes. You control such things as when Notes scans for unread documents, when your trash is emptied, and whether it saves a copy of the mail you send. Find these settings and options in the **User Preferences** dialog box (shown in Figure 22.1). To open the **User Preferences** dialog box, choose **File**, **Preferences**, **User Preferences**.

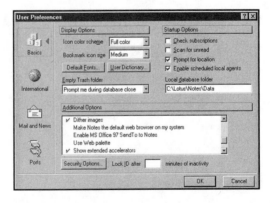

FIGURE 22.1   Keep in mind that some of the Preference settings won't take effect until the next time that you start Notes. Usually, you'll see an alert to that effect after you click **OK**.

More Information This lesson covers only the common, most basic options you can customize in **User Preferences.** If you need more information about customizing **User Preferences,** see *Sams Teach Yourself Lotus Notes R5 Client in 24 Hours* or *Special Edition Using Lotus Notes and Domino 5.*

Changing Basics Options

Click the **Basics** icon to access the **Basics** window in the **User Preferences** dialog box (refer to Figure 22.1). There you can work with the following options: Startup options, Local database folder, ID locking, Empty Trash folder, and so forth. Table 22.1 describes areas where you might want to make changes. For items you find in the properties box that are not covered here, please consult with your System Administrator.

Table 22.1   Basics Options

Option	Description
Startup options	Contains check boxes for commands that are performed automatically when you open Notes. Place a checkmark in the **Scan for unread** check box if you want Notes to look for unread message and documents. Put a checkmark in the **Prompt for location** box if you are a mobile user or if more than one person shares a workstation (See Lesson 20, "Setting Up for Mobile Use"). If you are set up to use subscriptions , select the **Check Subscriptions** checkbox to display new additions when you open Notes.
Lock ID file	A security measure that prompts you to type in your password if Notes has been inactive for a designated number of minutes.

Option	Description
Empty Trash folder	Governs when your trash folder is emptied. Choose whether you want to be prompted when you close the database, whether you always want it emptied when you close the database, or whether you want to empty it manually. (To learn more about using the trash folder, see Lesson 5, "Managing Mail.")
Additional options	Contains a list of options that control how you use Notes. A checkmark appears beside active options. Click an option to select or deselect it. Use the scrollbar on the right of this window to see all available options.
Security Options	Displays Workstation Execution Control Lists. You should not modify any of these options unless you are instructed to do so by your Domino System Administrator.
User Dictionary	Enables you to view words you've added to your User Dictionary during spell checking. You can add, update, and delete any of these words. (For more information on using Spell Check, see Lesson 4, "Creating and Sending Mail.")

Afraid of the Additional Options? If you're unsure of an option's meaning, read about the option in Notes Help system before you activate it. Also, check with your System Administrator or Notes Help desk before you make advanced settings if you are unsure of the results. If you do check an option and you don't like the results, open the **User Preferences** dialog box and deselect it.

Changing International Options

Most of the International settings are determined at the time that the
Domino server or the workstation is set up. For the most part, you will
leave the settings as they are pictured in Figure 22.2. However you might
want to change the Calendar information fields as described in Table 22.2.

Table 22.2   International Options—Calendar Settings

Option	Description
Week Starts on	In North America, the week begins on Sunday. Other parts of the world are different. This is where the first day of the week can be selected.
Calendar View Starts on	By default, the calendar view starts on Monday as seen in Lesson 9, "Using the Calendar." You can select a different day of the week if your work week does not begin on Monday.
Small Calendar Starts on	This affects the small calendar which appears in the Calendar Navigator Pane. The default setting here is Monday.

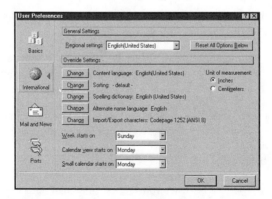

FIGURE 22.2   Most International Options never need changing as
they are set when Notes is installed on your workstation.

Changing Mail and News Options

As seen in Figure 22.3, you can change Mail options by clicking the **Mail** icon in the **User Preferences** dialog box. Table 22.3 describes some of the mail options you might want to change.

Table 22.3   Mail Options

Option	Description
Save sent mail	Controls whether Notes always keeps a copy of the mail messages you send, never keeps a copy, or prompts you so you can decide at the time you send the message whether to keep a copy of the message.
Audible notification	Controls whether Notes sounds a beep or any other sound upon receipt of new mail. You can select a different notification sound by clicking on the **Choose** button and then selecting the sound from the list.
Visible notification	Controls whether a dialog box is displayed in the center of your screen when a new message arrives in your inbox. Notes must be open (even if minimized) for visible notifications to work.
Sign sent mail	Tells Notes to always add a digital signature to your mail.
Encrypt sent mail	Tells Notes to always protect the mail you send so it can be opened only by the person to whom it's addressed.
Encrypt saved mail	Tells Notes to always protect the mail you save so others cannot view it.
Alternate memo editor	This advanced Mail feature enables you to use either Microsoft Word or Lotus WordPro for creating mail messages. In order for this to work, you must have the software installed on your workstation.

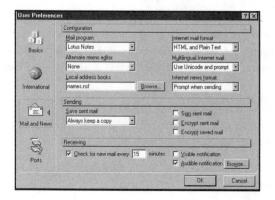

FIGURE 22.3 Mail options are changed in this section of the **User Preferences** dialog box.

Changing Ports Options

Port options determine how your workstation connects to the Domino server. Do not change these setting unless you are instructed to do so by your Domino System Administrator.

When you finish changing settings in the **User Preferences** dialog box, click **OK** to close it.

Using SmartIcons

SmartIcons (a Lotus term) are the icons located on the toolbar. Most of your Windows products contain a toolbar with icons that act as shortcuts or alternatives to using the menu. Some people find it faster to click a SmartIcon than to look through the menus to find choices such as opening a database or bolding text. Like menus and Action Bars, SmartIcons are *context sensitive*; that is, they change with the task you are doing.

Semper Fidelis The first six SmartIcons to the right of the first spacer are always available. They will not change as you move from task to task in Notes.

To help you understand the function of each SmartIcon, Lotus Notes has a feature that shows the SmartIcon's description. To see this brief description, hold your mouse over a SmartIcon. If the description does not appear, you might need to turn this feature on. Here's how to turn on the SmartIcon descriptions:

1. From your workspace, open the **File** menu and click **Preferences** and then **SmartIcon Settings**. The **SmartIcons** dialog box appears, as shown in Figure 22.4.

2. Under **Show**, select **Icon Bar** to show the icons, then select **Descriptions**.

3. Click **OK**.

FIGURE 22.4 To keep the options you select in the **SmartIcons** dialog box, click the **OK** button. Otherwise, click **Cancel**.

To learn the purpose of each SmartIcon, place your cursor on the SmartIcon; a description appears in a white box, listing the description of the SmartIcon. To have SmartIcons appear in color at all times (as opposed to color when you hold your mouse over the icon), choose **Preferences**, **User Preferences** from the menu. In the **Icon Color Scheme**, select **full color** from the drop-down menu.

You can change the default SmartIcon set (called the Universal Set) by customizing it for your needs. For example, you might find it convenient to have the Print icon on your toolbar. To add or remove the Print icon:

1. From your workspace, open the **File** menu and choose
   Preferences and **SmartIcon Settings** from the menu.

2. The **SmartIcon** dialog box appears, as shown in Figure 22.4.
   The left panel shows available icons; the right panel shows icons
   that are currently selected for your Universal Set (the set in use).
   Scroll through the left panel of available icons until you locate
   the Printer icon.

3. Drag the Printer icon from the left panel to the right panel.
   Position the icon on the right panel in the exact position you
   want it to appear on your toolbar. For example, placing this icon
   first on the list results in its appearing first (on the far left) on
   the toolbar.

4. Repositioning the Printer icon causes the icons to move down in
   the list so that your Printer icon is first on the list.

5. (**Optional**) To remove a SmartIcon from the toolbar, select it
   from the icons in the right panel and drag it to the left panel.

 Other SmartIcon Info If your monitor is a Super VGA
monitor, you can increase the *size* of your SmartIcons.
Click the **Icon Size** button and choose Large.

You might want to change the *placement* of your
SmartIcon palette. The default position for your
SmartIcon set is at the top of the screen. You can
select **Left, Right, Top, Bottom,** or **Floating**.

6. Click **OK** to save your changes and close the window. The
   Printer icon appears on the toolbar.

Floating Palette   When a floating palette is selected, the SmartIcon set appears in its own window rather than being anchored on the edge of the screen (as in Right, Left, Top, or Bottom). You can move the floating window around the screen by dragging its title bar; you can resize the window by dragging its borders.

Customizing the Welcome Page

Change your Welcome page by customizing it. Options for customizing the Welcome page are

- Create your own page

- Use a bookmark as your Welcome page

- Change the Welcome page template (Basics, My News, Notes, and Domino News)

To create your own page or customize a Welcome page style, click the drop-down menu located on your Welcome page next to the words **Welcome page**.

Choose from preset Welcome page styles. Any of these choices have customization options except the Basics page.

No Templates? No Options? Your Welcome page is customizable by your Notes administrator. It's entirely possible that a corporate Welcome page has been designed for your use and you may find that options mentioned here do not apply to your Notes desktop.

When you choose **Headlines with AOL My News** or **Notes and Domino News** click the **Options** button that appears next to the Welcome page style drop-down list to display the **Page Options** dialog box. If you select **Create new page style** from the drop-down list on the Welcome page, the **New page** dialog box appears. Both the **Create New Page** and the **Page Options** dialog boxes are the same with the exception of one field. Table 22.4 describes the options found for customizing your Welcome page.

Table 22.4   Customizing the Welcome Page

Option	Description
Basics Page	
Page Name	Title your page by completing the **Give your page a title** field.
Layout	Choose from one of the six frame layout styles for your Welcome page.
Delete	(Only available for My News and Notes and Domino News templates.) Selecting this deletes the template from your style list.
Content Page	
Select a Frame	Depending on your layout, click in one of the frames to set the definition for the frame in the Frame content section.
Frame content	Determines what displays in the frame select in the Select a Frame section. Choices include to do list, inbox, calendar Web page and so forth. Choosing Basic tasks gives you easy access to mail, calendar, and so forth. Database descriptions allow you to subscribe to a Domino database on your server. Quick Links allow you to list up to five Web page links in the frame.

To make a bookmark your home page, bookmark the page you want to use, right-click the bookmark, and select **Set Bookmark as Home Page**.

In this lesson, you learned how to customize user preferences, the Welcome Page and manage your SmartIcons.

Understanding Security and Access Rights

Lotus Notes and Domino security have several levels of access. Notes administrators and designers can determine the following:

- Who can access the server
- Who can access each database
- Who can access views and documents within a database
- Who can access fields within a form

Accessing the server is determined by your Notes ID and password. Whether you can access a database and what you can do within the database is determined by the Access Control List for each database. Notes security is a powerful, important tool for your company.

Passwords

Your first line of defense in securing your workstation and mail from unauthorized people is your password. When you access the Domino server the first time, you start a Notes session, which prompts you to enter your password For security reasons, neither you nor anyone else can see what you are typing—all you see are X's.

Your password can be any combination of keyboard characters, as long as the first character is a letter of the alphabet. The number of characters in your password is determined when your Notes ID (User ID) is created by your Domino administrator. Because passwords are case-sensitive, the password "INFONUT" is different from the password "infonut."

The User ID is a file created when the Domino administrator first registers you as a user. When you start up Lotus Notes on your computer for the first time, the User ID file transfers to your computer and by default is placed in the Lotus\Notes\Data directory or folder. You want to be careful to protect this file, because someone else could use it to pretend to be you on the Lotus Notes network. If your computer operating system is password-protected, that might be enough. If your computer is accessible to several people, however, or if you share a computer at work, you might want to move the User ID file out of your computer on to a floppy disk for safekeeping. If you ever suspect the file is lost (along with your stolen laptop), report it to the Notes administrator.

Lotus Notes has several features designed to limit access to documents, views, databases, and servers. For example, only authorized personnel can delete databases from the server, design applications, open certain documents, or read designated fields. The Notes administrator or the Application Designer controls most of this. What you are authorized to do depends on your status in the Access Control List of each database.

For example, a database that contains all of your company's customers might be accessible to everyone in the company, but it's very possible that different people see different views, forms, and fields and can see only a partial list of customers. Perhaps each salesperson can see only the customers assigned to her when she opens the database, yet the sales manager sees all of the customers when he accesses the database.

To determine your level of access for a particular database, click the database icon to select it; then, click the Access Key button on the status bar. The Groups and Roles dialog box appears, indicating your access level.

Each person is granted one of seven levels of access to a database:

- **No Access**—This denies you access to the database. You can't read any of the documents in the database, and you can't create new documents. In fact, you cannot add the database icon to your workspace if you do not have access.

- **Depositor**—You can create documents but can't read any of the documents in the database—including the ones you create yourself. You might be granted this access level to cast a ballot in a voting database, for example.

- **Reader**—You can read the documents in the database, but you can't create or edit documents. You might have this level of access to a company policy database so that you can read policies but can't create or change them.

- **Author**—As an author, you can create documents and edit your own documents. You can't edit documents created by others, however, even though you can read them.

- **Editor**—You can do everything an author does, and you can edit documents submitted by others. A manager who approves the expense reports submitted by others needs at least editor access to those documents.

- **Designer**—A designer can do everything an editor can but also can create or change any design elements of the database. To change the design of a form in a database, you must have Designer access. A designer also has the ability to create a Full Text Index.

- **Manager**—Can access everything a designer can. A manager also can assign and modify the Access Control List (ACL), modify replication settings, and delete a database from the server.

You probably will have at least reader access to the Directory (company Address Book), whereas you have manager access to your Personal Address Book and Mail databases.

Encryption

When you want to keep your email private, encrypt it. Encrypting scrambles your message so that only the person receiving it can read it.

Each Lotus Notes user has a unique *private* and *public* key that Notes stores as part of the ID file. The public key is also stored in the person document for each user in the Public Address Book. When someone sends you an encrypted mail message, Notes uses your public key from the Public Address Book to encrypt the message. Now, no one but you can read it. At the delivery end, Notes uses your private key from your ID file to decrypt the message so that you can read it.

Encryption can be an important tool for laptop users. If you travel with Notes databases on your laptop, consult your Notes administrator about how to encrypt databases on your laptop and whether he recommends it.

Signatures

Two "signatures" are available in Notes. One is the signature you attach to your letterhead. The second is an encoded and internal Notes function that prevents a user from masquerading as someone other than herself. To apply a signature to a message, the sender must have a Notes ID and know her password. For example, Jane, a Notes designer, can change her mail memo form to appear with Dorothy's name at the top and in the "from" field. She can send this message out, appearing to be Dorothy. Jane cannot *sign* the message as Dorothy, however, without knowing Dorothy's password and without having Dorothy's Notes ID. This is why you should protect your password and ID.

When a signature is applied in Notes, you see a message in the status bar that says "Signed by Jane Calabria." This assures you that Jane created the message (unless, of course, Jane was foolish enough to distribute her password and ID to someone else).

Web Access to Notes Mail

If you have access to your Notes mail file via the Internet using a Web Browser (Microsoft Internet Explorer or Netscape Navigator) you can access your mail when you are at a computer on which Lotus Notes is not installed, but which has Internet access. Check with your Notes administrator to see if your company has these capabilities. If you have this ability, when you access mail from a browser, you will be prompted to enter a username and password.

Your username is the same as the name that displays in the Enter Password dialog box when you log into Notes (such as Joe Doaks/Philly/Stillwater). You can use just the common name portion of this name, as in *Joe Doaks* or your shortname, *jdoaks*.

Your password is probably set and supplied to you by your Notes administrator and it *might* be the same as the password you use when you start the Lotus Notes client. However, it is possible that you will need to set your own password. Additionally, you might want to change your Internet password once your administrator supplies it to you. Check with your Notes administrator before you change or set your Internet password and follow these steps to set or edit your Internet password.

When Is a Password Not a Password? Your Internet password is not the same as your Notes password, even if both passwords use the same letters. In other words, changing one password does *not* change the other.

Open your **Company Address Book** (Directory). In the **People** view, open your Person Document and click the **Edit Person** button on the Action Bar. On the **Basics** page, type your desired password in the **Internet password** field. Click **Save** and **Close**. The password you set is stored in encrypted format, so be certain to type the password carefully. If you make a mistake, you will not be able to identify your typo when you place the Person document in edit mode again because your password is encrypted. If you think you made a mistake, edit the Person document and delete the password, retype if and save it again.

APPENDIX B

Email Etiquette

Because so many people use email, it's necessary to follow certain "rules" concerning what is proper or acceptable—*email etiquette.*

Check out these points of etiquette so you can responsibly and effectively use Lotus Notes Mail:

- **Always include information in the subject line**—Don't send email without including a clear and concise description of your message in the Subject line. It lets your recipients know what the message is about before they open it.

- **Beware of the written word**—Although email is fairly secure, it's not entirely secure. Someone might forward your message to others. Also, sarcasm doesn't translate well from the spoken word to the written word. You might be taken seriously or offend someone when you were only joking.

- **Send meaningful email**—Some companies do not allow any personal use of email. Even if they do, you should still be thoughtful about the number of messages you send people and the importance of those messages. People might not appreciate unsolicited jokes, thoughts for the day, gossip, and cartoons.

- **Give thought to sending attachments**—You can attach files from other programs within your Lotus Notes Mail. However, it takes time for the recipient to open and read an attachment. Send an attachment only if the recipient needs to make changes to or have a copy of that file for his records or the file is too large to cut, copy, and paste into your mail memo. Also, include information in your memo so the receiver knows what the file contains before he opens it.

- **Don't send email to the world**—Don't create large distribution lists. If you need to distribute information to a large group of people, ask your Notes administrator for possible alternatives. A discussion database application, a repository application, or a TeamRoom application might be better for sharing information.

- **DON'T USE ALL CAPS**—Typing in all uppercase letters implies that you're shouting.

- **Use Reply to All**—When you answer an email message that includes several names in the To or cc fields, use the Reply to All feature if your answer would be of use to all those people. Otherwise, some people will be dropped from the conversation and you (or the person to whom you're replying) will have to resend the reply to them. Conversely, don't use Reply to All if you only need to respond to the sender.

- **Keep your messages short**—The shorter the better. Some people often skip over email when the message contains more than a screen full of information.

- **Remember that you are using company property**—Unlike mail that's sent through the post office, your email is company property. Unless your company policy allows it, email topics that are personal, not work-related, or highly confidential should not be exchanged over the company's email system.

- **Don't print out your inbox**—This is more a common sense than an etiquette issue. If you print your email for reading purposes, aren't you defeating the purpose?

 Don't Risk Your Job! Remember that many large corporations have company policies regarding email; ask your company for a copy of these policies so you don't violate any rules that might cause problems for you at work.

APPENDIX C

Using Actioneer for Notes®5.0

Wouldn't it be great to create To Do's and Calendar entries even when Notes is not running? That's what Actioneer is all about.

Actioneer is a separate, add-in program that's routinely installed with Lotus Notes (check with your Notes Administrator if you don't have it on your computer).

The Actioneer program might be set up on your computer to automatically start when Windows opens, or you might have a shortcut icon on your Windows desktop that you use to start the program. If not, you can always start Actioneer by clicking the **Start** button on the Windows taskbar and choosing **Programs, Actioneer, Actioneer for Lotus Notes, Actioneer for Lotus Notes** from the Start menu.

Don't be surprised when you use Actioneer to be asked for a password when the program starts (see Figure C.1). Enter your Notes password. (To be sure this sharing of a password works properly before starting Actioneer for the first time, open Notes and choose **File, Tools, User ID**. Enter your Notes password and choose **OK**. In the User ID dialog box, make sure there is a check mark for the **Don't Prompt for a Password from Other Notes-Based Programs** option.)

FIGURE C.1   Enter your Notes password if Actioneer requests a password.

Make Entries with Actioneer

After the program starts, an Actioneer icon displays in the System tray on the Windows taskbar (see Figure C.2). Double-click that symbol whenever you need to capture information for a Calendar entry, To Do, or a note for your Journal database (you can also right-click the icon and choose **New Action Note** from the menu, or press **Ctrl+Alt+N**).

 — Actioneer icon

FIGURE C.2 Double-click the Actioneer icon to open a window to enter Calendar or To Do information.

The Actioneer window pops up on your screen, ready for any information you want to enter (see Figure C.3). Enter your text in the action pad pane on the left. Actioneer interprets the information and suggests possible Notes destinations (**To Do**, **Appointment**, **Journal Entry**) in the destination pane on the right. You can enter additional information or change the data Actioneer displays. For example, assign a category or change a date. It's also possible to change the type of entry by clicking one of the destination buttons.

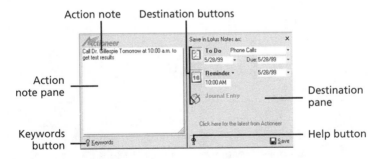

FIGURE C.3 You enter your text in the action pad pane and Actioneer automatically selects a possible destination.

Easy on Dates   You don't have to enter specific dates in Actioneer, because it automatically interprets words and phrases like "tomorrow" and "next Thursday." Actioneer keeps a folder of keywords that you might use so it can interpret dates from the text you enter or capture.

When the information for the entry is correct, click **Save** and Actioneer distributes the information directly to the assigned destination. The next time you open your Calendar, To Do list, or Journal database, you see your new entry (see Figure C.4).

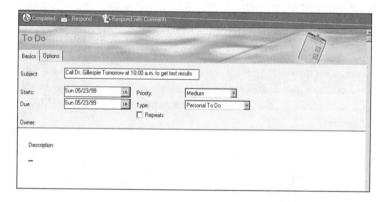

FIGURE C.4   The To Do you see in Notes was created in Actioneer.

Actioneer will also help you capture text from email or Web pages to make your entries. While you have the email or page open, highlight the text you want to capture and press **Ctrl+Alt+G**. The Actioneer window opens and the highlighted text appears in the action pad pane. Assign it a destination and click **Save**.

Getting Help for Actioneer

Actioneer has Online Help that provides information on how to use the program. To access Online Help do one of these three:

- Click the **Help** button on the Actioneer window.

- Press **F1**.

- Right-click the **Actioneer** icon in the Systems tray of the Windows taskbar and then choose **Help** from the menu.

The left pane of Online Help shows a set of book icons, which represent main topics (see Figure C.5). Double-click one of these books to see a list of topics. Then click the topic name to see that information in the right pane.

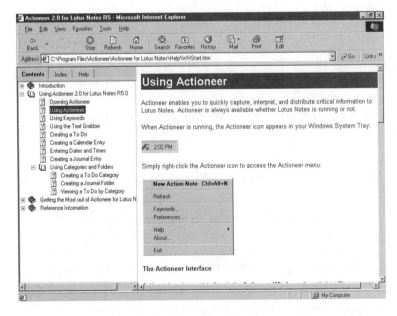

FIGURE C.5   Online Help, shown here in Internet Explorer, has two panes. On the left are the topics, and the right displays the details.

Online Help is displayed using Microsoft Internet Explorer or Netscape Navigator. Any problems you have viewing Online Help may be because you are using an older version of the browser software. Actioneer recommends using at least Internet Explorer 4.0 or Netscape Navigator 4.0.4, so you might consider upgrading.

Specifying Keywords

Doesn't it seem amazing that Actioneer can read your text and guess the category or date from what you've written? This occurs because of keywords. Keywords are dates, times, words, or phrases that Actioneer recognizes and interprets to select an appropriate destination. Click on the **Keywords** button or select **Keywords** from the Actioneer menu to see a list of the keywords Actioneer uses.

There is one keyword for every To Do category or Journal folder that exists in Lotus Notes. When you add a new category or folder, close Actioneer and start it again to have the category or folder added as a keyword.

Other keywords include "today" and "tomorrow," as well as the days of the week. Actioneer recognizes dates, as well, in different formats. It even recognizes "Next" in combination with a weekday, to figure the date for an entry. Times are also recognized in different formats.

Setting Preferences in Actioneer

Actioneer lets you set preferences to match the way you want to work with the program. Working with the ViaVoice utility, Actioneer can be speech-enabled (you must have ViaVoice installed first). Shortcut keys can be specified for opening an action note and activating the text grabber. You also decide if you want to open a new action note or close the action note on saving.

To open the Preferences dialog box (see Figure C.6), right-click the **Actioneer** icon and choose **Preferences** from the menu.

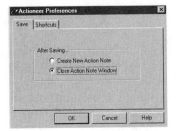

FIGURE C.6   The Save tab lets you decide what should happen after you click Save. The Shortcuts tab lets you set keyboard shortcuts.

The version of Actioneer that ships with Lotus Notes R5 is a scaled down version of Actioneer Pro. Actioneer Pro has the ability to

- Create customized keywords for all your To Do categories and Journal folders.

- Send email, task requests, and meeting invitations from Actioneer without opening Lotus Notes.

- Create new Personal Address Book contacts from Actioneer.

- Link contact records to To Do items and Journal entries.

For more information on Actioneer, visit their Web site at www.actioneer.com/welcome.

GLOSSARY

.nsf   A file extension for a Domino Database (as in Mail.nsf). The letters are short for Notes Storage Facility.

.ntf   A file extension for a Domino Database design template (as in perweb.ntf). The letters are short for Notes Template Facility.

@function   A commonly used or complex formula that is built into Notes.

About This Database document   A special document that describes the purpose of a Domino database. The document can be viewed from the Help menu.

Accelerator key   See *Hotkey.*

Access control   See *Access Control List.*

Access Control List (ACL)   A list of users, groups, and servers and their rights and access privileges to a Domino database.

Access control section   Within a Notes form, a section where the capability to edit can be restricted to specific individuals. An individual must already have the right to edit the document in the ACL before she can be granted the privilege to edit an access-controlled section. Other users can still read the section.

Access level   A security feature that defines the degree of access to a database granted to a user, group, or server. There are seven levels of access: No Access, Depositor, Reader, Author, Editor, Designer, and Manager.

ACL   See *Access Control List.*

Action Bar   Also called button bar, this nonscrolling region at the top of a view or form that contains predefined Actions for that form or view.

Action Buttons and Hotspots   Preprogrammed areas of a view or form that users click on to automate.

Address bar   The area of a window that shows the current file path or Web page address (URL). New file or address requests are entered here.

Address Books   See *Personal Address Book* and *Enterprise Directory.*

Agent (also called *macro*)   A program that consists of and performs a series of automated tasks. Agents can be initiated by the user or can run on a scheduled basis. It is comprised of three parts: 1. When it acts (the Trigger), 2. What it acts on (the Search) and 3. what it does (the action). Agents are written in the Lotus Formula language, LotusScript, JavaScript, or Java.

Alarm   In Domino, an automated notification that a triggering event has occurred. For example, a calendar event can notify a user that he has a meeting in 30 minutes, or a server event can trigger an alarm to the Domino administrator that a performance threshold has been reached.

Attachment   A file attached to a document or form.

Authenticate   In Domino, to exchange identifying information in such a way that the identity of both parties is established.

Authentication   In Domino security, the process by which clients and/or servers establish their identities to each other. Authentication can use certificates or in the case of a Notes client, a name and password, to establish identity.

Author access   A level of security (defined in the Access Control List) that permits a user or server to create and edit his own documents.

Authors field   A field that contains the name of the author of a document. When combined with author access to the database, an Authors field can be used to grant editor access to users who are not authors of the document.

Autolaunch   Automatically launches an attachment or embedded object in its native format when a Notes document is opened.

Bookmark folder   A folder on the bookmark bar that holds bookmarks linking to Domino databases, Notes views or documents, or Web pages.

Bookmark(s)   In Domino, a link that references a document or a location in a document on the Web or in a Domino database.

Broadcast meeting   A type of calendar entry that invites people to a meeting, but no response is required.

Browser   A graphical interface that lets users interact with the World Wide Web on the Internet.

Button bar   See *Action Bar.*

Button Hotspot   Also known as a pushbutton, actions that appear in the form of a clickable button which can be added to forms, subforms, pages, and documents. See also *Action.*

Calendar   In Domino, the calendaring views, forms and documents built into the Notes mail template, used to make and track events such as appointments, meetings and anniversaries. The calendar function also includes the scheduling of shared resources and tracking freetime for meeting scheduling and group calendaring.

Canonical format   The format in which Notes stores hierarchical names internally, with each hierarchical component identified by a one or two character code. For example, CN=John Smith/OU=East/O=Acme/C=US.

Cascading   Falling from. In Cascading *menu*, a collection of menu items that fall under a single prompt in a parent menu. The File, Database menu prompt is an example. In Cascading *actions*, a collection of actions that appear under a single action button in the Action Bar.

Category   In Domino, a word, number, or phrase used to group Notes documents in a view.

Certificate   A file that verifies the identity of a computer when two computers communicate. Certificates are used to verify the identity of an email sender and to exchange and authenticate identities with an Internet server.

Channel   Web site to which one can subscribe to receive information from the Internet, which uses Web pages that update themselves using *push technology.*

Checkbox   A small area on a form in which the user makes selections by clicking in that area. When clicked, a checkmark or X appears in the checkbox. Checkboxes are toggle keys: Click once to place a checkmark; click a checkmark to remove it.

Checkbox fields   In Domino, a keyword field type which presents a list of choices to the user in a checkbox format. Users make a choice by clicking the checkbox, which places an *x* in the box. This keyword field is used where multiple choices can be made, as in a checklist.

Child document   A Notes document created using a Response-type form. The child document inherits data from its parent document and is permanently associated with that parent. If the parent document is deleted, the child document will be orphaned unless it is also deleted.

Collapse   In Domino, to condense a view so that it displays only categories or only main documents (with the responses hidden). The term is also used when sections within documents are condensed so that only the section header is displayed.

Combobox field   A keyword field type which presents a list of choices to the user in a drop-down list format.

Command key   A keyboard shortcut for performing an immediate action. For example, to print a document, you can use Ctrl+P in Windows (Command+P on a Macintosh).

Common Name   The first element in the X.500 naming convention. Each name requires at a minimum the Common Name element (CN) and the Organization element (O). This field contains the user's full first and last names.

Compact   (in Domino) Compress a database by removing any white space created when documents are deleted.

Connection document   A Domino document that defines the connection properties between two servers. In order for two servers in separate domains to communicate, a connection document must exist in the PAB. It is required to transfer mail between adjacent domains.

Context Pane   The area of the Notes Window in which a document (such as a Mail Memo) is displayed while creating a response to that document, or a Mail Memo.

Context-sensitive   A term used to describe menus and help screens which change depending on the task or function being performed in the program.

Data directory   The top-level directory in which local Domino databases and templates are stored, along with DESKTOP.DSK files and CLS files. UNIX and OS/2 also store the NOTES.INI file in the data directory. By default, the directory is called DATA and is directly under the Notes or Domino directory.

Data type   The type of data a specific field on a Notes form can contain—for example, text, rich text, numbers, names.

Database Catalog   A database that lists information about databases on a Domino server, in a group of Domino servers, or in a Domain.

Database library   A database that lists information about selected databases on a workstation or shared databases on a server.

Database Manager   In Domino, a person who has been granted Manager access in the database ACL. The manager can edit the ACL and can delete the database, as well as performing all database design and edit functions.

Database replica   A database created using replication. A database replica has the same ID as the database from which it was created and can exchange information with the original database through replication.

Date/Time field   A field defined with the date/time data type. The field can only store data that is entered using date/time formats via user input or formulas.

DDE   See *Dynamic Data Exchange*.

Default   The setting, direction, or choice made by a program unless intervention is made by the user. Built into an application or program when values or options are necessary for the program to function.

Default Value (for fields)   The value displayed in an editable field when a document is first created.

Default value formula   A formula that computes a value for a field, requiring no intervention by the user. For example, a default value formula can insert today's date into a field that the user has the option of changing.

Default view   The view that is displayed when a database is first opened.

Depositer access   Level of security (defined in the Access Control List) which allows users or servers to create documents but not see or edit any documents.

Designer access   Level of security (defined in the Access Control List) that allows users or servers to modify the design of a database. Designer Access does not permit changes to the database Access Control List.

Desktop.dsk   A file that stores the options selected for the Notes client desktop.

Detach   In Domino, to save to a disk drive a copy of a file that appears as an attachment in a Notes document.

Dialog box   A box that is displayed on the screen so the user can provide further information when it is required before the system can continue.

Dialog list field   A keyword field type that presents a list of choices to the user in the Notes client. This field appears with the entry helper button by default. In a Web client this is presented as a combobox. See also *Combobox field.*

Dial-up   A type of connection in which you connect to a server or network using a modem over a telephone line.

Digital speech synthesizer   A device that translates what is on the screen into voice output, used as a way for the blind to get information from the computer screen.

Document   A type of form independent of all other forms. It stands alone. It does not respond to other forms. It is sometimes referred to as a *main document.*

Document ID   See *Notes identification number.*

Domain   In relation to the Internet, the last part of an Internet address (for example, .gov and .com). In networks, a group of connected computers that share the same security system, so a user has to use only one ID and password to access resources within the Domain. In Domino, an address book. See also *Domino Directory.*

Domino (also *Domino server*)   The server component in a Lotus Notes environment.

Domino application server   A Domino server used primarily to provide access to Domino databases for Lotus Notes clients.

Domino database   A container for both data and program code. (Note that this does not match the definition used for Relational Databases, which is a collection of related tables.)

Domino Designer   The software program used by application developers and programmers to create Domino databases.

Domino Directory   The Public Address Book stored on the Domino server containing names and addresses of people and servers in that Domino Domain. This Address Book is accessible to all individuals in the Domain.

Domino Enterprise Server   A Domino Server license type that provides the tools for scaling the Domino Application Server to a wider enterprise, with clustering, load balancing, and failover.

Domino Mail Server   A Domino server license type for a server whose primary use is for mail routing and hosting Notes mail databases.

Dual key encryption   An encryption using two sets of keys: one set for creating and reading digital signatures, and another set for encrypting and decrypting messages.

Dynamic Data Exchange (DDE)   A method of displaying data created in another application so that there is a link to the live data. When the data is displayed in Notes, the information is dynamically updated to reflect what is currently stored in the original application.

ECL   See *Execution Control List*

Edit mode   The condition in which a document can be modified or created.

Editable field   A field in which the user can enter or change values. The database designer can manipulate user input with formulas such as default value formulas, input translation formulas, or input validation formulas.

Editor access   Level of security (defined in the Access Control List) that allows users or servers to create, read, and edit documents in a database, whether or not they created the original document.

Electronic signature See *Signature, electronic.*

Email signature See *Signature, email.*

Embedded element Design or other objects embedded in forms and pages.

Encryption The scrambling or encoding of data to make it unreadable. Encrypted data must be decrypted to read it. Encryption and decryption involve the use of keys associated with or assigned by the software. Domino uses both public and private encryption keys and both single and dual key encryption methods.

Enterprise Directory A highly compressed directory containing entries from multiple Domino Domains. Used in large corporations to facilitate username lookups across Domains. Also used to allow mobile users to maintain a local copy of a corporatewide address book using minimal disk space.

Execution Control List (ECL) A list of settings that users control and maintain to enhance the security of workstation data. Accessed through the User Preferences dialog box.

Export To save a Lotus Notes document or view in a file format other than Notes (.nsf).

Extended accelerator key Keys used to access bookmarks and task buttons. To view the extended accelerator keys, press and hold down the Alt key.

Extranet A group of interconnected intranets with extended access usually protected by a firewall. For example, companies in business with each other can form extranets in order to share certain types of information as in the case of a manufacturer and a parts supplier. See also *Intranet.*

Field An area of a form which can contain a single data type of information, such as numbers, graphics, and rich text.

Field data type The classification of data a field is designed to accept. Examples of field data types are text, date/time, numbers, rich text, and names.

Field value The value stored in a field in a saved document.

File Transfer Protocol (FTP) A protocol designed for transferring large messages (files) between two points on the Internet, providing error-checking functions so that the entire data file arrives intact.

Folder A container similar to a view into which the user can place documents for later reference. The user can move documents into and out of a folder, whereas a view depends on a formula to determine which documents are displayed.

Folder pane The workspace area that shows the folders and views available in the opened database.

Form An item used for collecting and displaying information in a Domino application. Forms can contain subforms, graphics, fields, links, embedded elements, and so forth. Forms are used to create and display documents. There are three types of forms: Document, Response, and Response-to-Response.

Formula A collection of commands and variables to effect a result. Formulas can be written for numerous events in Domino such as view formulas, input validation, default value, and so forth.

Formula field Used to populate a subscription list. Subscription lists are used by the Headlines database.

Formula Pop-up Hotspot The collection of commands and variables (*formula*) that computes the text which appears on screen (*Pop-up*) when a mouse is held over an area of the screen (*Hotspot*).

Frames One of the panes of a frameset which can contain pages, documents, forms, links, views, and so forth.

Framesets A collection of frames. Each frame within the frameset can work independently of the other frames.

FTP See *File Transfer Protocol*.

Full-text index A series of files containing the indexes to text in a database, allowing Notes to process user search queries.

Full-text search Search option supporting word and phrase searches of Domino databases as well as advanced searches, such as logical expressions.

GIF See *Graphical Interchange Format*.

Graphical Interchange Format (GIF)   A graphics file format with widespread use on the Internet. GIF files are compressed graphic files that can be animated and have transparent backgrounds. See also *JPG, JPEG.*

Graphics   Graphics placed on a form appear in every document that uses that form. Graphics can be converted to imagemaps by adding hotspots. You learn more about graphics on Day 12.

Group   In Domino, a list of users and/or servers used for addressing, access control lists, and address books.

Groupware   A loosely defined term which refers to applications that allow groups of people to work together in a collaborative environment. Discussion databases are considered a Groupware application.

Hierarchical   Having a structure with gradations. See *Hierarchical naming.*

Hierarchical naming   A naming system in which an entity's name includes the names of the entity's antecedents. As used in Notes, your hierarchical name includes at least the name of the organization to which you belong, and may also include the names of sub-units within the organization and the country in which you reside. For example: Bob Dobbs/Sales/Stillwater/US. The benefit of hierarchical naming is that it increases security by providing a standard way of distinguishing between people who might otherwise have the same name. Thus Bob Dobbs/Sales/Stillwater is not the same person as Bob Dobbs/Acctg/Stillwater.

Hierarchical view   A view that displays response documents indented and directly beneath the documents to which they respond

Home page   The first page that displays when a user visits an Internet or intranet site. The home page of a site usually contains a company logo, a welcome message, and links to the other pages within the site.

Home server   The term used for the Domino server on which your mail database resides.

Hop   A mail stop along the delivery path of routed mail when the recipient's and sender's servers are not directly connected.

Hotkey   The underlined letter in a menu used to select a menu command. Also referred to as *accelerator key.*

Hotspot   An object or specific area on an object that has programming or a link attached to it. Hotspots can be attached to text or graphics. See also *Text Pop-up Hotspot, Action Buttons and Hotspots, Formula Pop-up Hotspot, Button Hotspot* and *Link Hotspot.*

HTML   See *Hypertext Markup Language*

HTTP   See *Hypertext Transfer Protocol*

Hyperlink   A block of text (usually colored and underlined) or a graphic that represents a connection to another place in a document or a separate document. Clicking the hyperlink opens the document to which it is linked.

Hypertext   Special text contained in a Web page that, when clicked, takes the user to a related Web page. Hypertext often appears as blue underlined text, changing to purple text when clicked.

Hypertext Markup Language (HTML)   A collection of instructions or tags that tell a browser program how to display a document—as in when to bold or italicize. HTML tags typically appear embedded within a document, set apart from the document text by angle brackets.

Hypertext Transfer Protocol (HTTP)   Protocol that defines how HTML files are sent and received via the Internet.

Imagemap   A special kind of graphics object that can contain multiple hotspots linking to other objects or URLs.

IMAP, IMAP4   See *Internet Message Access Protocol.*

Internet Message Access Protocol (IMAP, IMAP4)   a protocol allowing mail clients to access their mail over the Internet or intranet.

Internet Protocol (IP)   The system which defines the "location," or IP address, of the networks that comprise the Internet. See also *TCP/IP.*

Internet Service Provider (ISP)   A company that provides access to the Internet.

Internotes Server   A Domino Server process that retrieves Web pages and stores them in a Server Web Browser database so that users can retrieve the pages to their Personal Web Browser database without having to connect to the Internet.

Intranet   A restricted-access network that shares information intended for internal use within a company, although intranets can span the globe. Similar to the Web, intranet software allows the routing of HTML documents which are read using a Web browser. A major distinction between an intranet and the Web is access control. See also *Extranet*.

ISP   See *Internet Service Provider*.

Java   An interpreted programming language developed by Sun Microsystems. A Java program is delivered in textual, compressed, or tokenized form from an Internet server to a computer. The Java interpreter or *Java virtual machine* (such as the one which comes with Internet Explorer) interprets and executes the program, just as though it were stored on the receiving computer's hard drive. Java makes possible the transmission of logical and often user-tailored content (such as a desktop stock ticker), whereas HTML by contrast is merely a system for the format and display of text and graphics.

Java applets   Small, self-contained applications that can be embedded into forms.

JavaScript   A scripting language that permits access to the Document Object Model (DOM) and runs on both Notes and Web clients.

Joint Photographic Expert Group (JPG, JPEG)   One of two graphics files formats in use on the Internet. See also *GIF*.

JPG, JPEG   See *Joint Photographic Experts Group*.

Keyboard shortcut   A combination of keys that performs a command in lieu of selecting an item from the menu. For example, Ctrl+P is the keyboard shortcut for printing.

Keyword field   A multiple choice field which presents users a list of choices in checkbox, combobox, dialog list, listbox, and radio button format.

Labels   In database design, text accompanying a field which indicates the use or intended contents of the field. By convention field labels are usually positioned to the left or above the field.

LAN   See *Local area network*.

Letterhead   The manner (style) in which your name, date, and time at the top of a mail message.

Library   See *Database library*

Link   A pointer to a block of data, graphic, or page in an external file or document. On the Web, a link can reference another Web page, a file, or a program, such as a Java program. In Domino, links can open other views, databases, or documents without closing the object containing the link.

Link Hotspot   In Domino, an area which, when clicked, links to other Domino objects or URLs. Link hotspots can be text, graphics, or regions on a graphic object.

Local area network (LAN)   A network that connects a group of computers located within an immediate area, such as the same building. Computers are connected to each other by network cable.

Location document   A document, stored in the Personal Address Book, which contains settings that determine how Notes communicates with Domino server(s) from a specific location. Useful for working in Notes at a specific location.

Lotus Notes   A groupware product by Lotus Development Corporation consisting of server products and client products. Previous to Release 5 of Lotus Notes, all server and client products were referred to as Notes products. In Release 4.5 of Notes, Lotus Development Corporation renamed the server products *Domino* and the client products maintained the name *Lotus Notes*.

Macro   See *Agent*.

Mail database   A Lotus Notes database in which you send and receive mail. Your mail database is stored on your home server. See also *Outgoing mail database*.

Manager access   A level of security (defined in the Access Control List) which gives all rights to a database, including the right to modify a database Access Control List and delete a database. All other access levels (Designer, Editor, Reader, and so forth) fall under the level of Manager; the Manager has the rights defined in all those other access levels.

MIME   See *Multipurpose Internet Mail Extensions*.

Modem A piece of hardware, either internal or external, that allows a user to send data via telephone lines.

Multipurpose Internet Mail Extensions (MIME) An Internet standard that permits data transfer. An Internet browser or Internet mail viewer associates a MIME type with a file type, which gives information about which program should run when the file is opened over the Internet.

Names field A field of Names data type. It can hold the names of people, servers, and groups.

Navigation buttons In notes, browser-like buttons that enable navigation among open database documents or Web pages. Functions include Back, Forward, Stop, Refresh, Search, and Go.

Navigation pane The left pane of a Notes screen that displays either icons for all views, folders, and agents in a database, or the currently selected navigator.

Navigator In Notes, a menu made up of hyperlinked rich text, or hotspots. When clicked, the links or hotspots perform certain actions or access other documents. Netscape has a Web browser called Netscape Navigator.

Nested table Tables that reside within (or inside) other tables.

Network News Transfer Protocol The protocol of Usenet Newsgroups. Defines how newsgroup lists and articles will be transferred between NNTP servers and between NNTP servers and newsreaders.

Newsgroups Online discussion groups on the Internet. Messages posted to the newsgroup can be read and responded to by others.

Newsreader An NNTP client program that allows a user to browse, subscribe to, and unsubscribe from newsgroups, also to read, create, and print newsgroup articles.

NNTP See *Network News Transfer Protocol*.

No access In Notes, a database access level. Entities having no access to a database cannot, in general, see or add to the contents of a database or, for that matter, even add a shortcut for the database to their desktops. An exception to this rule is "public" documents. Users assigned "No Access" can still be permitted either to create or to read "public" documents in the database.

Notes client   Software designed for use by Lotus Notes users. Allows the user to access a Domino server, send mail, and browse the Web.

Notes Identification Number   Every element in a Notes database has two unique identification numbers: a universal ID (UNID) and a Notes ID. The UNID is unique across all replicas of a database. The Notes ID is unique within a single copy of the database. An element retains its UNID when it is replicated to another copy of the database but gets a new Note ID in each copy of the database.

NOTES.INI   A text file that consists of a list of variables and their values, each recorded on a separate line in the form *variable=value*. Notes and Domino refer to the settings in NOTES.INI when loading into memory and periodically while they are running to determine how to do various things.

Number field   In Notes, a field designated to hold a numerical value.

Operands   In programming, the data that will be "operated on" by the operator.

Operators   The "verbs" in a formula. In programming, operators manipulate data or perform certain operations (add, subtract, multiply, and so on) on operands. In "2 + 2" the + is the operator, the 2s are the operands.

Outgoing mail database   A Notes database that temporarily stores mail while it is en route to its final destination. Unlike most Notes databases, it does not use the NSF file extension. Rather, its filename is mail.box or, if in a Domino server uses multiple outgoing mail databases, mail*n*.box (where *n* is an integer).

Pages   In Web browsers, individual HTML documents that can display text, links to other documents, forms, and graphics.

Pane   A portion of a window, usually divided from the remainder of the window by a movable border.

Parent document   In Domino, a document from which information is derived or inherited by another document, such as a response document. All response and response to response documents have a parent document.

Passthru server   A Domino server used to receive incoming calls from mobile Notes users, authenticate those users, and allow them to access and authenticate with target servers to which they are not directly connected.

Permanent pen   A toggle feature of the Lotus Notes client software that allows users to enter text in rich text fields using a font and/or font color different from the default font, without affecting the default font settings.

Personal Address Book   A database designed for each Notes user which contains contact information entered by that user and which is protected by the users password and Notes ID.

POP3   See *Post Office Protocol Version 3.*

Post Office Protocol Version 3 (POP3)   An Internet protocol that defines a standard method for post office servers and mail users to communicate with each other so that the users can retrieve from the servers any mail waiting for them there.

Preview Pane   A window in which you view documents selected in the view pane without opening those documents. This pane is sizable (adjustable).

Private folder   A folder that users can create for their own, exclusive use.

Private key   The secret half of the public/private key pair that every Notes certifier, user, and server has. It is stored in the Notes ID file. Because it is private and unique to its owner, the private key makes possible Notes authentication, electronic signature, and mail encryption. See also public key

Private view   In Notes, a password protected view of Notes documents that is accessible only to the user who created it. Sometimes also known as a *personal view.*

Properties   Settings that control the behavior or appearance of Notes elements, documents, or databases.

Protocol   In networking, the established rules that servers and applications follow in order to communicate across networks. For example, the Internet Protocol (IP) describes how two computers will connect and exchange information over the Internet. FTP and HTTP are also examples of protocols.

Proxy server   Intermediary servers, providing controlled access through a firewall. Instead of allowing direct connections, proxy servers connect to the intended destination and handle data transfers.

Public key   The public half of the public/private key pair that every Notes certifier, server, and user has. Your public key is unique to you and the certificates in your ID file attest to that fact. You publish your public key in the Domino Directory so that others can use it to encrypt documents that they want to send you and to decrypt your signature on documents you send them.

Pull-down menu   A list of related commands or actions that expand when activated by the mouse or keyboard.

Radio button   Small round checkboxes that allow users to indicate their choice of items in a list.

Read access list   A list of authorized readers of a document or of documents created using a given form. Reader access lists can be defined in two places, either on the Security pane of Form and Document Properties boxes or in fields of Readers data type in forms and documents.

Read marks   See *Unread marks.*

Reader access   In the Access Control List of a database, the access level that allows users to read the contents of the database.

Readers field   In Notes, the readers field contains a list of individuals and groups who will be allowed to read the document in question.

Replicator   A Domino server task that replicates databases between servers.

Replicator page   The page in Notes where the user manages the replication process.

Role   Database-specific group or variable created to simplify the maintenance of a database. Roles allow a database manager to define who has access to restricted fields, documents, forms, and views without having to change the design of the database.

Screen reader   A device that reads what is displayed on the computer screen. See *Digital speech synthesizer.*

Search engine   A special program that allows users to find information on the Internet by typing in a keyword or phrase. The search engine searches the Internet for pages containing the keyword or phrase. The search engine then returns a list of Web addresses to the browser which are active links to pages on which the keyword or phrase was found.

Sections Collapsible areas of a document that arehelpful in managing large documents. When collapsed, sections display one line of information when expanded sections reveal their entire contents.

Serif/sans serif Serifs are the short, horizontal bars at the tops and bottoms of text characters. If a typeface has serifs, it is known as a serif typeface or *serif font*. If it does not have serifs, it's known as a *sans serif font*.

Server A computer whose purpose is to store files or programs and provide file, program and resource access to clients.

Shared Field A special kind of Notes field that exists independently of any form and can be re-used on multiple Notes forms. Shared fields streamline the Notes application development process by eliminating the need to recreate the same field in multiple forms.

Shared views Views that are public and accessible to multiple users.

Shared, Private on First Use View A view that is shared or private on the First Use, but reverts to another behavior (private or shared) on subsequent uses.

Shortcut keystroke A keystroke or combination of keystrokes that allow a task to be performed without using a mouse.

Sibling document In a hierarchical view or folder, all documents at a given level under a parent document are "siblings" of each other.

Sign The act of attaching an electronic signature to a document. The signature assures that the document originated with the signing party and that the signed document is unaltered since signed.

Signature, electronic An encryption method that allows Notes users to verify the identity of the author of a document or of a section in a document. At times, Domino automatically applies signatures to documents; other times, users can manually apply signatures.

Signature, email Text or object appended to the end of a mail message used in the way you would close a letter with your handwritten signature. Signatures can contain a name, email address, phone number, postal address, and other pertinent information.

Simple Mail Transfer Protocol (SMTP) The Internet's mail transfer protocol. SMTP hosts connect to each other over.

SmartIcons   Lotus' name for icons located on the Notes client and Designer software toolbars.

SMTP   See *Simple Mail Transfer Protocol.*

Stacked icon   In releases of Notes prior to R5, a database icon that represents more than one replica of a database. A stacked database icon has a small button in its upper-right corner that, when clicked, displays a list of the represented replicas.

Static text   The unchanging text on a form. The title, field labels, and so on.

Subform   A form fragment, stored as a separate design element, that becomes part of another form when the other form is called into use. Subforms can appear in forms based on conditions (formulas). For example, if a user places an *X* in a field indicating she is a first-time visitor to your site, a subform opens in the current form asking her to supply registration information.

Subscription   A Web page, channel, or Active Desktop item whose information is updated on a computer at preset intervals determined by the user. Subscriptions also apply to newsgroups.

Surfing   Browsing the Internet, similar to browsing or "surfing" channels on cable TV.

System Administrator   The person who oversees and manages a network. The administrator can grant a user permission to access certain files and resources, troubleshoot problems with the network, and control each computer on the network. The administrator has the ability to track each user's activities on the network.

TCP/IP   See *Transmission Control Protocol/Internet Protocol.*

Template   A Notes database that usually contains only design elements and is intended to provide the starting design of a production database.

Text constants   A fixed value (text) that does not change.

Text field   In a Notes form, a field that can hold and display text. Rich text fields in Notes can hold attachments, graphics, and code in addition to plain text.

Text Pop-up Hotspot   Text that appears when a user holds their mouse over or clicks on a specially marked or highlighted object. Text pop-ups are used to provide additional information to the user about the object. Text pop-ups are popular for parenthetical or extraneous information. See also *Link Hotspot, Button Hotspot, Formula Pop-up Hotspot*, and *Action Buttons and Hotspots*.

Transmission Control Protocol/Internet Protocol (TCP/IP)   The protocol that defines how data should be sent from point to point over the Internet. Following TCP protocol, data is broken into packets which are flushed through the Internet in the general direction of their recipient. There, they are collected and reorganized into their original sequence. Because TCP and IP protocols work hand-in-hand, people refer to them together as TCP/IP.

Twistie   The name of icon which, when clicked, expands and collapses a Domino document section.

UI   See *User interface*.

Uniform resource locator (URL)   A pointer to the location of an object, usually the address of an Internet resource. URLs conform to a standard syntax which generally looks as follows:

```
http://www.lotus.com
```

Unread marks   Characters (stars) in a Domino database that indicate when a document has not been read. Unread documents also appear in red text in a view. Once documents have been read, the unread marks disappear and the document text appears in black in a view.

URL   See *Uniform Resource Locator*.

User ID   A file that uniquely identifies every user and server to Lotus Notes and Domino

User interface (UI)   The onscreen environment that gives the user the ability to control and view the actions of an application.

Using This Database document   A special document that describes how a database works. The document can be viewed from the Help menu and it provides users with instructions on using the database.

View   In Notes, the method for grouping and sorting documents for display in table format, like a table of contents. Documents are selected for views based on their characteristics (for example, Field contents, Subject, Name, Date, and so on).

WAN   See *Wide area network.*

Web   See *World Wide Web.*

Welcome page   The opening screen in the Lotus Notes client. This page is customizable, contains a search bar, and links to major tasks such as sending mail and using the calendar.

Wide area network (WAN)   A network (usually private to a single company) that connects users and network components spread over a large geographical region.

Window tab   A tabbed page that represents an open window in Notes. Used to switch back and forth between open windows.

Workgroup   A group of people working together and sharing computer data, often over a company intranet.

Workstation   A computer used for work by an individual. Workstations can be standalone computers or networked computers.

World Wide Web (or *Web*)   A component of the Internet. It is a collection of HTML documents accessible through the Internet.

INDEX

items (To Do), 144
  accepting, 149
  appearing in calendar, 147
  assigning, 147-149
  calendar entries, converting to, 151
  counter-proposals, 148-149
  creating, 144
  declining, 149
  delegating, 148-149
  encrypting, 148
  generating from existing items, 151
  messages, converting to, 150
  private, 147
  responding to, 149
  reviewing replies, 147
  saving, 148
  sending assignments, 148
  setting, 145-147
  signing, 148
  viewing status of, 151

J-L

Keep Page command (Actions
  menu), 168
keyboard hotkeys, 196-197
keyboard shortcuts, 192
keys
  Delete, 213
  private, 285
  public, 285
keyword fields, 193
keywords (Actioneer), 294
Keywords button, 294

LAN (Local Area Network), 253
Launch button, 221
launching
  attachments, 219-221
  Mail Address Assistant, 155
  Notes Minder, 111
length (email messages), 289
length of day (calendar), setting, 106
less than or equal to sign (<=) search
  operator, 96
less than sign (<) search operator, 96
letterhead, 102. *See also* stationery
Letterhead tab, 102
levels of access, 284-285
limiting access, 284
line spacing (paragraphs), 197
Link Message command (Special
  menu), 214
Link Messages, 82, 214-215

Link Messages command (Special menu),
  82
links, 202-203
  anchor, 202
  creating, 202
  database, 203, 206
  document, 203-205
  My Author Profile, 233
  My Interest Profile, 231
  view, 203, 206
  viewing, 205
list boxes, 17
List by name option (Select Address
  dialog box), 48
List SmartIcon, 198
lists
  Change Calendar Entry type, 116
  paragraphs, formatting, 197
  Select Folder to Place
    Shortcut In, 111
  To Do, 11
Load Search button, 189
loading searches, 98
Local Area Network (LAN), 253
local databases, 28, 269-270
Locally Encrypt This Database Using
  drop-down list, 270
Location button, 28, 251-253, 268
Location button menu commands (Edit
  Current), 253
Location documents
  creating, 253
  displaying, 28
  editing, 173
  Home (Notes Direct
    Dialup), 253-255
  Travel, 256
locations
  choosing, 6
  folders, specifying, 65
  Home, 253
  Office, 253
  Travel, 253
Locations view, 253
Lock ID command (Tools menu), 22
Lock ID file options, 273
Lock ID SmartIcon, 22
locking User ID, 22
Look In option (Select Address
  dialog box), 48
Lotus Applications command (Programs
  menu), 6, 111
Lotus Applications menu commands
  Lotus Notes, 6
  Notes Minder, 111

U-V